Re-centering Cultural Performance and Orange Economy in Post-colonial Africa

Taiwo Afolabi · Olusola Ogunnubi ·
Shadrach Teryila Ukuma
Editors

Re-centering Cultural Performance and Orange Economy in Post-colonial Africa

Policy, Soft Power, and Sustainability

Editors
Taiwo Afolabi
University of Regina
Regina, SK, Canada

Olusola Ogunnubi
Carleton University
Ottawa, ON, Canada

Shadrach Teryila Ukuma
Benue State University
Makurdi, Nigeria

ISBN 978-981-19-0640-4   ISBN 978-981-19-0641-1 (eBook)
https://doi.org/10.1007/978-981-19-0641-1

© The Editor(s) (if applicable) and The Author(s), under exclusive license to Springer Nature Singapore Pte Ltd. 2022

This work is subject to copyright. All rights are solely and exclusively licensed by the Publisher, whether the whole or part of the material is concerned, specifically the rights of translation, reprinting, reuse of illustrations, recitation, broadcasting, reproduction on microfilms or in any other physical way, and transmission or information storage and retrieval, electronic adaptation, computer software, or by similar or dissimilar methodology now known or hereafter developed.

The use of general descriptive names, registered names, trademarks, service marks, etc. in this publication does not imply, even in the absence of a specific statement, that such names are exempt from the relevant protective laws and regulations and therefore free for general use.

The publisher, the authors, and the editors are safe to assume that the advice and information in this book are believed to be true and accurate at the date of publication. Neither the publisher nor the authors or the editors give a warranty, expressed or implied, with respect to the material contained herein or for any errors or omissions that may have been made. The publisher remains neutral with regard to jurisdictional claims in published maps and institutional affiliations.

This Palgrave Macmillan imprint is published by the registered company Springer Nature Singapore Pte Ltd.
The registered company address is: 152 Beach Road, #21-01/04 Gateway East, Singapore 189721, Singapore

Acknowledgements

This volume was inspired by the work of one of the editors (Dr. Taiwo Afolabi) at Theatre Emissary International (TEMi), Research Hub in Nigeria in over a dozen countries across four continents, and recently at the Centre for Socially Engaged Theatre (C-SET) at the University of Regina, Canada. Thus, special thanks to all the organizations, festival organizers, and partners that TEMi has worked with over the years.

Just like every major work, this volume would have been impossible without the amazing work and incredible support of many people. First, the editors would like to appreciate every contributor in this volume for their insightful contributions. Special thanks to Ambassador Cynthia Schneider for her contribution and Professor Sunnie Ododo, General Manager/CEO of the National Theatre Troupe of Nigeria for their chapters. Both of them bring immensely rich experience within the arts world and policy realm to enrich the work. Also, our gratitude goes to Sandeep Kaur, Ms. Shreenidhi Natarajan, and Aurelia Heumader at Palgrave for their editorial support. We also thank Deanne Collins for providing timely proof editing assistance for the book. Special thanks to the University of Regina providing Accountable Professional Expense Accounts (APEA) funds to cover some editorial cost.

Finally, we would like to appreciate our wives—Damilola Afolabi, Dr. Funmilayo Ogunnubi and Nelly Mnena Ukuma.

Introduction

Africa's fifty-four states are diverse, resilient, and rich in culture and traditions. It is no doubt that the continent has had its share of phenomenal events that have created a turn in its growth and development—slave trade, colonialism, civil wars, military coups, etc. Also, 'the danger of a single story', the shameful realities of African politics, and the social-economic experiences of many Africans have given the continent a negative reputation and poor image in the world. Among other things, the above realities have created a generalized evaluation of the continent which negatively affects the identities, realities, and inter-relations of Africa in international spaces. Unfortunate examples of racism, police brutality, unfavourable visa regimes, and undue politico-economic influence on Africans or people of African descent are still prevalent today.

Yet, African cultural resources and traditions are still sought after. From the tangible to the intangible aspects of culture including but not limited to the Safaris, cultural festivals, architecture, performances, and film industry. African cultural resources remain so attractive that even the return of looted artefacts from colonial times has become a controversial debate especially in Europe. These cultural facts, artefacts, and materials serve as a poster for the world about the continent. While this in itself can be problematic, it is worth exploring how such cultural resources and performances, and creative practices can be converted to become an enabling tool for advancing transformation on the continent. Thus, in this collection, the interest is on the role of national theatres, national cultural centres, cultural policy, festivals, and the film industry as creative and cultural performances hubs for exercising soft power, enhancing diplomatic ties, advancing policies, and promoting sustainability. Further, how can existing cultural and non-cultural infrastructures, sometimes referred to as the Orange Economy, open opportunities for more nuanced narratives about the continent? In what ways can cultural performance and creative practice be re-centred in post-colonial Africa and in post-global pandemic era? And what existing structures can cultural performers, diplomats, administrators, cultural entrepreneurs, and managers leverage to re-enact cultural performance and creative practice on the continent?

This volume is positioned within post-colonial discourse to amplify narratives, experiences, and realities that are anti-oppressive especially within critical discourse. Africa's enormous cultural capital has barely served the interest and satisfaction of its people. The relevance of Africa's creative industry as a leverage of 'soft power' and diplomacy provides new perspectives of how we seek to better appreciate the continent's cultural resources in different forms because cultural resources in all its forms are sustainability enabler locally and internationally (Keitumetse, 2014). This is also important in how the continent's cultural resources are perceived, celebrated, and developed in a sustainable manner that impacts positively on the African people and draws the attraction of the global audience. Relatedly, it is important to also assess the role that cultural leadership plays in sustaining creative practices as well as the soft power perspective attached to this.

Organizing the Material

The book's discourse is divided along three themes: Policy, Soft Power, and Sustainability.

Part I: Culture and Policy

The essays in this part focus on specific policy undertakings within the culture sector in Africa. Alla El Kahla and Iyadh El Kahla set the ball rolling with a case study from Tunisia. In their essay, 'Tunisia Music Culture Policy: Perspective/Challenges of a State's Project', the authors offer an historical lens into Tunisia's musical cultural policy established since post-independence in 1956. In Chapter 2, Ogunbode Olufemi Timothy, 'Community Museums for National Integration in

Nigeria, 1960–2020' provides a historical survey of Museum in Nigeria. Ogunbode proposes that community museums can be a strategy to preserve Nigerian communities' shared past in sculptural arts. Taiwo Afolabi, Tunde Onikoyi, and Stephen O. Okpadah's chapter, 'Film and Cultural Diplomacy in Post-colonial Africa: Nollywood and the Nigeria Cultural Policy', investigates the role of Nollywood in re-centring Nigeria's cultural diplomacy and argues that the Nigerian film industry has been marginalized in the construction of the 1988 Nigeria Cultural Policy. The authors submit that there is a need for a robust framework in the cultural policy that will raise consciousness of Nollywood as a viable cultural representative and cultural diplomat. In Chapter 4, Osedebamen David Oamem interrogates Pan-Africanism and cultural policy management through a formative evaluation of both Nigerian and Ghanaian cultural policies. Oamem recommends an integration of Pan-Africanism's objectives in the cultural policies of both African states. Djamila Boulil's chapter titled, 'Dutch-Moroccan Cultural Cooperation? A Discourse on Network of Cultural Policy', offers some insights to African cultural leaders and those interested in establishing the continent's cultural heritage and creative practice on the international field into how the world views many African countries. Boulil's longitudinal study is a case of long-term exchange between the Netherlands and Morocco. Both countries are chosen due to shared history that dates back over 400 years and the Netherlands has a robust cultural programming for Morocco and some other countries within the region. Boulil's work helps the readers better understand how cultural policies drive international cultural cooperation as evident in programming, funding, and other initiatives. Finally in this part, Sunnie Ododo, the General Manager of the Nigeria's National Theatre, articulates ways in which Nigeria's National Theatre and National Troupe are promoting cultural diplomacy. Ododo historicizes how through legislations and policy, the National Theatre was created and since its inception, it has been carrying out its role.

Part II: Creative Practice, Soft Power and Diplomacy

In Chapter 7, Silas O. Emovwodo, Maybe Zengenene, and Laurent Andriamalala's essay, 'Rewriting Africa's Single-Story Narrative: Lessons from the Darmasiswa Indonesia Scholarship Program', examines the Darmasiswa Scholarship Program, a soft power diplomatic tool employed by the Indonesian government in its post-colonial relations with other nations. Through the case study approach, the authors opine that the art and culture exchange programmes play a vital role in the mobility of ideas and knowledge exchange, strengthens diplomatic ties between Indonesia and participating nations. This helps to erase negative stereotypes about.

In Chapter 8, Kasim Adoke and Ishaq Saidu examine the theme of cultural diplomacy and Orange Economy in Africa focusing on the context of Nigeria's Nollywood. According to the authors, culture and identity play a significant role in challenging established state-centric approaches to diplomacy and demeaning stereotypical narratives about Africa. This will depend on the capacity of a country to commoditize its cultural products. The authors use this premise to examine how cultural diplomacy enhances soft power in Africa through the instrumentality of Nollywood.

In Chapter 9, Olusola Ogunnubi and Dare Leke Idowu continue with the subject of the appropriation of Nigeria's soft power through Nollywood and Orange Economy. The chapter agrees with the Adoke and Saidu that narratives about Africa have assisted to present a disparaging perception about the continent. According to both authors, Nigeria's cultural and creative resources have undeniable economic and foreign policy prospects that can be appropriated to address demeaning stereotypes about the country.

In Chapter 10, Olusola John's interesting study titled 'Pleasure While Flying: Inflight Entertainment as a Medium for Cultural Production and Dissemination' examines the production and distribution process of IFE for passengers and the promotion of cultural and economic values embedded in these entertainment packages for the national cultures of the originating country of the aircrafts. In his submission, inflight entertainment provides not only pleasure but has become covert instruments for promoting and exporting culture across borders.

In Chapter 11, Diana S. Stoica uses folk tales as cultural vehicle of images and codes to examine the definition of soft power (will) from an African context by focusing on a collection of Sudanese folk tale collection of characters and symbols by Leo Frobenius. This chapter presents two main arguments the first being that the three characters in the folk tales express an African epistemological ideology on power and secondly that soft power presents an alternative African agency with the tendency to take advantage of the term for the recognition of the 'African Self'.

Susan Rasmussen, in Chapter 12, compares cultural performances at two urban festivals in Niger's Agadez to look at the types of power conveyed by the event's respective cultural performances and their significance as cultural products. She asks the question of how these cultural performances are re-invented to upend existing local structures. Based on an extensive field research in Niger, her study finds that the two festivals share glaring similarities and remarkable differences at the same time suggesting 'diverse ways cultural performance re-invent already existing structures to revitalize creativity'. More important, her findings challenge assumptions of hierarchical connections between cultural, state, and civic power showing that the substance of local cultural influence is not entirely hegemonic but one that includes multiple voices and appropriations.

In Chapter 13, Joseph Kunnuji uses ethnographic data collected from in-depth interviews and biographical sketches of a key participant to trace the problematic origin of the National Troupe of Nigeria (NTN) and examine the soft power relevance of the Troupe formed to create a national cultural identity for the country. The chapter's main argument is that although the NTN is popular at state organized events, its full potential as a soft power tool is yet to maximized. Kunnuji goes on the suggest ways through which Nigeria could develop the performing and creative arts for cultural diplomacy.

In the last chapter for this part, Olusola Ogunnubi, Uchenna A. Aja, and Oladotun E. Awosusi offer an examination of the themes of Afrophobia and cultural diplomacy in Nigeria–South Africa relations. Focusing their attention on the role of the creative industries in mitigating perceived mistrust among both countries, the authors argue that an emphasis on mutually admired cultural products from their citizens is antidote for curbing periodic xenophobic outburst and reprisal attacks. In sum, they submit that through people-focused cultural diplomatic interactions, the scourge of Afrophobia in the continent can be curbed.

Part III: Cultural Performance and Sustainability

In Chapter 15, Emmanuel Chima's 'Tumaini Festival: Cultural Production and Transnational Exchange at Dzaleka Refugee Camp in Malawi' investigates how cultural production as an interactional transformative practice, has brokered a transnational exchange through the annual festival held at Dzaleka refugee camp. Chima's uses his analysis to reflect on the divisive elements of geopolitics and nationalism rooted in colonial history.

In the next chapter, Cynthia Schneider, the former US Ambassador to The Netherlands, reflects on her cultural and creative collaboration in Mali. In her essay titled. "The Brave Musicians and 'Bad-Ass Librarians' of Timbuktu: Culture Fuels Recovery from Conflict", Schneider shows that Timbuktu shows that while reviving culture cannot solve every problem, Mali's culture, specifically music and heritage, plays an essential role in creating conditions for recovering from conflict, countering extremism, and building a multi-ethnic peace.

In the penultimate chapter, Patricia N. Nkweteyim's essay titled 'Tapping into Africa's Environmental and Cultural Heritage: The Role of Theatre for Development' explores ways in which both environmental and cultural heritage have become important diplomatic asset for the continent. Nkweteyim uses the survey method on Cameroon, fondly known as 'Africa in Miniature', as a model, to establish the fact that if African citizens could embark on the 'We the people' approach for sustainability in community development, the image of the continent and its citizen can be boasted in the world.

In the final chapter (Chapter 18), Adewonuola A. Ajayi offers a unique perspective into ways chess (as an African cultural and leisure tool) can further develop African/Black School curriculum. Hence, Ajayi's 'Problematic Leisure: The Consequences of Engaging European Chess in African/Black Schools' Curriculum' argues for an African-centred pedagogy that aims to cultivate a positive cultural identity for African/black students by ensuring that African history, culture, and social realities permeate the entire education process.

CONCLUSION

For far too long, Africa's case studies and contexts of cultural performances are either silenced through the gatekeeping hegemony of knowledge production or not taken seriously for one reason or the other. In other words, this book's focus is on the development of Africa's cultural resources for cultural export and as soft power conceived not from a Euro-western context but from an Afrocentric focus that pays attention to pan-Africanism and Ubuntu (Madise & Isike, 2020). This post-colonial narrative which is not evident in existing studies will help to look at the role of culture in shaping positive perception and the agenda of sustainability in the continent. The contributions in this volume will therefore focus on examining the connection between soft power, nation branding, and the creative industry in Africa and their intersectionality with sustainability and diplomacy. Specifically, we have considered topics that examine the implication and value of creative industry for transforming the negative imagery about Africa and its people while also addressing the tangible soft power credits that are critical for sustainable development.

The chapters in this volume are, therefore, an attempt to give the agency to African scholars to contribute to the discourse on the value of culture and creative practices for reshaping perceptions about Africa. Some of the questions this book seeks to address is the soft power inherent in the cultural performance of African arts and the role of cultural exchanges and the mobility of ideas from the African continent. By reimagining the spaces of national theatres and Africa's ever-growing film industry, we also hope the contributions will consider the connection of arts, culture, and tourism with international relations and sustainability.

Also, the editors are also particularly interested in studies that examine the new concept of Orange Economy in relation to Africa. For instance, what are the opportunities that Africa's Orange Economy offer for the continent's development and for reshaping stereotypes about the region? This scholarly consideration will likely lead to a further exploration of the connection between Orange Economy, Cultural Policy, and Soft Power in Africa. Although the research in this area is still scanty, we hope that this book will open up more critical scholarly efforts that examine the emerging themes and discourses by providing explanatory nuances reflecting the African realities as much as possible.

Taiwo Afolabi
Olusola Ogunnubi
Shadrach Teryila Ukuma

References

Keitumetse, S. O. (2014). Cultural resources as sustainability enablers: Towards a community-based cultural heritage resources management (COBACHREM) Model. *Sustainability, 4*, 70–85. https://doi.org/103390/su6010070

Madise, D., & Isike, C. (2020). Ubuntu diplomacy: Broadening soft power in an African context. *Journal of Public Affairs, 2020*, e2097. https://doi.org/10.1002/pa.2097

Contents

Part I Culture and Policy

1 Tunisia's Musical Policy: Draft Law, Birth, and Development — 3
Alla El Kahla and Iyadh El Kahla

2 Community Museums for National Integration in Nigeria, 1960–2020 — 25
Olufemi Timothy Ogunbode

3 Film and Cultural Diplomacy in Postcolonial Africa: Nollywood and the Nigeria Cultural Policy — 41
Taiwo Afolabi, Tunde Onikoyi, and Stephen O. Okpadah

4 Pan-Africanism and Cultural Policy Management: A Formative Evaluation of Nigeria and Ghana's Cultural Policies — 59
Osedebamen David Oamen

5 Dutch-Moroccan Cultural Cooperation? A Discourse on Professional Network — 71
Djamila Boulil

6 Promoting Cultural Diplomacy: Nigeria's National Theatre and the National Troupe in Perspective — 97
Sunday Enessi Ododo

Part II Creative Practice, Soft Power and Diplomacy

7 Rewriting Africa's Single-Story Narrative: Lessons from the Darmasiswa Indonesia Scholarship Program 111
Silas O. Emovwodo, Maybe Zengenene, and Laurent Andriamalala

8 Cultural Diplomacy and the Orange Economy in Africa: A Case Study of Nollywood 125
Kasim Adoke and Ishaq Saidu

9 Nollywood, the Orange Economy and the Appropriation of Nigeria's Soft Power 141
Olusola Ogunnubi and Dare Leke Idowu

10 Pleasure While Flying: Inflight Entertainment as a Medium for Cultural Production and Dissemination 159
Olusola John

11 Fighters, Hunters and Blue-Blood: A Postmodern Reading of African Folk Tales and the Soft Will to Africanize 169
Diana S. Stoica

12 Beyond Entertainment: Power and Performance in Two Urban Festivals in Niger 191
Susan Rasmussen

13 The National Troupe of Nigeria Post-Ogunde: A Cultural Diplomacy Fad or Farce? 209
Joseph Kunnuji

14 Afrophobia and Cultural Diplomacy in Nigeria-South Africa Relations: The Role of the Creative Industries 229
Olusola Ogunnubi, Uchenna A. Aja, and Oladotun E. Awosusi

Part III Cultural Performance and Sustainability

15 Tumaini Festival: Cultural Production and Transnational Exchange at Dzaleka Refugee Camp in Malawi   255
Emmanuel Chima

16 The Brave Musicians and "Bad-Ass Librarians" of Timbuktu: Culture Fuels Recovery from Conflict   265
Cynthia Schneider

17 Tapping into Africa's Environmental and Cultural Heritage: The Role of Theatre for Development   275
Patricia N. Nkweteyim

18 Problematic Leisure: The Consequences of Engaging European Chess in African/Black Schools' Curriculum   289
Adewonuola A. Ajayi

Index   301

Editors and contributors

Kasim Adoke holds B.Sc. (Political Science) from Usman Danfodio University Sokoto, M.Sc. in International Relations from Nassawa State Keffi, Nigeria. He is a Ph.D. candidate (International Relations) at Ahmadu Bello University, Zaria Nigeria. He recently presented a paper titled *Towards the Application of Social Contract Theory in Nigeria's Democratic Governance and National Development* at Social Sciences Annual International Conference at Kaduna State University, Kaduna Nigeria from 4th to 6th July 2021. He has contributed to national discourse on a number of topical issues on national dailies including Daily Trust and The Nations. His interest includes Nigeria's foreign policy, political philosophy, regional organizations, and climate change.

Dr. Taiwo Afolabi holds the Canada Research Chair in Socially Engaged Theatre; is the Director of the Centre for Socially Engaged Theatre (C-SET), and an Assistant Professor at the University of Regina. He is an artist, qualitative researcher, theatre manager, applied theatre practitioner, and educator with a decade of experience working across a variety of creative and community contexts in over dozen countries across four continents. He researches, creates works, performs, and teaches at the intersection of performance and human ecology. His research interests lie in the areas of theatre and policing, social justice, decolonization, art leadership and management, migration, and the ethics of conducting arts-based research. He has co-edited two books and published articles in various books and reputable journals. He is a senior research associate at the University of Johannesburg (South Africa) and the founding artistic director of Theatre Emissary International.

Uchenna A. Aja is affiliated with the department of political science, University of Ilorin, Ilorin Nigeria. He obtained his B.Sc. and M.Sc. degrees from the University of Nigeria, Nsukka and University of Ilorin, Ilorin, respectively. His research interest spans issues on Security Studies, Insurgency & Terrorism, Transnational Organized Crimes, Peace and Conflict Processes, and South–South Cooperation.

Adewonuola A. Ajayi is a M.Sc. student of cultural Anthropology in Obafemi Awolowo University, Nigeria. My interest in decolonizing the games and leisure space led me to inventing an African strategy board game (titled Nubia) that has received endorsements from three international cultural institutes namely the Center for Black and African Arts and Civilization (CBAAC), the Center for Black Culture and International Understanding (CBCIU), and the Institute of Cultural Studies (ICS). I am also author of *More than Leisure: The Case for the Adoption of an African Chess Variant as a Tool for African Culture Showcase and Propagation* (2021).

Laurent Andriamalala holds a master degree from Media and Communication Airlangga University, Indonesia. His research interest is in sustainability and the SDGs as it is the key to fast tracking development in developing countries of the world.

Oladotun E. Awosusi teaches International Relations and Strategic Studies at Legacy University, Banjul, The Gambia. He holds M.A. (Hons.) in History and Strategic Studies and B.A. (Hons.) in History and International Studies from University of Lagos and Ekiti State University, Nigeria, respectively. His research interest covers; African geopolitics, border diplomacy/studies, peace and security studies.

Djamila Boulil comes from a Dutch and Algerian background. She has a bachelor's in sociology and a master's in cultural leadership. Her research focuses on organizational networks in the arts, especially in peripheral areas. Believing in the benefits of mixed methods, she uses quantitative, qualitative, and social network methods of analysis in her work. She currently teaches at the University of Groningen, helping a new generation of art professionals acquire technical skills, and does commercial impact research, helping current art professionals prove the wonderful effects their projects have on their surrounding social environment.

Emmanuel Chima is a third-year Ph.D. student in the School of Social Work at Michigan State University. His research focuses on experiences surrounding forced displacement, particularly youth transitions and ageing. His current research centres on the community at Dzaleka Refugee Camp in Malawi. He is a fellow in the US Department of Education Foreign Language and Area Studies (FLAS) programme; Association for Gerontology Education in Social Work (AGESW), and the Andrew W. Mellon Foundation Ubuntu Dialogues.

Silas O. Emovwodo is a research associate at Theatre Emissary International (TEMi) Nigeria. With a master of Communications from Airlangga University, Surabaya, Indonesia, his practice and research interests include creative industries, media and migration and the diaspora, environmental sustainability and the SDGs, and social media activism.

Dare Leke Idowu is an assistant lecturer in the Political Science and International Relations Programmes of Bowen University, Iwo, Nigeria. He holds a B.Sc. Ed. (combined honours) and M.Sc. in Political Science from Obafemi Awolowo University, Nigeria. His research interests are Cultural Diplomacy, Peace and Conflict Studies, Digital Activism and Social Change, Gender and Social Movements in Africa. His recent articles have been published in *The Roundtable Journal, The Commonwealth Journal of International Affairs*, Rowman and Littlefield, Palgrave Macmillan, and the Conversation Africa.

Dr. Olusola John is an experienced coach and mentor with over 15 years of working with various groups of people from young people to leadership teams from the development space, to the Business start-up entrepreneurs. He recently concluded a training and coaching project for the German Government GIZ program for returnees to Nigeria. He has focused on problem-solving in the areas of leadership crisis, change management, and emotional intelligence. This has taken him to some African countries for similar assignments with proven results. He is also a workshop facilitator, conference speaker, and leadership and organizational skills development trainer. He is also experienced in conflict management and public service delivery. He is a certified Emotional Intelligence; Certified Career Coach; and NLP Coach. Among the communication roles held include social media visibility branding for PeopleSmart, France, and the Public Relation Officer of the Aeronautical Information Management Association of Nigeria (AIMAN).

Alla El Kahla is a final phase Ph.D. candidate in ethnomusicology at Martin Luther University Halle-Wittenberg (MLU), Germany. Currently, he occupies a Research-Teaching assistant position at the ethnomusicology chair at MLU and a DAAD's (Deutscher Akademischer Austauschdienst: The German Academic Exchange Service) Ph.D. finalization grant holder. In his doctoral research, he extensively investigated from an ethnomusicological perspective the practice of al-istikhbār: an idiom of performance in Tunisian musical tradition, shed light upon, and dissected the roots of Tunisian-Maghreb Geo/socio-cultural features pertinent to it. He is also interested in musical culture in the Mena-Region with an emphasis on musical life relevant to its historical dynamic under Western colonization/occupation in the twentieth century vis-à-vis the state of music in Mena-Region societies as well.

Iyadh El Kahla is a doctoral candidate in cultural policy at the University of Hildesheim, Germany. He majored in Arts and Crafts and specialized in music education, with musicology as a minor in 2016, at the Higher Institute of Music, Tunis University, Tunisia, and then obtained a master's degree in Cultural studies in 2019 from the same institute. His dissertation proposes to conduct extensive research on Tunisian Post-revolution cultural policy, emphasizing the interpretation of culture in the context of non-dictatorship, particularly the challenges facing the musical sector as an integral component of the Tunisian cultural policy concept.

Joseph Kunnuji holds a doctorate in Ethnomusicology. He is currently a Senior Lecturer in Ethnomusicology and African Musics at the Odeion School of Music, University of the Free State, Bloemfontein, South Africa. In his exploration of African musics, Kunnuji combines teaching, research, and performance to demonstrate the contemporary relevance of indigenous African practices. Inspired by West African Ogu music, Kunnuji's compositions and performances blend popularized jazz and indigenous African elements to create musical syntheses. His research interests include reimagining marginal and historical musical practices within his vicinity. He blends his teaching, performing, and academic activism in striving towards unearthing some of the lesser-known Africa's musical heritage and pushing for their traction both in the academe and the broader society.

Patricia N. Nkweteyim is a lecturer at the University of Buea and teaches Use of English, Theatre, as well as Media and Cultural Studies. She has articles in academic journals, poems in anthologies, and one published play to her credit. Her areas of interest include Theatre for Development, Children's Theatre, Sustainable Development, Culture and Environment, Gender and Women's Issues, and New Media. She desires to contribute to knowledge and nation building through collaborative and interdisciplinary studies, research, and publications, as well as training the young to grow up to become responsible citizens. She has founded and runs the D-Light Foundation.

Dr. Osedebamen David Oamen, B.A. (Hons.) Dramatic Arts, Obafemi Awolowo University, Ile-Ife, M.A. and Ph.D. in Theatre Arts, University of Ibadan, Ibadan with research focused arts Management and cultural policy evaluation. He is a senior lecturer in the Department of Theatre and Media Arts, Ambrose Alli University, Ekpoma, Edo State, Nigeria. He has over fifty published works in international and national journals and books. He is an Arts and Cultural Manager, Playwright, Storyteller, and Poet.

Sunday Enessi Ododo (Ph.D.) is a professor of Performance Aesthetics, Theatre Practice, and Theatre Technology who is the General Manager/CEO, National Theatre, Nigeria. He is the proponent of 'Facekuerade Theory', which derives from maskless transformational practices of traditional Ebira masquerade (eku). He is on the team of World Scenography project. He was vice president of both the Association of Nigerian Authors (ANA) and the Society of Nigeria Theatre Artists (SONTA). He served as the 8th President of SONTA (2013–2017). He is a Fellow of the Society of Nigeria Theatre Artists (SONTA) and the Nigerian Academy of Letters (NAL).

Olufemi Timothy Ogunbode hails from Ogbomoso, Ogbomoso South Local Government Area of Oyo State. He is a product of Schools of

History of Obafemi Awolowo University, Ile-Ife, Osun State, and University of Ilorin, Ilorin, Kwara State. He is currently a Principal Curator in the Museums Department of the National Commission for Museums and Monuments, Akure, Ondo State where he works till date. He has published articles in reputable Journals within and outside Nigeria in the areas of Medical, Strategic, and Cultural History performances. The highlighted areas summarized his research interests' scholarship till date.

Dr. Olusola Ogunnubi (Ph.D. Political Science) is a research fellow with the University of the Free State, South Africa and a research scholar at Carleton University, Canada. He received his Ph.D. in Political Science from the University of KwaZulu-Natal, South Africa. His research interest is mainly concerned with the power dynamics of Africa's regional powers. His current research focuses on the intersection between religion, foreign policy, and the state with specific attention to Nigeria's religious soft power.

Stephen O. Okpadah is a Chancellor International Ph.D. Scholar, University of Warwick, Coventry, the United Kingdom. He has published numerous articles in international journals and chapters in books. He is a co-editor of *Committed Theatre in Nigeria: Perspectives on Teaching and Practice* (Lexington Books, 2020); *Locating Transnational Spaces: Culture, Theatre and Cinema* (IATC and the University College of the North, Canada, 2020); and *The Road to Social Inclusion* (UNESCO/Janusz Korczak Chair's Book Series, 2021). He won the 2021 Janusz Korczak/UNESCO Prize for Global South in emerging scholar category, he is a Non-resident Research Associate with the Centre for Socially Engaged Theatre (C-SET) at the University of Regina, and serves as the director of research at the Theatre Emissary International.

Tunde Onikoyi teaches African Screen Media, Cinema, and Post-colonial Studies in Adeleke University Nigeria. He is a member of Jury, African International Film Festival, and Editorial Board Member of *African Studies Review*, the flagship *Journal of African Studies*. His essays have appeared in renowned publications including, *African Theatre*, *Journal of African Cinemas*, *African Studies Review*, *Journal of Media and Communication Research*, and *Journal of Pan African Studies*. He co-edited *The Cinema of Tunde Kelani* (2021) with Taiwo Afolabi, and is working on a book on Nollywood cinema. He is writing his doctoral thesis in the University of Regina, Canada.

Susan Rasmussen Professor of Anthropology within the Department of Comparative Cultural Studies at the University of Houston, has conducted field research in rural and urban Tuareg (Kel Tamajaq) communities of northern Niger and Mali and among African immigrants in France. She has published articles on religion, medico-ritual healing, gender, ageing and intergenerational relationships, and verbal art, and six books on topics of female spirit possession, the poetics and politics of the life course, local healers in cultural encounters, smith/artisans' ritual roles, and acting and plays. More broadly, her interests include the connections between symbolism and power and culture and memory.

Dr. Ishaq Saidu is an experienced banker, professional accountant, economist, and academic instructor. He obtained his Ph.D. and M.Sc. in Economics from Usmanu Danfodiyo University Sokoto Nigeria and Bayero University Kano Nigeria, respectively. He holds Certificate in Public Policy Economics from Oxford University, London. He has published in both local and international journals. Besides his core competence in economics, he is a social writer and enjoys interdisciplinary academic contributions.

Cynthia Schneider, Ph.D. served as ambassador and is distinguished professor in the Practice of Diplomacy at Georgetown University, teaches, publishes, and organizes initiatives in diplomacy and culture. She co-directs the Laboratory for Global Performance and Politics at Georgetown, as well as the Los Angeles-based MOST Resource (Muslims on Screen and Television). Additionally, she co-directs the Mali-based Timbuktu Renaissance. She speaks and publishes on topics related to arts, culture, and media and international affairs. She was a member of Georgetown's art history faculty from 1984 to 2005, and published on Rembrandt and seventeenth-century Dutch art. From 1998 to 2001 she served as US Ambassador to The Netherlands, and led initiatives in cultural diplomacy, biotechnology, cyber security, and military affairs. She has a B.A. and Ph.D. from Harvard University.

Diana S. Stoica West University of Timisoara, was born in Baia Mare, Romania in 1980. She has a Bachelor in Advertising, a Master in International Development Studies and defended her Ph.D. thesis in Political Studies with an interdisciplinary approach, in 2021. Her main interests as a researcher are the African development narratives, the African social change, post-colonialism, decoloniality, the knowledge production, and Southern Epistemologies, as well as the African and global foundations of tourism and hosting philosophy, being inspired by the love for nature, knowledge, arts, and cultures from Africa, inherited from her father, a passionate geologist.

Shadrach Teryila Ukuma (Ph.D.) has been teaching Theatre and Cultural Studies at Benue State University, Nigeria since 2013. He won the Würth Foundation Global South Postdoctoral Fellowship in Cultural Management and taught International Cultural Management at the Heilbronn University of Applied Sciences, Campus Künzelsau, Germany, in the Winter Semester of 2021. He has also given invited lectures in the Universities of Warwick (UK), Bielefeld, and Hildesheim (Germany). His research interests include Cultural Performance, Cultural Management, Transculturality, and Cultural Sustainability. Since 2015, Dr. Ukuma has been serving as the Director of Kyegh Sha Shwa Cultural Festival (www.kyeghshashwa.org) which he co-founded.

Maybe Zengenene is intrinsically motivated and dedicated scholar in the field of religion, politics, gender, and violence. She is a member and advocate of interfaith dialogue on violent extremism (iDOVE).

List of Figures

Fig. 5.1	MA NL 2014	82
Fig. 5.2	MA NL 2015	83
Fig. 5.3	MA NL 2016	84
Fig. 5.4	MA NL 2017	85
Fig. 5.5	MA NL 2018	87
Fig. 5.6	MA NL 2019	88
Fig. 5.7	The Distribution of the Disciplines in 2014–2016 and 2017–2019	90
Fig. 18.1	Two chess pieces	293
Fig. 18.2	Nubia African chess	297

List of Tables

Table 1.1	The evolution of the budget of the Ministry of Culture. Figures in billion Tunisian dinars (TD)	12
Table 1.2	Number of permanent teachers and Male/Female students between (1998–1999)	17
Table 5.1	Disciplines, Art Forms and Colouring Scheme in the Networks	79
Table 5.2	Dutch Cultural Events in Morocco Registered in the DutchCulture Database in the Previous Dutch Policy Period	79
Table 5.3	Dutch Cultural Events in Morocco Registered in the DutchCulture Database in the Current Dutch Policy Period	80
Table 17.1	Proposed sustainable solutions for Africa's development	283

PART I

Culture and Policy

CHAPTER 1

Tunisia's Musical Policy: Draft Law, Birth, and Development

Alla El Kahla and Iyadh El Kahla

INTRODUCTION

Since the end of World War II, cultural policy has been the wave to shape and build a collaborative and peaceful world. Tunisia was part of this step and had been intensely engaged in elaborating the concept of cultural policy since the beginning of the seminars within UNESCO, see report on Tunisian cultural policy (Saïd, 1970, 56). Thereby, Tunisia

---

The transliteration of Arab words is as per the Arabic transliteration paradigm of the Library of Congress. This transliteration aims at making lecture consistency easier and relevant to foreign terms/words to non-Arab speakers. Then, all transliterated words employed in this chapter will be italicized.
Little material has been published regarding Tunisia's musical policy; however, the references' list presents alternative material that supports this chapter's information and provides background knowledge of it.

A. E. Kahla (✉)
Department of Musicology, Institute for Music, Media and Linguistics, Martin Luther University of Halle-Wittenberg, Halle (Saale), Germany
e-mail: alakalaak1991@gmail.com

© The Author(s), under exclusive license to Springer Nature Singapore Pte Ltd. 2022
T. Afolabi et al. (eds.), *Re-centering Cultural Performance and Orange Economy in Post-colonial Africa*,
https://doi.org/10.1007/978-981-19-0641-1_1

took on a share of the report titled "Prior Reflections on Cultural Policies"[1] on December 18–22, 1967, in Monaco (UNESCO, 1969, 52). The UNESCO report hinged on two important points:

> (1) Cultural policy is a set of conscious and deliberate social practices, interventions, or non-interventions to satisfy particular cultural needs through the optimal use of all the materials and human resources available in a given society at a given time. (2) Specific cultural development criteria should set economic and social development. (UNESCO, 1969, 8)

The report's recommendations took an active part within the Tunisian cultural policy's framework. This policy is based mainly on domains of cinema, fine arts, music, and theater; hence, each domain implemented its own policy/strategy. Music and theater, particularly, were the most important sectors in applying the Tunisian national strategy of culture.

Tunisia's cultural policy hinges on a philosophy based on the idea of democratization of culture, following the influence of the French cultural policy model. This policy was implemented by the leadership's belief, especially by President *Al-Ḥabīb Burqībah*, who saw culture as a fundamental ingredient/component for creating new Tunisian citizenship (Secretariat d'état à l'information, 1974, 1–28). That is why a "Ministry of Culture" was created in 1961. Since then, a national cultural policy has been put into place to promote Tunisian culture.

Afterward, the foundation of the Tunisian musical policy, whose imprint remains hitherto, is the work of a person who has marked the Tunisian musical and cultural scene: *Ṣālaḥ Al-mahdī*.[2] He represented an important actor who ensured the conception and implementation of the Tunisian musical policy. As of the national independent Tunisian state's

---

I. E. Kahla (✉)
Institute for Cultural Policy, University of Hildesheim, Hildesheim, Germany
e-mail: iyadh94@gmail.com

[1] The original report's title in French is as follows 'Réflexions Préalables sur les Politiques Culturelles'.

[2] (1925–2014) Tunisian musician, an ethnomusicologist, occupied different positions within the Ministry of Culture, such as a head of Tunisia National Conservatory in 1957, Chair of the Arts Department from 1975–1961, and Director of the Department of Music and Dance 1966.

announcement in 1956, he accompanied the establishment of vital institutions and relevant legislation necessary to form and organize the music sector in post-independence Tunisia.

In this context, the study regarding Tunisia's' cultural policy, particularly the musical policy, involved archival research from 2018 to 2020 in archival institutions, in Tunisia, tracing then factual data, such as constitutional amendments, cultural law texts, and decrees on cultural reforms. Moreover, interviews were conducted with music/cultural connoisseurs who adopted different standpoints on the music policy's dynamic in the post-independence context. Indeed, findings of archival documentation encountered will assist in understanding the scenario's change in Tunisian musical policy—to approach a historical perspective in the period mentioned above—to conceive the challenges and impacts of this state-applied politic on the development of the music sector as an integral component of the Tunisian government cultural strategy. Findings of available archival documentation tracked down allow to outline the Tunisian cultural policy's main lines, encompassing the music sector from 1958 to 1987. Tunisia's musical policy has not undergone an in-depth analysis of its dynamics in the post-independence period (1956–1987), especially its relevance as a reference backdrop to the prevalent music status as an integral cultural element of the Tunisian state and society.

The chapter proposes to demonstrate the birth and elaboration of the Ministry of Culture's governmental body and its evolution from 1961 until 1987, through the administrative implantation whose objective was to spread culture everywhere in Tunisia. Thus, this chapter is structured into two parts that highlight Tunisian cultural policy's vital priorities, particularly the musical policy. *Part 1* highlights the ensemble of decrees structuring the ministry's work and its organizational chart from 1961 to 1987. This central part reviews and details the different structures underlying cultural politics, by placing the ministry's philosophy within a cultural framework.

Part 2 proposes providing an in-depth glimpse/observation addressing how the musical policy was implanted and by which methods and instruments.

The Ministry of Culture

In this section, the Ministry of Culture's emergence and evolution is discussed, using primary legal law texts. The investigation for this study started from the examination of these texts; literature is still absent apropos of it. Therefore, the purpose of this study is to fill in and analyze how the various ministers in charge have acted to develop the work within the ministry which began with the name "Secretariat of State for Cultural Affairs and Information" in 1961. In 1969, it became the "Ministry of Cultural Affairs," then in 1970, "Ministry of Cultural Affairs and Information"; in 1973, it was again named "Ministry of Cultural Affairs," and in 1979, was changed again to "Ministry of Information and Cultural Affairs"; finally, in 1981, it was changed back to "Ministry of Cultural Affairs."

The secretariat required a legal status exhibiting the administrative attribution in this regard. Thus, the first decree appeared on December 11, 1961, as no. 61–426 (Official Gazette of the Republic of Tunisia, 1961, 1653). Hence, the decree's Article 2 includes an outline of the secretariat's duties as follows:

> (1) the promotion and harmonization of cultural activities through the elaboration and execution of a program for the development and dissemination of culture among the nation, (2) the enhancement of national cultural heritage, (3) popular and primary education in all its aspects, (4) the management of public libraries, museums, and the conservation of sites and historical monuments, (5) relations of a cultural nature with foreign countries and especially with the following international organizations involved, in any capacity, in the field of culture, (6) the promotion of, by appropriate means, artistic, literary, and theatrical activities, and (7) the control of, within the framework set by laws and regulations, all bodies or institutions private, whose purpose is to promote or disseminate works of art and spirit. (Official Gazette of the Republic of Tunisia 1961, 1654)

This decree presents the spirit of Tunisian cultural policy exercised by the Minister *Shadlī Al-qlībī*,[3] whose attributions were changed only once during *Burqībah*'s presidency.

Later, Decree No. 75–773 of October 30, 1975, promulgated under Minister *Maḥmūd Al-mis'dī*[4] and stated that the Ministry of Culture

---

[3] (1925–2020) a Tunisian politician. Director General of the national radio in 1958, he became the first Tunisian Minister of Cultural Affairs (1961–1970, 1971–1973, 1976–1978) under the presidency of *Al-Ḥabib Burqībah* and then Director of Cabinet of the President from 1974 to 1976.

[4] Tunisian author and intellectual served as Minister of Education (1958–1968) and Minister of Culture (1973–1976).

was gradually establishing sub-departments. The ministry also began employing a strategy to disseminate information about culture to all Tunisian citizens (Official Gazette of the Republic of Tunisia, 1975, 2335). Decree No. 75–773 contributed to defining alternative attributions of the Ministry of Cultural Affairs. In this context, the decree focused on defining the Ministry of Cultural Affairs' mission, that is, the structure and development, implementation, and execution of the country's cultural policy. This policy is reflected in Article 2 that exhibits the following essential guidelines:

> (1) to ensure and safeguard the continuous promotion of national culture, (2) to seek, preserve, and make accessible the elements of this culture, whether they relate to the past or present, such as historical or artistic monuments, works of art, literature, and popular arts. (3) To help develop the highest, most lively, and authentic forms of this culture, and (4) ensure their dissemination throughout the nation. (Official Gazette of the Republic of Tunisia 1975, 2336)

Furthermore, Decree No. 75–774 (Official Gazette of the Republic of Tunisia, 1975, 2336–2340) outlined the ministry organization and the administrative framework.

However, even if a decree retains the same mission as Article 2 of Decree 61–426 of December 11, 1961, a vital action should be added: supporting cultural actions abroad and ensuring cooperation with international organizations (Official Gazette of the Republic of Tunisia, 1961, 1653). For example, UNESCO has taken precedence in the cultural strategy formulated by the ministry. Concerning the organization of the ministry, it is noted that it includes a cabinet, office of inspection, technical services, human resources, literature department, art department—including sub-departments for theater, fine arts, cinema, and music and dance—the department of national cultural entertainment, and the board of cultural activities and national cooperation with UNESCO.

The appearance of Decree No. 81–1126 of September 1, 1981, strengthened the Ministry of Cultural Affairs' organization (Official Gazette of the Republic of Tunisia, 1981, 2098–2099), and a new decree under the no. 83–1084 of November 17, 1983, announced the reorganization of the Ministry of Cultural Affairs (Official Gazette of the Republic of Tunisia, 1983, 3026–3030). This decree was a continuation of its predecessor of 1975; it refers to the maturity that Tunisia has gained since the first conference on Venice's cultural policies in 1970 to the one in Mexico City in 1982.

In the central administration, three directorates are created: the administration of financial and planning services, the Department of Maisons du Peuple, i.e., for folk houses, culture and entertainment, and the department of public reading. For the first time, another mission was added, that of implementing foreign cultural policy. For the first time in the framework of diplomatic missions, Decree No. 84–797 of July 21, 1984, established a special status for cultural attachés working abroad (Official Gazette of the Republic of Tunisia, 1984a, 1680). The decree exhibited the path that would be followed subsequently as follows: The decree's Article 1 states that the Minister of Cultural Affairs will designate cultural attachés from among executives with cultural influence to promote Tunisian culture abroad. In Article 2, the decree defines the duty of the cultural attaché's mission, which will carry out its functions within the diplomatic missions' framework abroad for three renewable years after spending at least one year in Tunisia. In Article 3, it is noted that although the cultural attaché is under the ambassador's administrative authority, it is under the authority of the Minister of Cultural Affairs for its cultural mission (Official Gazette of the Republic of Tunisia, 1984a, 1680). This occurrence represents a revolution at the Ministry of Cultural Affairs' heart, with a national and international cultural policy being developed simultaneously for Tunisia's diplomacy benefit.

Influential Ministers

Two ministers have marked their fingerprints in shaping Tunisia's cultural policy and helping to brand the Tunisian cultural policy as an example in the region. This section defines both personalities and their impact on reinforcing Tunisia's cultural policy. The two eminent figures are *Shadlī Al-qlībī* and *Bashīr Bin Salāmah*. Both have worked on legislative and institutional levels to develop the importance of culture in many aspects of political, social, and economic life. They led the foundations for regulations that are still in practice today.

Shadlī Al-Qlībī's Three Ministries' Mandates (1961–1970; 1971–1973; 1976–1978)

Shadlī Al-qlībī was in charge of getting this new body of the government up and running. He was responsible for achieving an objective defined in President Burqībah's speech entitled, "Culture, a Civilizational Challenge,"[5] delivered in *Al-kāf* on September 15, 1968 (The Ministry of Culture, 1984b, 297). The aim was to improve the cultural sensitivity of people in Tunisia. This objective has served to define the objectives of Tunisian cultural action, its philosophy, and its means of action.

The book entitled, *Al-thaqāfa Rihān Hadārī,* i.e., Culture as a Stake in Civilization (Al-qlībī, 1978), is a collection of *Shadlī Al-qlībī*'s speeches delivered at different regions in Tunisia. One of *Shadlī Al-qlībī*'s fundamental ideas is that cultural development can pave the way for global development, particularly in its economic, intellectual, and spiritual aspects. In this context, Tunisia's cultural policy was based on three axes: revitalizing heritage, disseminating culture within the nation, and spreading Tunisian culture abroad, hence emphasizing the importance of cultural cooperation with the Maghreb and other countries. Revitalizing the legacy implied preserving the great monuments of Tunisian culture. This translated into managers' training to research the ancient history of Tunisia from Carthage to Rome and preserve Tunisia's heritage, i.e., amphitheaters such as that of Carthage[6] or *Al-jam*[7] or other historical sites and monuments, to prevent people from forgetting Tunisia's intangible heritage.

This also applied to collecting written heritage, i.e., manuscripts and their preservation in appropriate places in the National Library. It also involved attempts made to reunify traditional folk arts using the Tunisian radio and the establishment of a directorate of music and folk arts for collecting and cultural preservation and widespread knowledge of heritage.

The second axis of *Al-qlībī* cultural policy is the diffusion of culture. To that effect, a national committee of culture and regional cultural committees were created by Decree No. 63–114 of April 19, 1963, to make programs at the national and regional levels for stimulating cultural action (Official Gazette of the Republic of Tunisia, 1963, 526). Besides, the role of these committees was to coordinate the efforts of organizations and individuals. The same work, "Culture as a Stake in Civilization,"

---

[5] The original title in Arabic is as follows, "Al-Thaqāfa Rihān Hadārī.".

[6] The first state established by the Phoenician sailors on Tunisia's coasts in 814 BC.

[7] It is famous for its amphitheater, the largest in the Roman Empire (between 27,000 and 30,000 spectators) after the Colosseum in Rome (45,000 spectators) and that of Capua in Italy.

includes a speech delivered on behalf of "Cultural Advancement" at the National Conference of Regional Cultural Committees held in *Sūsah*, in August 1966 (Al-qlībī, 1978, 55–56). *Al-qlībī* affirms that artistic work in the region relies on several tools apart from regional structures, such as Maisons de la Culture (Houses of Culture). He mentioned also the significant rise in the number of libraries, which increased from 10 at the dawn of independence to 180 in 1966 (Al-qlībī, 1978, 61). The third important part of *Al-qlībī*'s policy is Tunisia's cultural outreach abroad to make the national culture known beyond its borders. This work was carried out mainly through a troupe of popular national artists that accompanied President *Burqībah* in his diplomatic missions to present a refreshing image of the blend of authenticity and modernity of Tunisia.

> This troupe is a mix between the best men and women in singing, dancing, and playing instruments. It took part in representing Tunisia in its cultural days organized worldwide. In Europe, they played in Bulgaria in October 1963, France in June 1968, Yugoslavia in January 1969, Belgium in February 1972, Hungry in June 1972, Czechoslovakia in January 1976, Sweden in May 1977, Poland and West-Germany in April 1978 and the Soviet Union in 1987. In Asia, the troupe played in, Syria in Mai 1975, in Kuwait in February 1976, Bahrein in November 1978, Qatar in November 1978, Pakistan in January 1982, Japan in September 1982, South Korea in September 1982, and Sultanate of Oman in 1986. This troupe also presented Tunisia in Africa: Egypt in December 1969, Algeria in February 1971, Morocco in April 1975, Senegal in Mai 1976, and Nigeria in 1977. (Ministry of culture, 1994, n.d.)

This foreign policy of the Ministry of Culture initially aimed to strengthen relations with African countries because of Tunisia and their shared history and common values.

Moreover, relations with the Maghreb countries were the primary focus of *Al-qlībī*'s policy, which can be evinced by his remarks in an interview entitled, "*Al-Maghrib, Al-Arabī, Al-Kabīr Wa Al-Thaqāfah*" (The Great Arab Maghreb and Culture), published by the magazine *Al-fikr* (knowledge) in November 1962 (Al-qlībī, 1978, 94–100). He believed that Tunisia must cooperate with the Maghreb to help revitalize their heritage by collecting Maghreb manuscripts, to publish them. The primary objective was to strengthen channels for dialogue and to show continuity between past and present. The interview emphasized how the culture, memory of a nation, and awareness of the past are necessary to build the future.

THE CONTRIBUTION OF BASHĪR BIN SALĀMAH'S MANDATE (1981–1986)

The government's philosophy toward culture can be summed up in a quote of Prime Minister *Muḥamad Mzālī*, "Culture is not only an aspect of development and one of its consequences. Rather, but it is also a development factor that is associated with growth" (Salāmah, 1986, 1). The concept of combining culture with the country's socio-economic development was a political feature of this period. This design has evolved and led to several vital choices in the cultural life of Tunisians. With its creation in 1961, the Ministry of Culture had altered and affected Tunisians' cultural consumption habits, thus changing their mentality and integrating them into the twentieth-century conditions.

The link between Carthage's history and the arrival of Islam is thus highlighted, as is the desire to open up and learn from the world's civilizations, which contributed to forging Tunisia's culture and reinforcing its identity. The close friendship of *Bashīr Bin Salāmah* with the Prime Minister benefited the agenda of his policy and led to its implementation. This minister benefitted from unique and favorable conditions. The Ministry of Culture was granted a considerable development and management budget, contrasting previous financial policies. A document from the Archives and Documentation Branch of the ministry provides information regarding the raise by more than double of the development budget from 1981 to 1986; it also shows the huge amount of the investments by the state in the cultural sector in the following years (Ministry of Culture, 2009, n.d.). The following shares the specifics (Table 1.1).

Minister *Bin Salāmah* extended the concept of culture to the Tunisians' daily practices and lives, both public and domestic. Ben Slama (1986), in his book, La Politique Culturelle en Tunisie, summarizes Tunisia's cultural policy in that period regarding its attachment to the ideas conceived for culture since independence. The axes around which *Bashīr bin Salāmah* built his cultural policy were training, encouragement of artistic activity, cultural infrastructure, and state support to construct cultural facilities.

Table 1.1 The evolution of the budget of the Ministry of Culture. Figures in billion Tunisian dinars (TD)

Year	Development Budget	Management Budget	General Budget
1981	1,442	5,476	6,918
1982	1,350	6,093	7,443
1983	2,207	7,571	9,778
1984	2,800	9,900	12,700
1985	3,800	12,376	16,176
1986	4,119	13,320	17,439

MUSICAL POLICY

This section proposes to bring the national musical policy into focus, which was put in place by *Ṣālaḥ Al-mahdī*. This policy was part of the national cultural policy through the ministry's governmental body: The department of music and dance. *Ṣālaḥ Al-mahdī* had a big project for the music and implanted it into every aspect of the Tunisian life/daily from school to radio to festivals. This section also attempts to understand this policy through the mechanism employed by the Ministry of Culture. The music policy has seen two phases: The first one is by implanting a network of conservatory in every region in the country and the second phase was initiated by creating the higher institute of music and its sisters in 1982, and this opened a larger opportunity to study music on a college-level internationally.

THE DIRECTION OF MUSIC AND DANCE

This direction is the pillar of the musical policy conceived by *Ṣālaḥ Al-mahdī*. This position was created for him in 1966; a parallel can be seen in France, where the composer Marcel Landowski was appointed to an equivalent position. Compared to France, Tunisia has not experienced a debate attributed to music, to an entire department not associated with cultural action. Indeed, being a musician and responsible for several cultural departments, *Ṣālaḥ Al-mahdī* brought music an attachment and importance reflected in creating music, popular arts, and the dance department. The functions of this service became precise for the first time in Decree No. 75–774 of October 30, 1975, establishing the attribution of the Ministry of Cultural Affairs (Official Gazette of the Republic of Tunisia, 1975, 2336–2340). In Article 10 (Official Gazette of the

Republic of Tunisia, 1991), a board designed for the arts is created. Music is included as a department of the arts directorate, related to dance and popular arts. This department of music is in charge of:

> (1) The preservation and development of the national heritage in music, dance, and popular arts. (2) The promotion of music, dance, and popular arts by supporting national research, creation, and production in different artistic fields. (3) To participate in the organization and regulation of the artistic profession regarding these areas. (4) Controlling the artistic organization of concerts and performances relating to music, dance, and popular arts, as well as national and foreign orchestras. (5) To ensure, in co-operation with the department in charge of national cultural activities, the organization and technical and artistic planning of national or regional festivals of music or popular arts, including in the cultural activities programs. (6) The organization of technical and artistic national participation in international festivals of the genre, in relation to the cultural promotion abroad and national cooperation with UNESCO. (7) The National Sound Archives' preservation and supply of audio recordings. (Official Gazette of the Republic of Tunisia 1991, 2042–2046)

Ṣālaḥ Al-mahdī has developed the mission of this department to cover every field related to music. For the first time in Tunisia, the national music sound archive has been one of the department's primary responsibilities. Since the ministry's status has changed under *Burqībah* (1956–1987) and *Bin 'Alī* (1987–2011) regimes, the music department has undergone significant changes throughout the years. In Decree No. 83–1084 of November 17, 1983 (Official Gazette of the Republic of Tunisia, 1983, 3026–3030), concerning the Ministry of Cultural Affairs, the mission of the music department underwent some changes.

The new organization chart shows that the department of music does not have authority over all institutions. The music department no longer provides the sound archive, which is the Higher Institute of Music in Tunis's responsibility. A seventh function is granted to the department of music: to organize training sessions of development and updating of personnel working in music, dance, and popular arts in collaboration with the department of specialized teaching and artistic training of executives. The second change consists of a few terms: an ensemble of musicians who play takes the name of troupe instead of orchestra. Political orientations toward culture change and the ministry's mission becomes somewhat reduced and no longer tackle the fundamental principles developed after independence.

The music and dance department becomes a direction in Decree No. 93–2378 of November 22, 1993, organizing the Ministry of Culture (Official Gazette of the Republic of Tunisia, 1993, 2042–2046). The missions of the department change and become as follows: (1) ensure the safeguarding and development of the national heritage relating to music, dance, and popular arts and its dissemination and popularization both within and abroad; (2) to encourage emerging performances and support creation in music, dance, and popular arts; (3) participate in the organization and regulation of the profession in these areas; (4) ensure the preparation and technical and artistic organization of national and regional festivals of music, dance, and popular arts; and (5) strengthen national participation abroad in the spheres of music, dance, and popular arts (Official Gazette of the Republic of Tunisia, 1983). The direction of the music and dance associates the service of training and the established musical professions, in the Decree No. 96–1875 of October 7, 1996, relating to the organization of the ministry of the culture (Official Gazette of the Republic of Tunisia, 1996, 2125–2131). The word "training" no longer exists, and the department becomes responsible for musical professions exclusively (Official Gazette of the Republic of Tunisia, 1983, 3384–3385).

Diploma of Arab Music and Instrument

Decree No. 58–16 of January 23, 1958, (Official Gazette of the Republic of Tunisia, 1958, 125), created a diploma of Arab music and a diploma of instrumental music. This was an initiative of the Ministry of National Education and, in particular, of the fine arts department chaired by Ṣālaḥ Al-mahdī; it altered the lives of many people, empowering them with the opportunity to be a musician and a teacher at the same time. This decree, unprecedented in the Arab world, has revolutionized music education in Tunisia. Article 2 of the Decree No. 58–16 (Official Gazette of the Republic of Tunisia, 1958) mentions the necessary subjects to achieve this diploma, by specifying, in Article 5 of that decree, the minimum required standard of five out of 20 for each subject. The subjects each candidate is required to take are the following: an exam on musical notation, sight-reading, a musical dictation, transposition, and finally the scansion of different Arabic prosody meters, with a question on the history of Arabic music or one of its prominent persons.

For the musical instrument diploma, it is necessary to have successfully passed the Arabic music diploma first. Then to pass the diploma, one has to pass three steps: firstly, the performance of a music piece, either Western or Arabic, depending on the type of the instrument; secondly, sight-reading of a sample of Arabic music; and finally to test skills and the instrumentalist's musical knowledge in improvisation, demonstrating both the candidate's technical and musical skills.

Conservatoire National De Tunis

The conservatory was the first institution dedicated to music in the post-independence Tunisian republic. After independence, music policy emerged in Tunisia and is nowadays named after the first director and founder of music policy-making *Ṣālaḥ Al-mahdī*. After its nationalization by *Ṣālaḥ Al-mahdī*, who was a former teacher at the conservatory during the colonial period, this institution became the center of artistic education in Tunisia.

The institution underwent a series of premise changes and settled at 20 avenue de Paris, Tunis, right in the city's heart, downtown Tunis. This establishment obtains the administrative character endowed with civil autonomy and financial autonomy in 1984, with law number 84–84 of December 31, 1984, (Official Gazette of the Republic of Tunisia, 1984c, 2961) on the finance law for the year 1985, including Article 7 on the creation of the National Conservatory of Tunis. This institution knows the passage of the majority of Tunisia's future artists, as it provides essential training in the theoretical and practical dimensions of music.

The project conceived for this conservatory and other conservatories in different regions is to provide training to obtain a diploma in Arabic music, which will allow the teaching staff to be integrated into the Ministry of National Education. One of the objectives of the establishment is to cover the lack of music teachers throughout the country. This conservatory came under the supervision of the State Secretariat for Culture and Information after its creation in 1961. Since the conservatory's establishment, there have been many prominent executives at the helm of this institution such as *Ṣālaḥ Al-mahdī*, and *Aḥmad Ashūr*[8] among others. The conservatory offers a range of Western and Arabic instrumental training, alongside theoretical instruction.

The National Music Conservatory plays a central role in the reform of the music policy of independent Tunisia. The conservatory assisted in the training of musicians, in developing the Tunisian Symphony Orchestra in 1969, which, in conjunction with the conservatory, is one of the fundamental pillars of *Ṣālaḥ Al-mahdī*'s policy on enhancing the musical life of the country. On another note, enrollment continues to grow each year and reached 509 students in 1998–1999, including 239 students who are boys and 270 girls, with a budget of 50 thousand Tunisian dinars.

Regional Conservatories

Ṣālaḥ Al-mahdī had the intention to democratize music. The objective is additional to the fundamental logic of institutional development of facilities specialized in music. After the city of *Sfāqis*, the regional conservatory in *Sūsah* opened its doors in 1974. followed by *Binzart* in 1981, *Ḥamām Al-anf* in 1982, *Aryānah* and *Munastīr* in 1985, *Nābil* in 1987, *Jandūbah* in 1988, *Gābis* in 1989, *Gasrīn* and *Bājah* in 1990, *Zaghwān* 1993, *Gafsah* in 1995, and *Silyānah* in 1998.

This decentralization policy was implemented under both regimes: *Burqībah* and *Bin 'Alī*. Eight conservatories were established at the end of *Burqībah*'s presidency in 1987, then 20 until 2006 (Mbarek, 2018, 105). However, the existence of these conservatories was threatened by disappearance during the term of the Minister of Culture *'Abdilbāqī al-ḥirmāsī* (1996–2004).

The number of students continues to grow at all conservatories, reaching, in 1998–1999, a total of 3500 students, and in 2010, 4500 students (Mbarek, 2018, 103). Thus, the number of students and teachers in these institutions is going up. According to a document of the sub-directorate of training and development, related to the ministry of culture, the number of permanent teachers was around 44 in 1998–1999 (Ministry of Culture, 1998–1999, n.d.). Table 1.2 shows the results in depth.

---

[8] (1945–2021) Tunisian composer and conductor of Tunisian Symphony Orchestra from 1979 to 2010, also ex-lecturer at the Higher Institute of Music of Tunis.

Table 1.2 Number of permanent teachers and Male/Female students between (1998–1999)

Institution	Number of permanent teachers	Number of students Female	Number of students Male
Conservatoire National de Tunis	12	270	239
the National Popular Arts Music Center	12	214	367
Regional conservatory of Ṣfāqis	06	401	501
Regional conservatory of Sūsa	03	81	98
Regional conservatory of Binzart	01	81	61
Regional conservatory of Ḥamām Al-anf	02	97	68
Regional conservatory of Aryāna	02	63	67
Regional conservatory of Munastīr	02	112	130
Regional conservatory of Nābil	01	13	16
Regional conservatory of Jandūba	–	09	13
Regional conservatory of Gābis	–	55	103
Regional conservatory of Gasrīn	01	06	02
Regional conservatory of Bāja	–	–	–

(continued)

Table 1.2 (continued)

Institution	Number of permanent teachers	Number of students Female	Number of students Male
Regional conservatory of Zaghwān	01	57	73
Regional conservatory of Gafsa	–	23	38
Regional conservatory of Silyāna	–	14	32
Regional conservatory of Mahdia	01	60	63
Regional conservatory of Qirwān	–	28	45
General Total	44	1584	1916

ACADEMIC INSTITUTIONS OF MUSIC

The Minister of Culture in the 1980s: *Bashīr Bin Salāmah* had the idea of founding a higher institute of music, which he believed was essential for the Tunisian music scene and academia. The objective was to give the profession of a "musician" a respectable and honorable dimension, similar to that in the Western world, as young musicians were only found performing at traditional weddings.

The Higher Institute of Music of Tunis: The establishment of the Higher Institute of Music of Tunis, in the University of Tunis on November 1, 1982, by *Bashīr Bin Salāmah* is regarded as a revolution in the fundamental music policy established by *Ṣālaḥ Al-mahdī*. This change occurred at a time of major cultural reforms. Substantial financial investment has made possible the integration of music and musicology as a scientific discipline in university training, enabling the development of a category of Ph.D. candidates specializing in research of music and musicology.

Decree No. 84–862 of August 11, 1984, has regulated the mode the institute works on (Official Gazette of the Republic of Tunisia, 1984b, 1720–1722). The decree was signed on July 26, 1984; this decree, in the second article, defines the vocation of the Higher Institute of Music to be an institution of higher education and to provide the necessary support for the development of its activities, with an administrative character that has legal personality and autonomy. Article 2 of the Official Gazette of the Republic of Tunisia (1984b) states the following:

> (1) To train specialists in the field of music- composers, instrumentalists, singers, researchers, music critics, and music education teachers. (2) -To promote music culture and develop innovative ideas for music-making and conduct fundamental and experimental research. (3) To contribute to the conservation, research, study and promotion of the musical heritage. (4) Ensure the upgrading of operatives working in the music field. (Official Gazette of the Republic of Tunisia 1984b, 1721–1722)

The decree defines the conditions of admission and the organization of the studies, the academic staff, and the administrative and financial tasks, including the academic director, the director of studies and internships, and the head of the administrative and financial affairs department. The decree mentions the three central bodies composing the Higher Institute of Music of Tunis: a board of the institute, a regular scientific committee, and a disciplinary advisory board.

The Higher Institute of Music commences the path in small steps. It represents the second phase of the musical policy established after independence and through *Bashīr Bin Salāmah*, who attributes three major projects to the institute that will enhance its role within the cultural policy, especially in the country's musical life. According to Ben Slama, the purposes of this project are:

> (1) The foundation of a specialized research center equipped with a music library and sound and visual documentation as well as a laboratory for comparative analysis, to conduct field research and collect the Tunisian musical heritage, at the same time as the creation of a research center for the study of the Tunisian musical heritage, Arabic and safeguard it. (2) The creation of a workshop specializing in the manufacture and repair of musical instruments. (3) The creation of a musical orchestra composed by the students of the institute. (Ben Slama, 1986, 52)

This institution commenced with 13 students and contributed to change the appearance of the Tunisian music scene. The institution offered an outstanding education that includes specialized training courses through masterclasses, symposiums, and seminars, which allow students with practical experience in the field, enabling them to carry out surveys and research, as described in Article 7 of Decree No. 84–862 (Official Gazette of the Republic of Tunisia, 1984c, 1722). In 1988, during the regime of *Bin ʿAlī*, the students of the Higher Institute of Music were on strike to protest against the change in the administration of the institute, rejecting *Maḥmūd Gṭāṭ* (Tunisian musicologist), who was temporarily replaced by *Alī Bin ʿArbī*. Newspapers followed the reasons and consequences of this strike; students were concerned about the value of the graduate degree, as the only existing doctor and lecturer in the establishment was *Maḥmūd Gṭāṭ*. After this crisis, the institute continued to grow, particularly in terms of the number of students, which increased each year and reached 162 in 1999–2000.

Graduated students were a vital addition to the artistic and musical scene in Tunisia; they represented enrichment in several orchestras such as the Symphony Orchestra Tunisia, *Al-rāshīddiah*, the radio orchestra, and the national orchestra of Arab music. Under the regime of *Bin ʿAlī*, the Higher Institute of Music of Tunis along with the Higher Institute of Dramatic Art and the Higher Institute of Animation for Youth and Culture developed a master's degree program besides a Ph.D. in culture sciences (i.e., a mixed curriculum of cultural studies and social sciences). This curriculum represents a significant change in the history of the institution and for students. Indeed, it was not possible earlier to obtain diplomas specializing in music and musicology in Tunisia, hence the need to go abroad.

Decentralization of the model of the Higher Institute of Music of Tunis: Before the 2000s, and under the regime of *Bin ʿAlī*, the model of the higher institute of music was decentralized through the creation of two new higher institutes of music in *Sūsah* and *Sfāqis*, by the Decree No. 99–559 of March 8, 1999, on the creation of institutions of higher education and research (Official Gazette of the Republic of Tunisia, 1999, 439). This process of decentralization of higher music education continued with the Decree No. 2001–1912 of August 14, 2001, establishing institutions of higher education and research, especially the Higher Institute of Arts and Crafts of *Gābis*, which delivers, among others, a master's degree in music and musicology (Official Gazette of the Republic of Tunisia, 2001, 2570). In 2005, new schools, offering the degree in music and musicology by Decree 2005–1971 of July 14, 2005, were initiated: the Higher Institute of Music and Theater of *Al-kāf*, where music and theater were taught in the same institution for the first time, and the Higher Institute of Arts and Crafts of *Gafsah* (Official Gazette of the Republic of Tunisia, 2005, 1739). These new establishments provide Tunisia with six new institutes which provide music and musicology training, covering the country's entirety, offering proximity to all the republic students who want to study music and musicology.

Conclusion

The chapter provides insight through the institutionalization of Tunisia's independence on March 20, 1956, regarding cultural policy as a post-independence project example, especially the national policy concerning the music sector. The journey that Tunisian cultural policy took was quite significant. Culture played and still plays a central role in shaping the Tunisia of tomorrow. The Tunisian ministry of culture is still the essential governmental body for the state to share culture in different forms throughout the country. This governmental institution attested a significant evolution through its different administrations, departments, and directorates, strengthening appropriate roles/tasks as an essential governmental body to benefit the Tunisian people.

Music, as an integral cultural element, was a significant part of the Tunisian cultural policy project. That is why the role played by *Ṣālaḥ Al-mahdī* was successful in preparing the Tunisian music scene to the needs of the twentieth century and opening up a new chapter for a national musical policy; it was one of the firsts strategies concerning music politic in a developing country. Hence, this policy played a central role in mapping the cultural politic at the international level, an example of post-independence cultural politic after 75 years of French colonization.

The chapter addressed Tunisia's cultural policy as a model example for the country's cultural extent, such as African, Maghreb, Mediterranean, and Arab. This policy inspired a political will by President *Burqībah*, the founder of the modern independent Tunisian state; he believed that culture was an essential ingredient to shape the Tunisian citizenship of tomorrow and be proud of Tunisia's identity emblem. The example of the inauguration of some ensembles, such as the troupe of popular arts, played a role to highlight this policy as the cultural ambassador of the Tunisian identity, with their tours worldwide. Both ministers *Shadlī Al-qlībī* and *Bashīr Bin Salāmah* marked the importance of the political intervention that sets the state as the regulator of this policy and creates it.

The music sector represented the most key ingredient of this cultural policy toward building a new image of the Tunisian culture as an independent sovereign state. The credit of this policy goes to *Ṣālaḥ Al-mahdī*, who also influenced the Maghreb neighbors of Tunisia by his ideas, implementing a network of music schools to create a professional scene capable of spreading the country's success. Another influence of this policy was on the state, as a relatively high amount of the budget was invested for its success. This triggered competition with other countries, especially with Algeria and Morocco, to enhance their budget for the culture sector. We believe that the route the Tunisian model took after independence was created as an example of policy for the African continent: How culture can shape and brand the country's image as an instrument of soft power.

References

Al-qlībī, S. (1978) *Al-Thaqāfa Rihān Hadārī* [Culture as a Stake in Civilization], STD.
Ben Slama, B. (1986) *La politique culturelle en tunisie*, Tunis: Ministère de la Culture.
Mbarek, S. (2018) *Le statut du musicien en Tunisie État des lieux de la politique musicale: approche sociologique*, l'Harmattan.
Ministry of Culture. (1994) *History of participation of the troupe of popular arts*.
Ministry of Culture. (1998–99) *Annual report of the ministry of culture*, Idārah Al-raskalah Wa Al-takwīn [Department of institutionalization and Training].
Ministry of Culture. (2009) *Jadwal Taṭṭwar Mīzāniwat Wizārat Al-thaqāfah* [Table of budget development of the Ministry of culture], Tunis: Al-idārah Al-far'iyyah Lil Arshīf Wa Al-tawthīq [Sub-department of Archives and Documentations].
Official Gazette of the Republic of Tunisia. (1958) *Vol February 4th*, Official Printing House of the Tunisian Republic.
Official Gazette of the Republic of Tunisia. (1961) *Vol December 11th*, Official Printing House of the Tunisian Republic.
Official Gazette of the Republic of Tunisia. (1963) *Vol April 19th*, Official Printing House of the Tunisian Republic.
Official Gazette of the Republic of Tunisia. (1975) *Vol October 30th*, Official Printing House of the Tunisian Republic.
Official Gazette of the Republic of Tunisia. (1981) *Vol September 1st*, Official Printing House of the Tunisian Republic.

Official Gazette of the Republic of Tunisia. (1983) *Vol November 17th*, Official Printing House of the Tunisian Republic.
Official Gazette of the Republic of Tunisia. (1984a) *Vol July 21st*, Official Printing House of the Tunisian Republic.
Official Gazette of the Republic of Tunisia. (1984b) *Vol August 11th*, Official Printing House of the Tunisian Republic.
Official Gazette of the Republic of Tunisia. (1984c) *Vol December 31st*, Official Printing House of the Tunisian Republic.
Official Gazette of the Republic of Tunisia. (1991) *Vol December 3rd*, Official Printing House of the Tunisian Republic.
Official Gazette of the Republic of Tunisia. (1993) *Vol November 22nd*, Official Printing House of the Tunisian Republic.
Official Gazette of the Republic of Tunisia. (1996) *Vol October 7th*, Official Printing House of the Tunisian Republic.
Official Gazette of the Republic of Tunisia. (1999) *Vol March 23rd*, Official Printing House of the Tunisian Republic.
Official Gazette of the Republic of Tunisia. (2001) *Vol August 24th*, Official Printing House of the Tunisian Republic.
Official Gazette of the Republic of Tunisia. (2005) *Vol July 15th,* Official Printing House of the Tunisian Republic.
Saïd, R. (1970). *La Politique culturelle en Tunisie.* UNESCO.
Secrétariat d'état à l'information. (1974) *Habib Bourguiba propos et réflexions*, STAG.
UNESCO. (1969). *Réflexions préalables sur les politiques culturelles.* UNESCO.

CHAPTER 2

Community Museums for National Integration in Nigeria, 1960–2020

Olufemi Timothy Ogunbode

INTRODUCTION

West Africa is home to many popular, internationally renowned sculptural traditions. The sculpture and cultural artifacts of Nok, Ife, Benin, Owo, Igbo-Ukwu, Esie, Igala, Ikenga and Calabar, among others, played an important role in Nigeria's history (Onwuejogwu, 2007; Usman, 2014). The country is also one of the most socially and culturally diverse countries in Africa with more than 500 major and minor ethnic groups, notably the Hausa, Fulani, Yoruba, Ibo, Kanuri, Tiv, Edo, Nupe, Ibibio, Owo, Ikale, Ijaw and Okun (Onwuejogwu, 2007; Otite, 2002; Ogumor, 1993). It is home to hundreds of unique cultures, each with unique peculiarities in sculptural arts. These sculptures reflect traditional ways of life often

---

O. T. Ogunbode (✉)
Museums Department, National Commission for Museums and Monuments, Curatorial Unit, Akure, Nigeria
e-mail: Olufemmie2010@gmail.com

© The Author(s), under exclusive license to Springer Nature Singapore Pte Ltd. 2022
T. Afolabi et al. (eds.), *Re-centering Cultural Performance and Orange Economy in Post-colonial Africa*,
https://doi.org/10.1007/978-981-19-0641-1_2

preserved in local customs, lifestyle, handicrafts and other creative products. Through their attraction to society, cultural objects and sculptural materials, some of which are kept in museums and art galleries (Ekpo, 1977; Otite, 1990), have the soft power potential to unite Nigerians (Nye, 2017; Onwuejogwu, 2007; Otite, 2002; Ogumor, 1993).

Performative culture describes the speech act theory in cultural objects and sculptural materials as a dialogue among subject elements in a defined space for a harmonious society that shares a common purpose and goal (Ogunbode et al., 2017a, 2017b). This implies that, the diplomatic power which Ocampo & Lersch (2010) term communal power is inherent in these cultural objects and sculptural materials through the dialogue among component cultures in Nigeria. Cultural objects and sculptural materials are important due to their tangible appealing reality.

Thus, many cultural objects and sculptural materials do not merely describe reality, but also have an effect on reality because of their attraction to humanity. They represent the performance of acts of attraction rather than a report on its performance to people in Nigeria (Nye, 2017; Ogunbode et al., 2017a, 2017b, 2018). Performative culture is, therefore, the climax of an act that resides in the functionality of a work of art due to its structure. It also involves an interpretation of an object rather than a belief. Therefore, the symbols of an artwork can be said to epitomize the aesthetic, religious, ethical and social values of a society which are found in the cultural objects and sculptural materials of a group of people (Ogunbode et al., 2017a, 2017b, 2018; Odewumi, 2009). Art is a human structure and it functions over time in all spheres of human life. In other words, art is a skill or expertise in societies' agreed symbolic values (Odewumi, 2009). Performative culture is considered acceptable to a social system because it is a structure and it functions as a skill and an agreed symbolic value of the social system for structural and psychological functionalism (Ogunbode et al., 2017a, 2017b, 2018). Therefore, the social dimension of a community museum for national integration is an instrument that enhances the performative culture of cultural objects and sculptural materials for equilibrium in the social order of Nigerian states in the twenty-first century (Ogunbode et al., 2012, 2018, 2010).

Ogunbode et al., (2017a, 2017b) observe that, 'a life that neglects its culture; cultural objects and sculptural material is like a life divorced of reality (tangibility)[1] and actual performance in its cultural existence in a defined space.' Thus, such a life embraces cultural and sculptural suicide, mere reportage of a performance (description of reality) and not the performance of some sort. Hence, Ethnocide (destroying people) and Genocide (destroying race) of cultural objects and sculptural materials are unavoidable in such a life or system.

This consciousness of the performance of cultural objects and sculptural materials highlights the need for a reawakening of the cultural and creative arts of Nigerian reality as depicted in cultural objects and sculptural materials as far back 900 BC in contemporary times (Ogunbode et al., 2017a, 2017b, 2018). The emergence of the western knowledge system and the application of this system in modern-day Nigeria has done more harm than good in integrating Nigeria. Some Nigerians fail to appreciate cultural objects and sculptural materials such as Nok, Ife, Benin, Owo Igbo-Ukwu and Esie, among others, due to their Christian or Muslim beliefs that regard these materials as evil, the devil incarnate and symbols of a lack of civilization. They are thus not inclined to preserve them in museums or other cultural repositories for future generations. The reason lies in the failure to contextualize Christian and Islamic ideologies and doctrines within the Nigerian cultural framework (Ogunbode et al., 2017a, 2017b, 2018).

This situation has undermined Nigerians' shared past. The origins of Nigerian culture lie in Nok, Ife, Benin, Owo, Igbo-Ukwu and Esie, among others, which is people-oriented (Ogunbode et al., 2018; Usman, 2014) as these cultural objects and sculptural materials are derived from the people. Retrieving the unity of the past that was fostered by these materials has to be driven from within Nigeria rather than from abroad. When the British government amalgamated the territories that became Nigeria in 1914, its cultures were not amalgamated from within, but from outside. This bred cultural beliefs such as political power belongs to the North, Education to the West and Business to the East as reflected in the country's Constitution, the system of government (Parliamentary and Presidential), the electoral system and political parties and many other structures. Creating the Nigerian culture from within the system would showcase Nigerian creativity and promote national integration (Awolowo, 1947; Lugard, 1919; Ogunbode et al., 2017a, 2017b, 2018).

[1] Structure and function.

This chapter advocates for a campaign to establish community museums to exhibit Nigerian culture and educate people. Cultural objects and sculptural materials have been a medium for the development and identity of fragmented Nigerian cultures since 900 BC. Their reawakening would showcase the individual ingenuity exhibited in cultural objects and sculptural materials of the past, unlike cultural beliefs which are descriptive, dogmatic, pessimistic and reflect religious bias (Ogunbode et al., 2017a, 2017b, 2018).

Literature Review

There is a rich body of literature on museums and community museums (see, among others, Afigbo & Okita, 1985; Binkat, 2018; Ogunbode et al., 2017a, 2017b, 2018; Ocampo & Lersch, 2010; Karp et al., 2006; Okpoko, 2006; Filane, 2003; Kerri, 1994; Abadom, 1994; Okita, 1982; Nyangila, 2006). These works highlight the discourse on community, museums, objects, sculptures, exhibition, preservation, conservation and values, among others, while some have raised significant issues in relation to the art of functional museum practice for community sustainability. The role of Nigeria's National Commission for Museums and Monuments in interpretation of objects, documentation and inventory is also an important issue as it affects Nigeria's growth and development. While cultural objects and sculptural materials have thus received attention, more in-depth scientific appraisal is necessary.

Studies have also been conducted on national integration in Nigeria as a mere geographical expression (Awolowo, 1947). Lugard (1919) observed that 'Nigeria only exists on paper, ...the accident of British suzerainty' and Soyinka (2009) views national integration as nation space (see, among others, Onyeakazi & Okoroafor, 2018; Aluko & Usman, 2016; Ogunbode, 2012; Matlou, 2009; Oloruntimehin, 2007; Onwuejogwu, 2007; Otite, 1990, 2002; Awolowo, 1947). However, these studies did not focus on identifying, examining and discussing the role of community museums in national integration in Nigeria since independence. This chapter contributes to filling this gap in the literature.

Conceptual Clarification
Community Museum

Karp et al. (2006) state that community museums are an imaginative strategy that communities have developed to sustain their culture. This chapter adopts Karp's definition to argue that Nigeria should adopt this instrument as a creative strategy to sustain her cultural objects and sculptural materials. Nigerian culture is a collection of different nations and community museums could serve as a tool for national integration, the creation of nationhood and sustainability in the country. Karp notes that community museums are instruments to recreate identity and affirm the cultural objects and sculptural materials of traditional and contemporary culture, while Ocampo and Lersch (2010) observe that they act as a space for the exercise of communal power. The authors add that communal power is the sense of collective responsibility among the being-elements[2] that make up the whole. Each being-element has power, but a community museum renders the power communal by amalgamating these being-elements into a workable whole. Furthermore, Ocampo and Lersch (2010) validate the community museum as a tool for the construction of collective subjects (self-knowledge, creativity); communities may appropriate the museum to enrich their relations, develop awareness of their history, foster reflection and critical analysis, and to create projects to transform their collective future memories. This definition of community museums fits with the argument made in this chapter that they should be used to correct the notion of Nigeria as a collection of ethnic nations to the detriment of its existential wholeness. Its collective history is based on the coming together of all its parts to form a nation of diversified culture. Therefore, the community museum is a deviation from the traditional museum practice of making history for the community rather than the community making its own history by blending cultures that have self-knowledge and creative potential to promote nationhood. (Ocampo & Lersch, 2010)

---

[2] Individual culture

National Integration

Deutch and Foltiz describe national integration as efforts by the central authority to avoid ethnic bias, ties and affiliations in order to build national unity, stability and development. (Deutch and Foltiz, 1963; Aluko & Usman, 2016). For Shona (2013), national integration is 'the awareness of a common identity among citizens of a country....' This perspective is based on the understanding that there might be differences, but there is room for a common identity in a nation. In relation to this chapter, it is argued that the cultural objects and sculptural materials of different parts of Nigeria served as a common identity which integrated these components in times gone by, and could serve as an instrument for national integration to achieve a common identity through the activities of community museums (Shona, 2013; Aluko & Usman, 2016). Aluko and Usman (2016) observe that national integration is the hallmark of unity and development in any polity. A nation space like Nigeria is a multiethnic state and potent integration mechanisms are required to achieve unity and equilibrium. Again, in relation to this chapter, this potent integrative mechanism is community museums (Aluko & Usman, 2016). Finally, Onyeakazi and Okoroafor (2018) state that, national integration is the process of bringing various peoples of different cultural and social backgrounds together in a given social context or polity for their collective interests and good. This implies that bringing community museums into play for national integration in Nigeria is not the end but a means to an end because national integration is a process, a work in progress to achieve goodness for all.

Failed Cultural Beliefs

Cultural beliefs are portrayed as reportage[3] of performances of unity in Nigeria, 1960–2020. Such reportage has not succeeded in integrating Nigerians as Nation, while they describe reality, they have no impact on the reality (united existence) described in Nigeria in the past. Nigerian cultural beliefs that have failed to integrate the country include State Creation (currently 36 states); the Nigerian currency; Political Parties; National Dailies; Print and Electronic media houses, Unity

---

[3] Description of reality, but lacks potential to impact the reality to achieve integration.

Schools (nursery, primary, secondary, college, polytechnic and university); Abuja as the Federal Capital Territory (FCT); the National Youth Service Corp (NYSC); the Nigerian Civil Service Commission; National Anthem; National Pledge; Federal Character Policy; Nigerian Constitution; Federalism; and the National Assembly (Senate and the House of Representatives) (Akinade, 2004; Matlou, 2009; Ogunbode et al., 2018; Oloruntimehin, 2007). These cultural beliefs failed because they were concerned with describing Nigeria without a workable model for Nigerian unity and this stymied the country's development following independence in 1960 and generated conflict. The cultural beliefs are not acceptable to all and they thus did not create opportunities to combine different realities with different styles to make them attractive to all Nigerians. Furthermore, they lack tangibility and truth that are strong factors that create appeal (Ekpo, 1977; Matlou, 2009; Ogumor, 1993; Oloruntimehin, 2007).

Cultural Objects and Sculptural Materials

A cultural object is a heritage that encompasses the entire corpus of a community's national life (Webber & Donatius, 2008). The UNESCO World Heritage Convention 1972 described it as the manifestation of human ingenuity in the past or the present. Cultural objects have the potential to contribute to an understanding or appreciation of the human story which is an important aspect of continuing cultural traditions in the spiritual and emotional sense (Albert, 2008; Webber & Donatius, 2008). Sculptural materials refer to three-dimensional works of art that are created by carving, modeling or casting a cultural movable or immovable heritage. It Showcases the culture in order to safeguard the object depicted in the sculpture (Ogunbode et al., 2017a, 2017b, 2018; Odewumi, 2009).

In pre-colonial Nigeria, cultural objects and sculptural materials were instruments for unity and they remain active in the consciousness of Nigeria. When a Nigerian anywhere in the world hears about cultural objects and sculptural materials, the consciousness is awoken that, 'this is ours' because of the way in which the senses react to objects such as the Nok terracotta of a human head from Rafin Kura, Abuja Emirate, Shere and Jemaa, Nok terracotta of a beaded man from Katsina-Ala (Usman, 2014), Queen Amina of Zauzau, Ife bronze head, Ife bronze head representing Olokun, Ife bronze head of Wunmonije, Ife full length bronze statue, Ife terracotta head at Ita Yemoo (Usman, 2014), Oranmiyan staff, Esie soapstone seated figure (Usman, 2014), Benin bronze aquamaniles in the form of a leopard, Benin female bronze head representing the Queen mother, Benin bronze memorial head wearing ridged hair and beaded collar around the neck, Benin miniature bronze figure, Benin bronze medicine container with legs, Benin bronze Oba's flutter, Benin ivory Queen Idiah (Usman, 2014), Owo terracotta face from Igbo-laja, Owo terracotta of hand presenting a lizard from Igbo-laja, Owo terracotta human head from Igbo-laja, Owo wooden head of a ram (Osamasinmi) from Owo (Usman, 2014), Igbo-Ukwu bronze pot on a stand and Igbo-Ukwu bronze pendant depicting a ram's head with decorative features from Igbo Isaiah and Igbo-Ukwu bronze snail shell. Although the aforementioned cultural objects and sculptural materials date from 900 BC, their potential to integrate the diverse cultural groups which the objects depict could be realized through community museums (Ogunbode et al., 2017a, 2017b, 2018; Usman, 2014).

COMMUNITY MUSEUMS AS A VIABLE INSTRUMENT FOR NATIONAL INTEGRATION IN NIGERIA, 1960–2020

> The project to create museum springs from deep community interests and concerns, which are related to its disadvantageous position regarding global processes and the need to legitimize its values and experiences. These concerns build up gradually, like an underground current, and become apparent in critical moments, or when certain factors catalyze or trigger their manifestation. (Ocampo & Lersch, 2010)

Ocampo and Lersch (2010) identify three stages in the development of a community museum, namely consciousness of the need to unite on agreed terms among the community; creating and building a museum which reflects people's consciousness, whether great or small; and the development of daily museum activities and projects in line with the community's philosophy.

Ocampo and Lersch (2010) add that community museums' origins do not lie in plunder or expensive acquisitions; rather, they are the consequence of conscious decisions to support a collective initiative. The community museum emerges, not to display the reality of the other, but to tell the community's particular story. The aim of the community museum that is presented in this chapter is to make a Nigerian story. This can be achieved through consciousness of an agreed collective memory that represents all Nigerians. Ocampo and Lersch (2010) also assert that, in a community museum, the object is not the dominant value but rather collective memory which is revitalized through the recreation and reinterpretation of meaningful stories about the community. Thus, as a member of a Nigerian community, every Nigerian should use the community museum to remember how things were before, to relive events and practices in the twenty-first century. In the community museum, people invent a way of telling their stories, and in this way, they define their common identity instead of consuming identities imposed by outsiders. A substantial part of the Nigerian identity has been described from the outside, which is depicted in the cultural beliefs highlighted in this chapter. However, cultural objects and sculptural materials which date from 900 BC were created within the local system as collective memory (Ocampo & Lersch, 2010; Usman, 2014, Ogunbode et al., 2018).

To integrate Nigeria, Nigerians must create new knowledge instead of conforming to a dominant view and the prevailing interpretation of national history, which exclude the being-elements and eliminates them from collective memory. Nigeria must overcome a history of devaluation by valuing its stories and the daily events of its community life and by blending traditional and contemporary cultures to create a modern Nigerian. This will enable Nigerians to appropriate an institution created for the elite to legitimize and impose their values on the people (Ocampo and Lersch, 2010). By implication, the community museum becomes a tool to manage heritage through grassroots, community organizations in which communal power is asserted in the creation and interpretation of objects selected by the community and for the community. On the one hand, it serves to maintain or recover possession of the community's material (cultural objects and sculptural materials), and on the other hand, it enables the re-appropriation of intangible heritage by elaborating its meaning on the community's own terms. Through the museum, the community strives to exert power over patrimony and resist expropriation. This struggle is carried out through its own organizational forms, the communal assembly or others. In these grassroots organizations, community members determine what to present in the museum, how it should be run, and which priorities it should address (Ocampo & Lersch, 2010). In addition, a community museum controls communities' future by controlling their past. It is an instrument that enables community decision-making entities to exert power over the memory which feeds their future aspirations (Ocampo & Lersch, 2010).

The community museum is a process, rather than a product. It integrates complex processes of constitution of the collective community subject through reflection, self-knowledge and creativity; consolidates community identity by legitimizing its own histories and values; improves the quality of community life through multiple projects for the future; and promotes processes that strengthen the community's capacity for action through the creation of networks with similar communities. This is a collective process which comes to life within the community; it is a museum 'of' the community, not built from the outside 'for' the community. The community museum is a tool to foster self-determination, strengthening communities as collective subjects that create, recreate and make decisions that shape their realities (Ocampo & Lersch, 2010).

In order to foster national integration in Nigeria, the collective being-elements in the form of cultural objects and sculptural materials must be interpreted objectively. This will enable broader social circulation of the proposal for a new Nigeria that is no longer a 'mere geographical expression' and 'nation space,' but rather an expression of nationhood (Ocampo & Lersch, 2010; Soyinka, 2009; Awolowo, 1947).

Community Museums should safeguard the cultural objects and sculptural materials in Nigeria and in so doing, identify and preserve the values of each community that can enhance national integration in the country. Traditional cultural materials of different parts of Nigeria such as Nok, Benin, Esie, Igala, Igbo-Ukwu, Ikenga, Calabar and Owo, among others have been important sources of attraction for national integration since antiquity and this should be maximized to the fullest in contemporary Nigeria. Thus, national integration will come from civil society rather than from the government machinery. Cultural belief is mere propaganda that lacks self-knowledge. It is not credible and thus, cannot serve as a tool for national integration. Therefore, cultural beliefs should not be part of community museums unless they are converted to carry the Nigerian identity and ideology of cultural objects and sculptural materials (Nye, 2017; Odewumi, 2009; Bodley, 2007).

The role of the community museum is to create room for sourcing creative arts which depict the communal values of Nigeria. This will help to build national integration and ensure that cultural objects and sculptural materials in the galleries of these museums are used to educate people about the country, and its communities on the importance of unity. To achieve national integration, Nigeria needs to support talent among its citizens to create new cultural objects and sculptural materials in addition to the existing ones, as this will convey that modern Nigeria is an entity with identity, even though this is difficult to reconcile with the rigid cultural beliefs in the country (Awolowo, 1947; Nye, 2017; Webber & Donatius, 2008).

Community museums can promote consciousness that cultural objects and sculptural materials belong to a set of people who understand its collective values, thereby facilitating national integration. It is, therefore, important that citizens have a sense of belonging; that these materials are 'ours,' which supports the concept of cultural democracy. Furthermore, they need to be conscious of the need to work for the good of the whole (Nigeria). When they think about their cultural objects and sculptural materials, they should also think about Nigeria because each is a functional part of the country (Bodley, 2007; Webber & Donatius, 2008; Oloruntimehin, 2007).

A community museum safeguards cultural objects and sculptural materials by subjecting them to objective criticism and documentation in a digitalized format for preservation and conservation where necessary. Traditional and contemporary cultures will need to blend together to build a composite portrait of Nigerian nationhood and federalism that will be exhibited in all community and national galleries in the country (Nye, 2017; Bodley, 2007; Webber & Donatius, 2008).

The government and its agencies should also encourage the study of history at formal and informal levels. Community museums serve as an informal platform to teach history and in doing so, they should reflect its ups and downs, the good and the bad, and successes and failures. This will help citizens to decide whether they want to be an object of history or a subject of history. Nigeria as a state has failed to take history seriously and to learn from its lessons (Bodley, 2007; Carr, 1974; Rowse, 1963).

The galleries in community museums should be different from those found in the United States, Mexico, Canada, Turkey, Malaysia, Egypt and Israel, among others. Given their objective of promoting national integration, they should present blended displays of cultural objects and sculptural materials in different themes. Exhibitions could be ethnographic or archaeological (pottery, textiles, agriculture and religion, among others), natural and cultural. Monuments should be protected and replicated in museum galleries (Ogunbode et al., 2017a, 2017b, 2018; Webber & Donatius, 2008).

Finally, the National Commission for Museums and Monuments should be empowered to perform its statutory role in the management of cultural objects and sculptural materials, with appropriate laws (Ogunbode et al., 2017a, 2017b, 2018; Webber & Donatius, 2008).

Conclusion

This chapter advocated for the establishment of community museums to promote Nigeria's development and strengthen national integration. It proposed that the performative values of Nigerian cultural objects and sculptural materials should be harnessed in community museums to recreate Nigerian functional culture. Thus, the cultural dimension of national integration is community museums. The cultural objects and sculptural materials highlighted in this study dating from 900BC are imbued with community consciousness that stems from communal power.

The historical materialism philosophy in cultural objects and sculptural materials emphasizes transcendentalism poststructuralism in Nigeria. Therefore, showcasing its restructured cultural objects and sculptural materials in line with current realities in the country by blending the traditional and contemporary cultures to access a new Nigerian culture, will surely be a blessing to Nigerians and the world at large. Accessing a new culture will go a long way in enculturating and acculturating future generations into the consciousness and attitude of national integration. Finally, art and culture should be guarded with all diligence. Nigeria needs to view her cultural heritage from the Emic rather than the Etic perspective by believing in her beauty.

References

Abadom, M. (1994). The complementarity of museums and tourism. *Nigerian Heritage Journal of the National Commission for Museums and Monuments*, 3, 75–80.

Afigbo, A. E., & Okita, S. I. O (1985). *The museum and nation building*. New African Publishing Co.

Akinade, J. A. (2004). *Dictionary of Nigerian government and politics*. Macak Books Ltd, (MBL), Lagos, 1,3–6,9,17, 39, 50, 57, 80, 176.

Akinyele, R. T. From 'Geographical expression' to 'nation space': Nigeria and the challenge of nation building, 1–3.

Albert M. (2008). Framework for legislation on immovable cultural heritage in Africa. Webber Ndoro, Albert Mumma and George Abungu (eds.), *Cultural heritage and law protecting immovable heritage in English speaking countries of sub-saharan Africa*. 102–104.

Aluko, O. I., & Usman, S. (2016). Visiting the hippopotamus: National integration issues in Nigeria. *The Journal of the Romanian Regional Science Association*, 10(1), 70–71.

Awolowo, O. (1947). *Path to Nigeria's freedom* (London: Faber and Faber), 47–48.

Binkat, M. J. (2018). *Documentation in museum settings: Meaning, scope and procedures*. MATKOL Press. 15–20.

Bodley, J. H. (2007). *Culture*. Microsoft Corporation.

Carr, E. H. (1974). What is History? *Penguin Book*, 7–9, 21–26.

Deutch and Foltiz. (1963). in Ezeibe C. C. (2010). Federal character principle and national question in Nigeria. *International Journal of Research in Arts and Social Sciences*, 2, 81.

Ekpo, E. (1977). Two thousand years of Nigerian art. Federal department of antiquities. Lagos.

Filane, K. (2003). Museums in Nigeria: Historical antecedents and current practice. *Dakar—Art, Minorities, Majorities*. Aica press. 3–5.

Hawkes, J. (2001). *The fourth pillar of sustainability: Culture's essential role in public planning*. Common ground Publishing and Cultural Development Network.

Hirzy, E. (2008). *'Museum' Microsoft® Encarta® 2009 (DVD)*. Microsoft Corporation.

Karp, I. et al. (eds.) (2006). *Community museums and global connections: The union of community museums in oaxaca*. (Durham and London: Duke University Press), 7, 27

Kerri, H. O. (1994). Developing museums: The Nigerian experience. *Nigerian Heritage Journal of the National Commission for Museums and Monuments.*, 3, 59–68.

Matlou, P. M. (2009). Advancing and integrating African values, ethics and norms in the interest of Africans and Africans diaspora. Centre for black and African arts and civilization (CBAAC). *Occasional Monograph No.*, 10, 6–11.

Michael, O. et al. (1999). *Government for senior secondary schools*. Africana-Fep, Onitsha. 19.

Nyangila, J. M (2006). Museums and community involvement: A case study of community collaborative initiatives—national museums of Kenya, 69–74.

Nye, J. (2017). Soft power: The origin and political progress of a concept. *Palgrave Communications*. https://doi.org/10.1057/palcomms.2017.8

Obiefuna, B. A. C. (2009). Democracy in contemporary Nigeria: Lessons from Igbo culture area. *The humanities and Nigeria's democratic experience.* Faculty of Arts, NAU.

Ocampo, C. C., & Lersch, T. M. Sociomuseology IV, Cadernos de Sociomuseologia, Vol. 38–2010, 139–142

Odewumi, M. O. (2009). Junior secondary cultural and creative art, book 1. *Ayekooto Press., 60,* 64–68.

Ogumor, E. (1993). *Certificate art for junior and senior secondary school* (p. 129). University Press.

Ogunbode, O. T. et al. (2018). *Performative culture: National museum Akure as a spectator in some selected objects in Akure kingdom.* LAP Lambert Academic.

Ogunbode, O. T. (2010a). Museum and social harmony in Nigeria: A case of Akure objects. *Proceeding of International Conference on Research and Development., 3*(24), 35–40.

Ogunbode, O. T. (2010b). Environmental theatre a podium for Nigerian politicians. *International Journal of Communication and Performing Arts., 2*(1), 98–104.

Ogunbode, O. T. (2012). Museum in Nigeria and social harmony: A case of Akure objects. *International Journal of Arts and Culture, 3*(24), 34–40.

Ogunbode, O. T., et al. (2017a). Performative culture: National museum Akure as a spectator in cowry head cult in Akure KINGDOM. *Journal of Applied Sciences and Environmental Sustainability., 3*(8), 101–112.

Ogunbode, O. T., et al. (2017b). *Ethnocide and Genocide of the Relics of Nigerian's Mother Culture: Community Museum as a Way Forward' in Journal of Applied Sciences and Environmental Sustainability., 3*(8), 113–122.

Okita, S. I. (1982). Museums as agents for cultural transmission. *Nigeria magazine,* No. 143. Federal ministry of social development, youth and culture. 3–20.

Okpoko, A. I. (2006). *Fundamental of Museum Practice. Afro-Orbis., 1–4*(8–12), 66–67.

Oloruntimehin, B. O. (2007). Culture and democracy. Centre for black and African arts and civilization (CBAAC). *Occasional Monograph No., 5,* 22–26.

Onwuejogwu, M. A. (2007). The national Multi-ethnic nationalities of Nigeria and the problems of governance. Lecture Series. *National institution for cultural orientations (NICO).* Abuja.

Onyeakazi, J., & Okoroafor, E. C. (2018). National integration in Nigeria: A philosophical insight. *International Journal of Novel Researches in Humanities, Social Sciences and Management* Vol. 1, No. 1, ISSN 2141 825X, www.oasisinternationaljournal.org, 52

Otite, O. (1990). *Ethnic pluralism and ethnicity in Nigeria.* Ibadan. Shaneson C.I. Ltd.

Otite, O. (2002). Perspective on national integration in multicultural societies: A Nigerian overview. Isiugu-Abanihe, Isamah and Adesina (eds.), *Currents and perspectives in sociology.* Malthouse Press Limited. 163–174.

Rowse, A. L. (1963). What is History? Rowse, A.L. *The use history.* The English Universities Press Ltd. 8–15.

Shona, W. S. (2013). Reforming the law (Commission): A crisis of identity? *Public Law*, 20–29.

Soyinka, W. (2009) Lecture delivered at the centenary anniversary of the late chief Obafemi Awolowo in *This Day.* 20.

The Report by Sir F. D. Lugard on the amalgamation of Northern and Southern Nigeria, and administration, 1912–1919. Presented to the parliament by the command of His Majesty. (London: His Majesty's Statutory Office), December, 1919, 8.

Usman, P. M. (2014). Groundwork of Nigerian Arts. Haytee Press and Publishing Company. 1, 3, 7–16, 22–30, 34–53, 56–59, 62–98.

Webber N. and Donatius K. (2008). The Ranking of heritage resources and sites in legislation. Webber Ndoro, Albert Mumma and George Abungu (eds.), *Cultural heritage and law protecting immovable heritage in English speaking countries of sub-saharan Africa.* 37–38.

Workshop to Ratify and Adopt the Draft Laws of NCMM. News bulletin, national commission for museums and monuments. A monthly publication of NCMM, November 2012, Vol. 3, No. 11. 1.

CHAPTER 3

Film and Cultural Diplomacy in Postcolonial Africa: Nollywood and the Nigeria Cultural Policy

Taiwo Afolabi, Tunde Onikoyi, and Stephen O. Okpadah

INTRODUCTION

In an age of globalization and digitalization, the exposure of numerous people and their impression of other cultures are offered or made available through the creative outputs of the film industry. It is not surprising that

T. Afolabi · S. O. Okpadah
Centre for Socially Engaged Theatre, University of Regina, Regina, SK, Canada
e-mail: Taiwo.afolabi@uregina.ca

T. Afolabi
Department of Sociology, University of Johannesburg, Johannesburg, South Africa

T. Onikoyi
Department of Film, University of Regina, Regina, SK, Canada

S. O. Okpadah (✉)
Department of Theatre and Performance Studies, University of Warwick,

© The Author(s), under exclusive license to Springer Nature Singapore Pte Ltd. 2022
T. Afolabi et al. (eds.), *Re-centering Cultural Performance and Orange Economy in Post-colonial Africa*,
https://doi.org/10.1007/978-981-19-0641-1_3

people's first impression of the American culture is through Hollywood. Creative outputs such as video films, online streaming of movies, cinema and documentaries provide viewers with a rich plethora of visual contents to learn about other people, places and cultures without necessarily being present or on site. By and large, the film industry has become one of the lenses through which we attempt to understand, know, perceive and imagine others. This is due largely to the idea that it offers the possibility to exchange ideas and information about something, someone and some place. For instance, Taiwo Afolabi, one of the authors, had a first-hand experience of the global impact of Nollywood upon visiting Iran in 2017 as member of a team of global-theater-experts to discuss the potentials of the new independent theater sector. His contact person upon hearing that he was coming said she had to get acquainted with Nigerian culture by watching some Nollywood movies online. From the movies she saw, she learnt to offer greetings in pidgin; and pronounced some words that were familiar to Nigerians. He was really impressed as they shared personal experiences about interacting with other cultures through the cinema.

The idea of *exchange* aligns with, Milton Cumming's (2003) definition of cultural diplomacy as "the exchange of ideas, information, values, systems, traditions, beliefs, and other aspects of culture, with the intention of fostering mutual understanding" (p. 1). This portends that both the created content and the creative content are part of the exchange process and they represent a people, culture and location. This notion of representation was reiterated at the 2007 Zuma Film Festival (formerly known as the National Film Festival) held in Abuja (Nigeria's Federal Capital Territory) when John Oluwagbenga, the festival director noted that whether there is an awareness or not, individuals and institutions involved in developing creative contents such as film, music, performance, archeological discovery or preservation etc., are cultural diplomats. This is because, cultural diplomats use ideas, skills, talents and resources to foster exchange of ideas such as cultural and religious beliefs, values and tradition etc. For instance, cinema is one of the channels through which American pop-culture is produced and circulated globally.

Nollywood, globally recognized as the second largest film producer in the world is not an exception (PwC, 2017). Nollywood caters for over

---

Warwick, UK
e-mail: okpadahstephen@gmail.com

180 million population and it has garnered tremendous attention over the years due to its cultural and economic impact. For instance, in 2016, Nollywood contributed approximately $600 million to Nigeria's Gross Domestic Product (GDP) (PwC, 2017). In fact, Nollywood is considered a profit-driven industry. With such large production comes economic success, and the presence of the internet provides the opportunity for global transmission and, cross-interaction of culture and traditions. Against this backdrop, with an examination of the Nigerian Cultural Policy, this paper investigates the role of Nollywood in re-centering Nigeria's cultural diplomacy and argues that the Nigerian film industry has been marginalized in the creation of the Nigeria Cultural Policy. Some questions however need to be posed: What is the strategic importance and the role of film industry in the Nigerian cultural policy? How can the cultural policy enable Nollywood to become a channel for forming good public opinion and promoting proper self-image of Nigeria and its citizens?

THE MEDIUM OF FILM AND CULTURAL DIPLOMACY

The film industry is a full-fledged marker for cultural diplomacy because of its potentials to transmit socio-cultural ideas and form public opinion for various nations (Razlogova, 2020). In international politics film culture functions as a vehicle for soft power to advance the cultural visibility of a nation. This is because, although, there is an exchange of ideas of some sort, it does not necessarily mean such exchange is for the purpose of accomplishing mutual understanding. Cinema normally propagates, directs, influences, comments or even dominates others. From Riverwood (Kenya), to Bollywood (India), Hollywood (US) and Nollywood (Nigeria/Ghana) among others, film cultures engage in the business of exchanging cultural ideas. In this paper the focus is on Nollywood for three reasons: *personal* (authors are Nigerians), *functional* (Nollywood's continental economic and cultural impact) and *political* (the use of Nollywood films to amplify the success story from the Africa continent that can promote the African image).

The Conventional Nollywood that ushered in the VHS format in over two decades ago has grown into a global phenomenon (Denzer, 2016). From its global reach to its economic viability and cultural productions, Nollywood has emerged as a hub for millions to encounter some cultural realities in Africa. Nollywood's scope was further broadened when

Netflix, an international provider of on-demand video streaming, created a session for movies from Nollywood. Currently, there are over forty-five Nollywood movies on Netflix, while Youtube and iROKOtv (an online streaming site launched in 2011) offer numerous Nollywood titles. Each title is an opportunity to tell the Nigerian story (Hyanes, 2016, 2018), and share information about African people and their experiences and their place in the world. Through the movies they are offered the opportunity to express their identity and taking ownership of the African experiences because, one of the goals of cultural diplomacy is to use culture to promote positive self-image and the right perception (Brook, 2019).

Cultural diplomacy is a soft power strategy to exercise co-optive power (Nye, 1990). In his book, *Soft Power*, Joseph Nye, Harvard political scientist suggested three key sources for a country's soft power: "its culture (in places where it is attractive to others), its political values (when it lives up to them at home and abroad), and its foreign policies (when they are seen as legitimate and having moral standards and authority)" (Nye, 2004a: 11).These sources direct the public diplomatic strategy of a country. Nye would later identify three dimensions of public diplomacy: daily communications, strategic planning and "the development of lasting relationships with key individuals over many years through scholarships, exchanges, training, seminars, conferences, and access to media channels" (Nye, 2011: 43). In addition to the earlier identified attribute of cultural diplomacy which is exchange, Richard Arndt opines that cultural relations and diplomacy refer to those "aspects of intellect and education lodged in any society that tend to cross-border and connect with foreign institutions" (2015).

The notion of *border-crossing* is important to our analysis here. The art and act of sharing creative works and productions (in this context film) involves "crossing the border" which mostly happens virtually in recent times. Although, culture relations grow naturally and organically, "[cultural diplomacy involves] the promotion of cultural values to articulate national interests" (quoted in Tim Rivera, 2015, p. 10). Herein lies the transnational trend in filmmaking. Transnational Hollywood and Bollywood had been in the foray for decades. Perhaps this stems from the fact that the origin of these two film industries dates back to the early twentieth century. Hollywood and Bollywood have transported, American and Indian epistemes to the world. Transnational Nollywood cinema began in the twenty-first century as it witnessed an upsurge in this trend in filmmaking. Mathias Krings and Onookome Okome (2013) employed the term, "Global Nollywood" to refer to the transnational Nigerian film industry that goes beyond the frontiers of the Nigerian nation-state. (2013: 4).

To further concretize the development that characterized Nollywood, Jonathan Haynes theorized the shift initiated by a new crop of filmmakers as "New Nollywood." He captures this in his essay, *New Nollywood: Kunle Afolayan*: "It is a phrase being used to describe a recent strategy by Nigerian filmmakers to make films with high budgets, to screen them in cinemas both in Nigeria and abroad and to enter them in international film festivals" (Haynes, 2014, p. 53). Other filmmakers like Jeta Amata (*Black November*) and Chineze Anyaene (*Ije: The Journey*) have contributed to popularizing this trend in Nollywood. The Nigerian comedian turned filmmaker, Ayo Makun (popularly known as AY) contributed to the universalization of transnational Nollywood with his intercontinental filmmaking engagements. In films such as *30 Days in Atlanta* (2014), *10 Days in Sun City* (2016) and *American Driver* (2017), he employs the use of multiple national setting and crisis of lingua franca. In other words, he transports Nigeria's Yoruba, Urhobo and Pidgin languages to other national spaces. These exceptional efforts contributed to fostering Nigeria's diplomatic ties with the world. The success of all of the above no doubt cannot be divorced from the creation of the Nigeria's Cultural Policy. The promotion of values and national interests take place through the exchange and border-crossing of ideas and information.

THE NIGERIAN CULTURAL POLICY OF 1988

The Cultural Policy for Nigeria, promulgated in 1988, is "a well written document, which takes the cultural diversification of the diverse ethnic groups into consideration. It explores the role of government in the administration of culture for national development." The policy also focuses on "issues of development and the place of leadership which Nigeria finds herself in the polity of African nations (Yerima, 2010: 10). At the attainment of independence in October 1, 1960, the Nigerian government considered it significant to produce an indigenous based cultural policy that would spur and develop traditional Nigerian cultures. In 1977, the Festival of Arts and Culture was hosted by Nigeria. According to Uzoma (2013), venues for the festival included the "Mbari Cultural Centre, Owerri, Imo State; Ogun State Council for Arts and Culture,

Kuto, Abeokuta; Cross River Council for Arts and Culture in Calabar, and Oyo State Council for Arts and Culture, Mokola, Ibadan, built to complement the National Arts Theatre, Lagos during the FESTAC 77" (23). Unfortunately, after the FESTAC exercise, a fully-fledged cultural policy could not be created. The 1988 Cultural policy has eight cardinal points. The policy shall:

1. Promote creativity in the field of arts, science and technology, ensure the continuity of traditional skills and sports and their progressive updating to serve modern development needs as our contribution to world growth of culture and ideas.
2. Promote national cultural, and an educational system that stimulates creativity and draws largely on national tradition and values of respect for humanity, human dignity and respect for positive Nigerian moral and religious values.
3. Mobilize and motivate the people by disseminating and propagating ideas which promote national pride, solidarity and consciousness.
4. Establish and reinforce code of behavior compatible with our tradition of humanism and disciplined moral society.
5. Provide sustainable environmental and social conditions to enhance the quality of life, produce responsible citizenship and ordered society.
6. Enhance the efficient management of national resources through the transformation of the indigenous technology, design-resources and skills.
7. Foster national self-reliance, self-sufficiency, and reflect our cultural heritage and national aspirations in the process of industrialization (Cultural Policy for Nigeria, 1988: 4).

Adedokun and Osedebamen (2014), reveal further that in the cultural policy of Nigeria, "the state shall preserve and present oral tradition, folklore, poetry, drama, essays, novels and short stories through the theatre, film, video and audio tapes and in written form, and popularize them by producing them in Nigerian languages and promoting them through the school system, language centres, writers' workshops, book development councils, the media, etc." (182). It is explicit that from the foregoing, the medium of film is not fully represented in the 1988 Nigeria Cultural Policy.

Postcolonial Africa and the Marginalization of Nollywood in the Nigeria Cultural Policy

Africa's fifty-four states are diverse, resilient and rich in culture and traditions. The continent has had its share of phenomenal events that have created a downturn in its growth and development—slave trade, colonialism, civil wars, military coups etc. Also, "the danger of a single story," the shameful realities of African politics, and the socio-economic experiences of many Africans have created for the continent, a negative reputation and poor image in the global space. In fact, Africa could be likened to what the African economic scholar, Paul Collier termed *the Bottom Billion*. In his argument, "the plight of the 'bottom billion' is, they are caught in one (or often several) of four traps; (i) conflict; (ii) mismanaged dependency on natural resources; (iii) weak governance in a small country; and (iv) economic isolation among other very poor economies, with access to big markets available only at a high cost. Or as he puts it in the African context, landlocked with bad neighbours" (Collier, 2007: 1). Collier's observation among other realities has created a generalized evaluation of the continent which adversely affects the identities, realities and inter-relations of the African in international spaces. Yet, African cultural resources and traditions are still sought after from the tangible to the intangible cultural assets including but not limited to the Safaris, cultural festivals, architecture, performances and film industry. Nollywood is rooted in the flow of culture and capitals across West Africa. Through collaboration with other film cultures, Nollywood's foremost and emerging stars have raised standards of this creative industry in manifold ways. Nigeria and Africa's fast-changing cultures have arguably become visible through the lens of the camera (Matheson, Okpadah & Raj, 2020).

The film culture functions as a form of soft power- in international politics to advance cultural visibility (Cooke, 2016). For instance, Cooke underscores how soft power, is inherent in the film culture with a case study of BRICS group of emerging nations (Brazil, Russia, India, China and South Africa). With a focus on China's presence and influence in Hollywood, Cooke argues that cinema plays an important role in capturing soft power, and the BRICS in global politics. The case should not be different in Nigeria because video art is widespread and its uses are socio-culturally and economically significant (Haynes, 1997, Ogunleye, 2004, Adesokan, 2012). It also has "the ability to attract people to our side without coercion" (Nye, 1990, p. 166). For instance, many Nollywood films were made to promote Nigerian culture or cultural misunderstanding; document history or critique political realities on the continent with films such as *Saworoide* (1999); *Osuofia in London* (2003); *Somewhere in Africa: The Cries of Humanity* (2011); *Invasion 1897* (2014); *October 1* (2014); *93 Days* (2016), *Wedding Party* (2016) and *Up North* (2018) among others. This array of selected movies points to the opportunity for Nollywood to take on the role of effectively utilizing the soft power of film culture by selling to the world positive images, representation and perception of Nigeria. Although, the initial motivation of filmmaking in Nollywood may have been purely commercial, there is a need to leverage existing creative contents, histories of productions and current reach for "power of attraction" in international foreign relations (Nye, 2004a, p. ix). The soft power of culture has to be effectively instrumentalized. To achieve this goal, it is crucial to engage a robust legislation and policy to incentivize. Hence, in what ways can the Nigerian cultural policy promote re-centering Nollywood for effective and functional cultural diplomacy? The 1988 Nigeria cultural policy is a document prescribing guidelines, procedures, methods and practice of culture in the country. There was a draft of a revised cultural policy in 2008 with little or no difference. The goals of the policy are to mobilize and motivate the people by disseminating and propagating ideas that promote national pride, solidarity and consciousness. Its aim is.

> to create an evolution of national culture from a plurality or diversity perspective; promote an educational system that motivate and stimulate creativity and draws largely on indigenous values; promote creativity in the fields of arts, science, technology and ensure continuity of traditional skills and sports and updating them to serve modern development; establish a code of behavior compatible with our tradition of humanism and disciplined moral society; sustain environmental and social conditions that enhance the quality of life, responsible citizenship and an ordered society; enhance efficient management of national resources through the transformation of indigenous technology and skills; and preserve national self-reliance and sufficiency and reflection of cultural heritage and national

aspiration in the process of industrialization. (Cultural Policy for Nigeria, 1988: 5)

It is emphasized that the role of the Nigeria Cultural Policy is to protect, preserve and promote Nigerian Culture. According to the 1999 constitution, there are different legal and institutional frameworks to implement the cultural policy which include: the copyright act; National Institute for Cultural Orientation Act, National Council for Arts and Culture Act; National Commission for Museums and Monuments Act; the National Broadcasting Commission Act; The Nigerian Tourism Development Corporation Act; the Centre for Black and African Arts and Civilization Act; and National Gallery of Art Act.

Interestingly, there is little or no reference to cinema in the cultural policy and its role in promoting and preserving culture. It is important to note that the **National Film and Video Censors Board (NFVCB)** is the regulatory body set up by Act No.85 of 1993 to regulate the films and video industry in Nigeria. "The Board is empowered by law to classify all films and videos whether imported or produced locally. It is also the duty of the Board to register all films and video outlets across the country and to keep a register of such registered outlets among other functions such registered outlets among other functions across the country and to keep a register of such registered outlets among other functions" (NFVCB website). In other words, the NFVCB is saddled with the duty of making decisions on which video film is suitable for audience consumption or not in Nigeria. There is no clear articulation of cinema (Nollywood) as a critical tool for cultural diplomacy and ways to strengthen this creative cinematic industry. It is pertinent to note that during the colonial era, the Colonial Film Unit (CFU) was established to create a film culture in Nigeria. According to Haynes (1997: 3), "the British had a Colonial Film Unit which produced documentaries and propaganda, thereby introducing some cinematic technology and skills into the country…" The Federal Film Unit came in 1974 after the CFU with the attempt to indigenize the Nigerian film industry. This was precursory to independence. The FFU could not improve on the challenges of the CFU. In Shehu's (1992) argument;

> Instead of building a resourceful inter-African corporation, and commercial exchange in this lucrative industry, we are still tied around the mentality of colonial arrangement. Although the Nigerian Enterprises Promotion Act

1977 (Indigenisation Decree) was aimed at correcting these neo-colonialist tendencies in our filmmaking and distribution, any serious investigation will reveal that many of our film exhibition centres are owned by Nigerian fronts on behalf of the foreigners. (p. 20)

The indigenous Nigerian film policy is faced with the challenges signaled in the above quote. In 1979, the Nigerian Film Corporation was established and placed under the supervision of the Federal Ministry of Information and Culture. "It is a frontline film Agency aimed at laying a viable and sustainable film industry and cinema culture in Nigeria" (NFC, 2020). The Nigeria Film Institute, Jos, was also established to train actors, directors, costumiers, editors, makeup artists, cinematographers among others. However, the desired result of the institute has not been achieved. This notwithstanding, apart from the fact that the strategic importance and the role of the film industry in the Nigerian cultural policy is to preserve and propagate culture, Nigeria supports UNESCO's *Convention on the Protection and Promotion of Diversity of Cultural Expressions* in principle with significant efforts from individuals and citizens. The unprecedented growth and shift, of the Nigerian film culture calls for a film policy that can incentivize investors, leverage the global economy and promote industry personnel. The film policy in Nigeria should be designed to regulate and support measures for creation and development, production, distribution, conservation and promotion. It should also promote other aspects, such as access to credit, use of new technologies and external promotion.

Nollywood as the Postcolonial Cinema

The Nollywood film industry emerged as a popular cultural industry, as well as a (essentially) a postcolonial cinema. This is because the engagements associated with the filmmaking culture in Nigeria compels the industry's serious cineastes to address the myriad predicaments and problems that a failed state such as Nigeria can anticipate as consequences; following the consistent, incessant and obnoxious leadership, which was indirectly responsible for the crushed fabric of the Nigerian society. The question to be asked is: under what condition/context/scenario did Nollywood emerge? What particularly led to the evolution of Nollywood as a postcolonial film industry? The brief existence of celluloid filmmaking in Nigeria, and its eventual demise occurred as a result of the economic decline during the mid-1980s. A good number of prominent filmmakers including; Francis Oladele, Ola Balogun, Eddie Ugbomah and many others, experienced the hardship of the economic problems, during the period.

Following the horrendous economic quagmire, film production became challenging, as filmmakers were unable to sustain the status quo of entertainment. In order to remain in business filmmakers like Tunde Kelani decided to make films by making use of the rather substandard video camera. Not only was it assessable to most filmmakers, but it "was" as Valeri Orlando would put it, "very cheap and made film easier to produce" (Orlando, 2017: 60) Tunde Onikoyi also stressed that, "films were more than enough to satisfy the markets, as productions increased to about a hundred films and more in a week. Audiences in Lagos and elsewhere had the opportunity to stay in the comfort of their homes and treat themselves to films on their video players" (2021: 5). The economic, social and insecurity challenges were extremely problematic, and people were compelled to remain in their various homes to see their preferred movies. This strategy also contributed to the decline in the cinema-going-culture, including the high crime rates, and breakdown of law and order, even up to the 1990s.

Entertainment reemerged in the 1990s onwards. Although, of a low-quality, the video-technology represented an alternative means to entertainment for the state holders of the industry, and a postcolonial reaction to the decline of the more established cinema culture, which did not offer the audiences to opportunity to see most of the films produced, by the first generation of Nigerian filmmakers. While most of the filmmakers were not exactly trained filmmakers, there efforts have helped to sustain till today, a cinema culture which has managed to develop into a strong global cinema: both in transnational and international terms.

Postcolonial Nigerian Film/Cinema, and Cultural Policy: What is to Be Done?

The Nigerian film industry (Nollywood) is constantly recording giant strides. Not only has it become the Centre of attraction on the African continent, but it has become a major industry which is gradually attaining global visibility and recognition. From the production of local cinematic works, to continental cinematic projects, diaspora (or what Hamid Naficy has rightly termed "Accented Cinemas"(2001) films and global intended film, situated specifically at the Global North, are indeed ground-breaking accomplishments, which Nigerian film directors and filmmakers have all painstakingly created, in order to show the world that, not only can Nigeria films exhibit a lot about the Nigerian culture, arts and social realities, but has the potential to provide the world with enough details about the country, through creative apparatus of lasting substance.

While it is true that Nigerian cinema has become a popular cinema within a postcolonial condition and framework, the industry is not devoid of its generated intractable controversies, "about its place in the production of culture, in postcolonial Nigeria" (Saul & Austin, 2010). Critics have argued that the development and neglect of popular arts in Nigeria has always generated social debates, most of which are beclouding the significance of such productions and their place in the life of those who live with the debilities that they inscribe. Even though we may have reasons to show that in recent times, such attitudes are beginning to be altered, there are still dominant critiques refused to accept the social significance of these forms of expression in Nigeria and indeed Africa. Such historical abnegation can be attributed to the educational regime that colonialism offered to African nations. This is also partly connected to what Chinua Achebe (as Onookome Okome puts it) had earlier described as "anxiety of the postcolonial." (1).

The legislation of an art is very important, and Nollywood could benefit immensely from this state act. But in order to legislate a popular art such as Nollywood, it is important for the so-called cultural mediators to understand the dynamics of the production of cultural materials, in relation to the basic conception and knowledge about the postcolonial condition that warrants the production of the cultural materials. To legislate Nollywood, would mean to understand the basic objects of enquiries that foster the production of the films within the industry.

The goal of Nigeria's cultural mediators is obvious. It is to bring Nigeria to the world in a certain way. There is good reason to focus this effort on Nollywood, which is as socially and as culturally rich in Nigeria as it is popular across the continent. What is inscribed in the texts of Nollywood films are the cultural and political debates of the day. The debates may be localized but, they have deeper implications for the continent of Africa and its Diasporas. After the demise of celluloid filmmaking in the 1980s, Nollywood has risen rapidly from a corner of the social life of the people of Nigeria to the center of its cultural and economic attraction. When it fought its way into this space of attraction, it was met with stiff opposition from observers who consider it less than an art form. The situation, however, is quite different now, as Nollywood is constantly inscribed in the serious realm of Nigeria's postcoloniality.

Conclusion and Recommendations

Since there is no provision in the cultural policy that Nollywood can leverage upon, there is a need for a robust framework in the cultural policy that will raise the consciousness of Nollywood as a viable cultural representative. Such a framework will not only strengthen the vibrant film industry, but it will also empower practitioners to better understand their roles in rebranding and promoting better image of the country. Nollywood films have become a unique means of communication and can be reshaped as a tool, to promote positive social transformation. To achieve this goal, Nollywood filmmakers should be able to negotiate certain formations of guidance, defined by a cultural and film policy that, among other things, encourage filmmakers to mobilize and motivate the people by disseminating ideas which promote national pride, solidarity and consciousness.

A cultural policy for film in Nigeria needs to conceive film as an important means of communication and an equally important culture specific contribution. The objectives of the policy, in as much as film is concerned, must be richly unique. These objectives must be spelt out in details which are as follows:

1. Establish a strong and sustainable profit-oriented film industry.
2. Preserve rich cultural heritage.
3. Serve as a tool of national cohesion, public enlightenment, education and entertainment.
4. Expand Nigeria's sphere of influence through export of our cultural values.
5. Serve as a significant instrument for national integration, unity and international image building.
6. Encourage the production and exportation of Nigerian films in view of the potential of film as earner of foreign exchange.

Some guidelines, however, should be spelt out in the development of a well-funded cultural policy for film which in effect should energize the potentials of Nollywood films, and what they are expected to contain. Some projected guidelines might include exploiting our heroic past and cultural heritage in the production of films, designed for both local and external consumption, explore themes that emphasize the desirable-rather than the negative formations of our present social existence including; the belief in the capacity of our people to overcome extreme adverse conditions of nature and socio-cultural arrangements, development of indigenous heroes and heroines that can serve as models for our people in all areas of human endeavors- political leadership, military, science and warfare, education, science and technology moral character and trust, integrity, hard work and concern for the sanctity of human life and its protection, tolerance and so on. Also, there could be the deliberation of employment of film potentials in inculcating in the generality of our people the virtues inherent in our diverse cultures and people. In the same vein, there should be deliberate employment of film potentials to propagate the desirable aspects of our national character, values and cultures internally and externally and the employment of film potentials to counter racial bigotry and prejudices of our international community.

The above are suggested ideas for the construction of a template of Cultural/Film Policy. Innovative ideas can be provided to complement a system-text that aspires to promote the potential desires of a unique-policy-document. Nollywood films produced in the current times are improving by the day. The creators of New Nollywood are poised and determined to produce cinematic productions that meet global standards—as they are entered in film festivals at international level, nominated for awards, screened at both local and international cinemas etc. Nollywood films have become potent forces in value system and re-orientation that resonates well with the familiar modernity that defines the citizen's current existence. A potential policy will help show how film, remains a significant cultural tool, which can also be a vehicle for advancing cultural and human rights and empowerment. Our discussion in this paper, illustrate the ways in which Nollywood have been (can still be) able to safeguard and promote Nigeria's distinctive diversity, in homogenizing ethnic boundaries in the current postcolonial times.

REFERENCES

Adedokun, R., & Osademamen, D. (2014). Managing storytelling as performance and cultural enterprise, In S. Ododo., & S. Fosudo (Eds.), *Marketing contemporary Nigerian theatre and cultural entertainment* (pp. 170–182), SONTA.

Arndt, R. (2005). *The first resort of kings: American cultural diplomacy in the twentieth century.* Dulles: Brassey.

Brook, S. (2019). "Uncertain Embrace: The rise and fall of Canadian studies abroad as a tool of foreign policy". In *Promoting canadian studies abroad: Soft power and cultural diplomacy* (S. Brooks, ed). Palgrave Macmillan. 1–36

Collier. P. (2007). *The bottom billion: Why the poorest countries are failing and what can be done about it.* Oxford University Press.

Cooke, P. (2016). Soft power, film culture and the BRICS. *New Cinemas, 14*(1), 3–15.

Cumming, Milton. (2003). *Cultural diplomacy and the United States government: A survey.* Centre for Art and Culture.

Denzer, L. (2016). The Nollywood phenomenon. *Britannica*

Ekwuazi, H. (1992). *Film in Nigeria.* Jos: Nigerian Film Cooperation.

Elam, J. (2019). *The postcolonial theory.*Oxford Bibliographies

Federal Republic of Nigeria (1988). *Cultural policy for Nigeria.* Federal Government Printers.

Haynes, J. (1997). Nigerian cinema: Structural adjustments. In O. Okome & J. Haynes (Eds.), *Cinema and social change in West Africa* (pp. 1–25). Nigerian Film Corporation.

Haynes, J. (2014). New Nollywood: Kunle Afolayan. *Black Camera., 5*(2), 53–73.

_____. (1997). *Nigerian video films.* Jos: Nigerian Film Corporation.

_____. (2016). Nollywood: The creation of Nigerian film genres. University Press.

_____. (2018). "Keeping up: The corporatization of Nollywood's economy and paradigms for studying African screen media". *Africa Today.* 64(4): pp. 3–29

Krings, Matthais, and Okome, Onookome. (2013). *Global Nollywood. The transnational dimension of an African video film industry.* Indiana Minneapolis: University of Indiana Press.

Ndlovu-Gatsheni, S., J. (2013). Coloniality of power in postcolonial Africa: Myths of decolonization. Dakar: Council for the development of social science research in Africa (CODESRIA)

Naficy, H. (2001). *An accented cinema: Exilic and diasporic filmmaking.* University Press.

Nigeria gears up for 1st Zuma film festival. *AfrolNews* .http://www.afrol.com/articles/18287

Nye, J. (1990). Soft power. *Foreign Policy*. (80): 153–170 Retrieved 28th September, 2020 from https://doi.org/10.2307/1148580

———. (2004a). *Soft power: The means to success in world politics*. New York: Public Affairs.

———. (2004b). *Power in the global information age: From realism to globalization*. Routledge.

———. (2011). *The future of power*. Public Affairs.

Oral interview with Arnold Udoka. National theatre, Orile-Iganmu, Lagos, 5th April, 2016.

Ogunleye, F. (2004). A report from the front: The Nigerian video film. *Quarterly Review of Film and Video*, 21(2), 79–88.

Onikoyi, T. (2021). Interview with Tunde Kelani. *African Studies Review.*, 64(1), 1–25.

Okome, O. (2002). "Writing the anxious city: images of Lagos in Nigerian Home video Films", in *Under siege: Four African cities-freetown, Johannesburg, Kinshasa, and Lagos*, ed. Okwui Enwezor et al. Kassel: Hatje Cantz. pp. 315–334.

Orlando, V. (2017). *Quick takes, movies and popular culture: New African cinema*. Rutgers University Press.

Matheson, S., Okpadah, S., and Raj, P.E., (Eds.), (2020). *Locating transnational spaces: Culture, theatre and cinema*. IATC and UCN.

O' Brien, T. (2018). *The Bottom Billion: Why the poorest countries are failing and what can be done about it: Some insights for the Pacific?* Routledge.

PwC Report (2017). Perspectives from the global entertainment and media outlook 2017–2021. https://www.pwc.com/gx/en/entertainment-media/pdf/outlook-2017-curtain-up.pdf

Razlogova, E. (2020). World cinema at Soviet festivals: Cultural diplomacy and personal ties. *Studies in European Cinema*, 17(2), 140–154. https://doi.org/10.1080/17411548.2019.1686893

Rivera, T. (2015.) Distinguishing cultural relations from cultural diplomacy. *CPD Perspectives on Public Diplomacy*. Figueroa. https://uscpublicdiplomacy.org/sites/uscpublicdiplomacy.org/files/useruploads/u33041/Distinguishing%20Cultural%20Relations%20From%20Cultural%20Diplomacy%20-%20Full%20Version%20(1).pdf

Saul, M., & Ralph, A. (2010). *Viewing Africa in the twenty first century: Arts films and the Nollywood video revolution*. Ohio University Press.

Shehu, B. (1992). "Decolonisation of the film industry: Role of policy". In: Hyginus. Ekwuazi and Yakubu, Nasidi (Eds.), *No not Hollywood: Essays & speeches of Brendan Shehu* (pp. 19–34), Jos: Nigerian Film Corporation

Welcome to NFC. (2020). Retrieved 25th September, 2020 from www.nfc.gov.ng/

Yerima, A. (2010). "An appraisal of the Nigerian cultural policy". In: Emmanuel, Dandaura and Abdul Rasheed, Adeoye (Eds.), *Culture, identity and leadership in Nigeria,* (pp. 37–47). Ibadan: Kraft Books Ltd.

CHAPTER 4

Pan-Africanism and Cultural Policy Management: A Formative Evaluation of Nigeria and Ghana's Cultural Policies

Osedebamen David Oamen

INTRODUCTION

The bitter experiences of African slaves and those who had just been emancipated from slavery, whose hopes were dashed by the US Supreme Court's 1857 ruling that freed slaves could not become citizens of the United States, re-energized the struggle for Pan-Africanism. Colonized Africans' struggle to liberate themselves from the yoke of imperialist rule added momentum to this movement. The Pan-African Conference was held in London in 1900. Further congresses have been convened over the decades to address the political, economic and social challenges confronted by Africans in their place of birth and in the diaspora. Thus, "Pan-Africanism is … considered to be the struggle against slavery and

---

O. D. Oamen (✉)
Department of Theatre and Media, Arts, Faculty of Arts, Ambrose Alli University, Ekpoma, Nigeria

© The Author(s), under exclusive license to Springer Nature Singapore Pte Ltd. 2022
T. Afolabi et al. (eds.), *Re-centering Cultural Performance and Orange Economy in Post-colonial Africa*,
https://doi.org/10.1007/978-981-19-0641-1_4

systemic discrimination that blacks in the diaspora and Africa collectively faced" (Eugene Benigo Nwikina 2).

Imperialism and xenophobic practices also belittled African peoples' cultures. The assertion that "Xenophobia is historically and in modern times a very systemic, political, social and economic manifestation of imperialism" (Sechaba Khoapa 1) remains valid in the post-colonial era and Pan-Africanism is an effective instrument against such attacks. While it has become synonymous with the struggles of Black people of whatever kind, this chapter focuses on Pan-Africanism's cultural dimensions and whether these have influenced cultural policy's formative content, particularly in Nigeria and Ghana where the early members of the Pan-African movement were very active. This is important in promoting a twenty-first-century Pan-African ideology toward forging a new identity which goes beyond racial emancipation to assert Africans' social, economic, political and scientific identity.

Literature Review

Pan-Africanism's roots lie in diverse opinions and views that shaped its discourse. It is, however, a continuum that extends to the future of Black people because of its major impact on their struggles around the world. In common with all struggles in life, the voyage has not been a smooth one, but as the ship that brings Africans together, Pan-Africanism still sails the seas to promote Black people's social, political, economic and cultural liberation. "At first, the Pan-African movement was really a Pan-Negro movement, centered in America, to unite the Negro people of Africa and America in the fight against racialism and colonialism" (Ivan Potekhin 39). Its positive achievements enabled it to extend its efforts to other areas. "Pan-Africanism started as a political movement with its own ideological basis at the end of the nineteenth century and has since followed a very complicated, contradictory course as it originated in America" (Potekhin 37–38). During the course of its development, its ideology was further distilled, and it is now being drawn on in areas where it originally held no sway. Pan-Africanism's political struggle yielded outstanding results, not only in Africa but across the world. However, "The struggle for political power ... is the first step towards, and the necessary prerequisite, to complete social, economic and political emancipation" (Marika Sherwood 109). Given widespread racism, oppression and exploitation of Africans, it was "urgent to refute the 'theory' of white racial superiority and show that the Negro was a human being and that black skinned people were no worse than white-skinned people" (Potekhin 38).

The assumed inferior nature of Black people was grounds for whites to assume superiority. Furthermore, Black people's products and services were also deemed inferior. Such notions of superiority were fiercely resisted by the Pan-Africanist ideology. This is not to suggest that some Black people did not benefit from the racial and colonial ideology. Indeed, there were those that hid behind the flag of Pan-Africanism to undermine Africa's quest for unity, total independence and development (Potekhin 13). Direct or indirect support for colonial elements by Black people who ought to have spoken out against racism and colonialism was a setback for those at the frontline of Pan-Africanism. However, the movement persisted in its struggle for the political, economic and social emancipation of Black people. For many decades, culture was not part of the Pan-Africanist lexicon. However, it was anticipated that "A common language should be found which all could speak in addition of their own tongues" (Sherwood 7). The situation changed with the convening of the 1947/1948 conference in West Africa, "where cultural representatives were allowed to represent their people" (Sherwood 9). The Cultural Manifesto adopted at the first Pan-African Cultural Festival held in Algiers in July/August 1969 under the aegis of Organization of African Unity (OAU) placed culture firmly on the agenda of Pan-Africanism. Its contents were expected to form the nucleus of the national and foreign cultural policies of African countries and to promote "the forging of a new African identity in the twenty-first century" (Sherwood 3). Given Nigeria and Ghana's contribution to the Pan-African movement, it is assumed that their cultural policies would incorporate the recommendations of the Pan-African Cultural Manifesto. Nigeria's cultural policy was adopted in 1988, while Ghana's came into existence in 2004.

Theoretical Framework

This chapter draws on Pan-Africanist theories and the theories expressed in the Pan-African Cultural Manifesto of Algiers (1969) as well as the proceedings of the Inter-governmental Conference on Cultural Policies in Africa organized by UNESCO in Accra in 1975 in cooperation with the OAU, which declared "that all cultures emanate from the people, and that any African cultural policy should of necessity enable the people to expand for increased responsibility in the development of its cultural heritage" (UNESCO 1). These theories form the bedrock of the movement's objectives and continue to inform its contemporary focus. In the first instance, "Pan-Africanism is … a reaction to colonial enslavement in Africa and racial discrimination against the descendants of African slaves in America; it is an ideological and political means of fighting racism and colonialism" (Sherwood 39). While it initially excluded culture, it was later acknowledged that culture is an integral part of the struggle against racism and colonialism. This is because, "any people has the inalienable right to organize its cultural life in full harmony with its political, economic, social, philosophical and spiritual ideas" (OAU 1). Furthermore, "Culture is the sum total of experiences and concrete expressions, linked to the history of peoples. Thus culture, from our point of view, must embrace the particular expressions that characterized each major civilization. But our Africanity is determined by profound similarities and common aspirations" (OAU 2). Culture is thus an important factor in achieving African unity. The Pan-African Cultural Manifesto recognized that the African personality revolves around cultural values. "The idea of the African personality was propounded at the first conference of independent African States in 1958; this idea means recognizing that Africa has its own personality, its own history and its own culture and that it has made valuable contributions to world history and world culture" (Potemkin 4). Pan-Africanism's recognition of culture as an instrument of emancipation added value to the pursuit and realization of its objectives, as all human activity is linked to culture. The Manifesto also noted that, "African culture, art and science, whatever the diversity of their expression, are in no way essentially different from each other. They are but the specific expression of a single universality" (African Union 2). Thus, culture is the sum total of experiences and concrete expressions, linked to the history of peoples. While it must embrace the particular expressions that characterize each major civilization, Africanity is determined by profound similarities and common aspirations (OAU 2).

This profound view reveals the strength of African culture as a bond and an instrument to be used against the oppressor. Cultural similarities and aspirations were recognized as valuable African resources. The recognition of culture strengthened Pan-Africanism and was expected to enhance African nations' cultural relations. Thus, individual countries' cultural policies should seek to harness culture in the contemporary struggle against neocolonialism and racism.

Pan-Africanism and Culture Exclusion

The 1900 conference held in London at the instance of Henry Sylvester Williams—a Trinidadian who was studying to become a lawyer—was held under the auspices of the African Association. The African Association was later renamed the Pan-African Association with the following primary objectives:

1. to secure civil and political rights for Africans and their descendants throughout the world;
2. to encourage friendly relations between the Caucasian and African races;
3. to encourage African people everywhere in the educational, industrial and commercial enterprise;
4. to approach Governments and influence legislation in the interests of the black races, and
5. to ameliorate the condition of the oppressed Negro in all parts of the world (Sherwood 2).

These objectives clearly reflect that, when it was launched, the association did not concern itself with culture. The closest it came to doing so was in the sphere of education; however, this concerned education as an enterprise. One of the reasons for this omission could have been that the stakeholders were from different backgrounds and thus did not share a common culture. Furthermore, at the time, there was paucity of research on culture. It can hence be argued that culture was not deliberately excluded from the association's objectives.

Pan-Africanism and the Inclusion of Culture

It was at a conference held in Paris in 1946 as a result of non-representation of French-speaking countries that Nkrumah raised the need for a common language to bridge the language barriers separating the people of Africa. A conference in West Africa noted that "a common language should be found which all could speak in addition to their own tongues" (Sherwood 7). At the conference held in Lagos in 1947/1948, it was agreed for the first time that cultural representatives could represent their nations: "The peoples of West Africa will be represented at this Congress by their political, cultural, or educational organizations,

Trades Unions, Co-operatives or Farmers' Organizations, by their natural rulers, and any group of individuals who desire to attend" (Sherwood 9). This represented endorsement not only of cultural representatives, but also of culture as an instrument with the potential to support the Pan-African crusade against colonialism and racialism and promote continental unity. Recognition of culture's potential led to the adoption of the Cultural Manifesto of 1969 whose content was expected to inform individual nations' cultural policies. However, there is a paucity of research on the extent to which this has occurred. It is against this background that this chapter examines the extent to which Pan-African's stance on culture has influenced the cultural policies of longstanding members of the Pan-African Association, Nigeria and Ghana.

Pan-Africanism and Cultural Management

The negative consequences of cultural exclusion and the need for cultural inclusion informed the adoption of culture as an instrument in the struggle against Western racial and colonial oppression. The Pan-African Cultural Symposium held in July/August 1969 in Algiers gave birth to the Pan-African Cultural Manifesto. The Manifesto is divided into three parts, namely the realities of African culture, the role of African culture in the national liberation struggle and the consolidation of African unity, and the role of African culture in the economic and social development of Africa.

On the realities of African culture, the Manifesto recognized that culture makes a people who they are and gives shape to their lives. It is conceived out of thought, philosophies, science, beliefs, art and languages. These reflect people's social, political, economic and technical endeavors. The Manifesto highlighted the need to return to African values and to undertake critical re-evaluation to purge colonial elements and revalidate their universal benefits for science, and technical and social revolutions. It noted the evil nature of colonialism, particularly the slave trade and political domination which Africa united to overcome. Culture was presented as a social bond, a foundational means of communication even with the outside world. It is also a dynamic force that has the capacity to change in order to work with nature and improve society. The Manifesto noted that the culture imposed by colonialism depersonalized and alienated the African personality and communality and that this called for transformation of the African mind to enable economic and social development. Given that culture is the totality of a peoples' experience, the Africanity in African culture must be determined by common aspirations because "African culture and science, whatever the diversity of their expression, is in no way essentially different from each other." Based on this premise, the Manifesto stressed the need for the development of an all-encompassing African culture devoid of any borrowed elements. While the people were colonized, their innate African identity was not. The Manifesto emphasized the need to revive African languages that reflect the spiritual and material elements in the life of a people. It called for the strengthening of the indomitable African personality, which cannot be depersonalized because of its inborn sense of solidarity, hospitality, mutual aid, brother/sisterhood and human nature which inform the African body of knowledge, and that the future of Africa lies in African hands.

On the role of African culture in the liberation struggle and African unity, the Manifesto held that the only response to colonialism is a liberation struggle. Colonial dominance checked cultural and other development in Africa and raised an elite that sustained a colonial and racist culture. As noted below, despite this, African culture resisted colonial incursions:

> Cultural policy is, first of all, a reflection of the socio-political development of a country.
> During the 1960s culture in Africa served to the ideas of liberation and was used as.
> "decisive weapon in the fight for liberation and against colonialism, racism and.
> apartheid"… That period of African history produced the ideas of Negritude and Pan-
> Africanism (Kristina Bekeno 1).

Thus, the struggle for the liberation of Africa generated structures that developed African culture, which in turn contributed to the achievement of freedom.

On the role of culture in Africa's economic and social development, the Manifesto recognized culture as a liberating force that has the capacity to transform the social and economic environment for the national good and to meet universal standards of living. Hence, African culture should be revived and be utilized in science and technology to defend and preserve African dignity, while adapting to innovation and contemporary developments in order to promote social development. The Manifesto stressed the importance of education and political will, international collaboration and the development of African languages to accommodate scientific thought in order to achieve these objectives. The symposium agreed on 40far-reaching recommendations, which were expected to be incorporated into member states' cultural policies.

Formative Evaluation of the Influence of the Pan-African Cultural Symposium's Recommendations on Nigeria and Ghana's Cultural Policies

Given that Nigeria and Ghana were major, active participants in the Pan-African movement, to what extent did the symposium's recommendations influence their cultural policies? Nigeria adopted its cultural policy in 1988 while that of Ghana came into existence in 2004. While they were formulated long after the Pan-African Cultural Symposium, it was expected that they would reflect its recommendations. Nigeria's cultural policy has three chapters and sub-chapters, while Ghana's has eight chapters and sub-chapters. The objectives of both policies focus on the nation's cultural development. Nigeria's cultural policy does not make explicit mention of Pan-Africanism or anything related to it. The only section that relates to Africa is paragraph 3.2, which states that: "The policy shall serve to evolve from our plurality, a national culture, the stamp of which will be reflected in Africa and world affairs." This reflects Nigeria's relationship with the rest of the continent, which is expected with Pan-Africanism. In contrast, paragraph 3.2.15 of Ghana's cultural policy states that it aims "To promote the harmonization of African cultures in fulfillment of Ghana's objectives of promoting Pan-Africanism." If Africa is to achieve the identity it seeks in contemporary times, harmonization of African culture is essential. The preamble to the *Cultural Manifesto of Africa* states that, "all cultures emanate from the people, and that any African cultural policy should of necessity enable the people to expand for increased responsibility in the development of its cultural heritage" (OAU 1).

Of concern in relation to Ghana's cultural policy is that no provision is made for a cultural policy administration and finance framework, which is set out in the third part of Nigeria's cultural policy. This could hamper effective management of cultural policy in the country.

Eugine Banigo Nwikina observes that, "… the relevance of Pan-Africanism is in its essential doctrine of unity among Africans that is fostered by integration and connectivity" (6), in an era of continental competition, which permeates political, economic, scientific and social activities. Article 30, Part VIII of the Cultural Manifesto that deals with Inter-African Cultural Co-Operation states that:

> The African States acknowledge that it is vital to establish inter-African cultural cooperation as a contribution to the mutual understanding of national cultures and enrichment of African cultures, thus to take the form of a two-way exchange, firstly, among all the countries on the continent and, secondly, between Africa and the rest of the world through specialized institutions like UNESCO. (UNESCO 3)

Cultural integration within the ambit of Pan-Africanism could create a market for cultural goods and services as well as enable a collective stance to be adopted in international cultural spaces within and beyond Africa. To achieve this, there is a need to re-ignite the Cultural Manifesto's call for Africans to return to their cultural roots in order to liberate them from foreign cultural and socio-political entanglement. The desire to rejuvenate Africa's science of art and culture led to the foundation of FESTACT, which took place in Nigeria in 1977. Its objectives were:

> To ensure the revival, resurgence, propagation and promotion of Black and African culture and black and African cultural values and civilization; To present black and African culture in its highest and widest conception; To bring to light the diverse contributions of black and African peoples to the universal currents of thought and arts; To promote black and African artists, performers and writers and facilitate their world acceptance and their access to world outlets; To promote better international and interracial understanding; To facilitate a periodic return to origin in Africa by black artists, writers and performers uprooted to other continents. (OAU 4)

These objectives are expected to be part of every African Union member state's cultural policy with a view to propagating Africanity and dignity and respect for all Black people and Africans. Recognition of the importance of African arts and culture is the first step in harnessing it for the development of the continent and her peoples.

Findings

While Pan-Africanism is not mentioned in Nigeria's cultural policy, but is part of Ghana's cultural policy, the spirit of Pan-Africanism runs through both. This is particularly evident when it comes to intrinsic cultural policy management. However, the extrinsic element, which concerns the harmonization of Africa culture, has not been given the attention it deserves. Given that Nigeria and Ghana were active participants in the Pan-African movement, it could be expected that their cultural policies would reflect the recommendations of the Pan-African Cultural Symposium.

A review of the progress made by African nations who are expected to implement Pan-Africanism in their cultural policies reveals that, in its early stages, Pan-Africanism did not consider culture. Its inclusion was a ground-breaking moment due to the hold culture has on people and how it was manipulated to enable the colonial masters to gain a stranglehold on Africa. This calls fora reversion to the many beneficial aspects of African culture, without which the global space is incomplete.

Pan-Africanism recognized that economic, political and social emancipation were rooted in the culture of the people; thus, culture is a powerful tool for liberation. This recognition prompted the Cultural Symposium to seek ways to reclaim and sustain African culture and restrict racial and colonial culture that was severely dualizing it. However, it is not mandatory for African states to adopt the symposium's recommendations and many countries' cultural policies do not seem to recognize their importance.

Recommendations and Conclusion

Harmonization of African culture, through a comprehensive continental cultural policy which is the extrinsic element of the Pan-African Symposium's recommendations on culture, remains an important objective and it should hence be included in the cultural policies of African Union member states. Management of African culture must be sustained as, in redefining African identify, it is one of the instruments that enhance the struggle against the racial and colonial stranglehold on Africa.

Furthermore, as exemplified in Ghana's case, member states' cultural policies should indicate how they intend to manage or harmonize their cultural policy with the Pan-African recommendations. This is in line with the first sentence of Article 8 of the Charter of African Cultural Renaissance, which states that; "the experience of the previous decades recommends that an in-depth renewal of national and regional approaches in terms of cultural policy be carried out" (OAU 10). The 1969 African Cultural Manifesto noted that, "culture should be a constant search for the people's creative consciousness. Any African cultural policy should, therefore, be based on the necessity of enabling the people to become informed, educated, mobilized and organized so as to make them responsible for their cultural heritage and its development" (OAU 3).

Adoption of the recommendations of the 1969 African Cultural Manifesto would promote Africa's social, political and economic development and go a long way in addressing the scourge of neocolonialism.

The inclusion of cultural inclusion in Pan-Africanism acknowledged the important role it plays in the struggle for freedom. Indeed, culture is the axis of African civilization. The Pan-African Cultural Symposium of 1969 recognized the need for cultural policy as the principal instrument for cultural management in Africa. While Ghana's cultural policy commits the country to promote the objectives of Pan-Africanism, with Nigeria's cultural policy being silent on this issue, it is clear that both policies reflect the spirit and the letter of Pan-Africanism's cultural recommendations. These and other states' cultural policies that are informed by the recommendations have helped to strengthen cultural management on the continent against on-going racism and neocolonialism. Implementation of these principles is crucial in forging a new identity in twenty-first-century Africa. As the Pan-African Cultural Manifesto notes, "culture is the sum total of experiences and concrete expressions, linked to the history of peoples. Thus culture, from our point of view, must embrace the particular expressions that characterize each major civilization. But our Africanity is determined by profound similarities and common aspirations" (OAU 2). Forging a new African identity will depend on Africa's ability to manage her historical-cultural foothold and the foundation was laid by the Pan-African cultural recommendations whose formative content is expected to flow into member states' cultural policies. This is important because:

As African understanding of culture shows, the cultural policy has become an increasingly a decisive factor in country's consolidation, an instrument to improve country's image, to boost tourism potential, to establish cultural ties with other countries, but moreover, there is an understanding that culture is a strategic element of the country's development. (Bekenova 2)

The shift that is required for a new African identity to be achieved was set out in the Pan-African Cultural Symposium's recommendations. Had these recommendations been implemented, there would be no need to seek a new identity, but rather to review an existing one.

References

African Union. (2006). *Charter of African cultural renaissance*. African Union.
Bekenova, Kristina. (2017). Cultural policy in Africa: From liberation to an institution and development. *African Politics and Policy online Journal*, 1–5. www.africanpoliticsandpolicy.com/?p=8340 Retrieved on 4 May, 2019.
Federal Republic of Ghana. (2004). *The cultural policy of Ghana*. National Culture Commission.
Federal Republic of Nigeria. (1988). *Cultural policy of Nigeria*. Department of Culture.
Nwikina, Eugene Banigo. (2002). Pan-Africanism: Its relevance today. Organisation of African Unity. *Cultural Charter for Africa*. https://medium.com/@eugenebanigonwikina/pan-africanism-its-relevance-today-7. Retrieved on 4 April, 2021.
Pan Africanism. (1969). *Pan-African cultural manifesto*. Organisation of African Unity.
Sechaba, Khoapa. (2016). Xenophobia in Southern Africa: A Pan-Africanist perspective for modern times. *Open Access Library Journal, 3* (3). https://www.scirp.org/html/69094_69094.htm, 9.
Sherwood, Marika. (2012). Pan-African conferences, 1900–1953: What did 'Pan-Africanism' mean? *The Journal of Pan African Studies, 4* (10), 106–226. www.jpanafrican.org/docs/vol4no10/4.10Pan-African.pdf. Retrieved on 1 June, 2019.
Wikipedia, the free encyclopedia. "FESTIVAL OF ARTS AND CULTURE" (FESTAC). https://en.wikipedia.org/wiki/FESTAC_77. Retrieved on 23 April 2021.

CHAPTER 5

Dutch-Moroccan Cultural Cooperation? A Discourse on Professional Network

Djamila Boulil

INTRODUCTION: A MORE REALISTIC POINT OF VIEW

International cultural cooperation is a goal that many nations' cultural policies strive for (Fisher, 2007; Kieft, 2018; Wyszomirski et al., 2003). Rather than exporting national culture worldwide (*nation branding*; Minnaert, 2014; Paschalidis, 2009), international cultural relations became more and more focussed on creating equal relationships and supporting some type of understanding between countries who have these cultural bonds (Cummings, 2003; Gienow-Hecht & Donfried, 2010). Originally these bonds were forged as part of *cultural diplomacy* strategies, which refer to the usages of international cultural exchange as instruments to support economic, diplomatic, and political goals (Wallis, 1994). Although successful, this *instrumental use of culture* in cultural policy (Mulcahy, 2010), or *soft power* in governance (Nye, 1990), has

D. Boulil (✉)
Groningen, The Netherlands
e-mail: djamilaboulil@gmail.com

© The Author(s), under exclusive license to Springer Nature Singapore Pte Ltd. 2022
T. Afolabi et al. (eds.), *Re-centering Cultural Performance and Orange Economy in Post-colonial Africa*,
https://doi.org/10.1007/978-981-19-0641-1_5

been critiqued by many academics in arts and culture (Ang et al., 2015; Hadley & Gray, 2017). The claim is made that cultural diplomacy is a form of *neo-colonialism*, with one country using cultural export to oppress the other (Ang et al., 2015), and that making culture a tool for policymakers puts the autonomy of the cultural sector at risk (Hadley & Gray, 2017). However, recently a counterclaim was made that in the international field, when a wish for cooperation is added, the use of international cultural exchange could possibly yield positive results (Carter, 2015).

The social theory behind this claim is that cooperation leads to conversation which in turn leads to understanding (Sennett, 2012). This hypothesis has not been researched much in the field of international cultural relations. Although cultural diplomacy and international cultural cooperation have both been extensively studied, most studies are focussed on relations within Europe or on the relations of the geographical North with Asia. They also use mostly historical examples (Albro, 2015; Carter, 2015; Gienow-Hecht & Donfried, 2010; Iwabunchi, 2015; Jurkovà, 2015; Kang, 2015; Lowe, 2015; Rösler, 2015; Singh, 2010; Sun, 2015). The problem with these studies is that they do not use any information based on actual exchange but limit themselves to the content analysis of second-hand information, such as policy documents and other written reports.

In more recent years, Boulil (2019) and Hampel (2017) studied the actual relations that artists and others involved in international cultural exchange have, resulting in some interesting insights into the dynamics of international cultural relations. Using two different methodologies, Boulil (2019) the more quantitative social network analysis of the contemporary Dutch international cultural relations with two countries from the MENA region, and Hampel (2017) holding qualitative in-depth interviews with German and Indian cultural practitioners, they come to the same conclusion. Both Boulil's (2019) social network analysis and Hampel's (2017) in-depth interviews show that there is an interdependent network of relations that underly international cultural cooperation that extends way beyond what policymakers and historians write down.

These two studies nest themselves as practical applications of *art worlds*, all those involved in the production of culture as described by Becker (1986), or the existence of *cultural ecologies*, the interpersonal connections within those art worlds, that Holden (2015) advocates. Both Boulil (2019) and Hampel (2017), though looking at two very different cases, but both encompassing north–south cooperation, try to unveil international cultural actors and how they relate to each other. They include not only the policymakers' dreams through content analyses, but also the practical applications of how international cultural cooperation is approached by the sector itself (Boulil, 2019; Hampel, 2017). This chapter is a continuation of this holistic approach towards international cultural relations, considering all actors involved in the international cultural cooperation attempted by the Kingdom of the Netherlands with a part of Africa that they share no colonial past with the Kingdom of Morocco.

By using contemporary information on the international cultural exchange between the two countries, from quantitative export data, and comparing this to their policy goals, found in policy documents, this chapter will discuss the neo-colonial nature of the relations of the two nations as a result from the use of soft power or cultural diplomacy. It will also address the issue of sustainability in international cultural exchange by visualising and comparing the cultural ecology between the two countries from 2014 through 2019 in a simple social network analysis. The fact that the two countries are both located in the north of their respective continents makes that some effort is required for local cultural practitioners to exchange culture between themselves. So, first, it will take a closer look at the cultural relations between the countries by examining some historical and contemporary accounts of when the two nations cultural communities physically interacted.

SOME CONTEXT: AN ALIEN IN THE NORTH

The Dutch Moroccan cultural exchange was not chosen at random. Looking at their general colonial past, the Netherlands and Morocco seem to not cross paths. Where the Netherlands colonised parts of South America, South East Asia, and South Africa, Morocco struggled with other countries (Spain, France, and Great Britain) trying to take over their governance throughout the centuries (Benali & Obdeijn, 2005). The international relationships between the two countries do date back to the late sixteenth century, when some Dutch[1] merchants travelled to Marrakech to trade and to form an alliance between the two countries

---

[1] In this period, the Netherlands and Belgium were separated into two countries, making that some of these merchants would now be considered Flemish.

against the Spanish (Benali & Obdeijn, 2005). A cultural component to these relations was officially established in 2017 when Morocco was included as one of the target countries for the international cultural export of the Netherlands (Koenders & Bussemaker, 2016). This relationship was reciprocated by the Moroccan government in 2018 when they appointed a cultural attaché to their embassy in the Netherlands (Boulil, 2019).

Before this there were three short moments when Moroccan and Dutch culture mingled internationally, starting with two Dutch orientalists getting inspired by Moroccan "lunatics" at the end of the nineteenth century; authors J. Hendrik van Balen (1879) and Jacobus van Looy (1892; Benali & Obdeijn, 2005). They were part of an art movement inspired by the Middle East, called *orientalism*, that is more famously known as the basis of the *thesis of representation* by Edward Saïd (1978). As a founding father of post-colonialism, Saïd explains that negative cultural representations of the Orient, such as calling the Moroccans lunatics, were used as an opposite to the assumed positive culture of the West (*othering*; Saïd, 1978). However, no more examples of this critical theory can be found in the historical international cultural exchange between the Netherlands and Morocco. Apart from a short visit from Anton Pieck, a famous Dutch painter, in 1937, the Dutch art scene gives little to no attention to Morocco (Benali & Obdeijn, 2005).

What does make it an interesting case is that, despite the non-existent historical cultural relationship that the two countries have had on an international level, in the past century the Moroccan culture has had a big impact on the Dutch society. In the 1960s, a large group of Moroccan guest workers came to the Netherlands (Benali & Obdeijn, 2005). Temporary workers became permanent residents in the past decennia and currently about 2.3% of the Dutch population was either born in Morocco or has one or both parents born there (CBS, 2020). And, although the first generation of Moroccans in the Netherlands were poor, undereducated men from the Riff area who had little time for any other activities than their work, their sons and daughters are some of the more famous members of the Dutch artistic community (Benali & Obdeijn, 2005; Caubet, 2006). There is now not a Dutch person around that has not heard of Abdelkader Benali (author), Ali B. (musician), or Najib Amali (actor; Caubet, 2006).

Since the 1990s the Netherlands struggles with the integration of this and her other diasporas, but a certain pride for the multicultural Dutch citizen is reflected in the Dutch international cultural policy of that time (Verhoef, 2015). In 1992 the Dutch, marketing their famous tolerance, made their multicultural population[2] an official part of their international nation branding strategy (D'Ancona, 1992). But, while creative members of the Moroccan diaspora are still a proud part of Dutch society, in the twenty-first century their Moroccan contemporaries are faced with a different type of Dutch "tolerance". In 2019, a group of three Moroccan dancers is stopped by the Dutch border security for problems with their visa (Belhaj, 2019). They are put in a detention facility with illegal immigrants and sent back to Marrakech a week later. The dancers never made the stage of the competition they were invited to join. An interview with several representatives from the Dutch artistic community shows that this treatment is not uncommon for African artists that want to perform in the Netherlands (Belhaj, 2019). The Moroccan embassy in the Netherlands actively tries to keep in contact with the Moroccan diaspora in the Netherlands by hosting (cultural) events (Personal correspondence, 2020b). They corroborate that getting a visa is a big threshold for them as well. Sadly, further analysis of neo-colonial practices in of this form of cultural diplomacy was not possible, as the activities of the embassy are more in the informal sphere and leave no paper trail that the embassy could provide (Personal correspondence, 2020b).

Meanwhile on the African shores, Dutch and other international artists are welcomed with open arms. International cultural partnerships are celebrated, as they are viewed as a good tool to support the Moroccan cultural community (Van Hamersveld & Vaughan, 2010). Although contemporary Dutch cultural policy claims the need for international cultural exchange as well (Koenders & Bussemaker, 2016), the execution of the two countries could not be more different. Where the Moroccans state that letting international artists and other cultural actors into the country could benefit their cultural sector (*cultural import*),[3] the Dutch believe that sending their cultural artists abroad is the best way to stimulate their cultural sector (*cultural export*; Boulil, 2019). Combining this with the only recent interest in cultural exchange with each other and the lack of information of cultural activities of members of the Moroccan artists in

---

[2] About 25% of the Dutch population has a migration background of one generation or less (CBS, 2020).

[3] This strategy is not unique to North Africa and is quite common for most countries outside the geographical North (Boulil, 2019; Hampel, 2017).

the Netherlands, the rest of this chapter will focus on the part of the cultural exchange that is happening on Moroccan soil.

Methodology: Finding Cooperation in Export

The focus is on the Moroccan Dutch cultural ecology that happened in the period 2014 through 2019 in Morocco. This consciously leaves out the year 2020, when the exchange was highly affected by the outbreak of COVID-19. Additionally, the data of the, mostly cancelled, 2020 Dutch cultural export is still being collected (Chang, 2020), and it will take well into 2021 before it becomes available. This sample does allow for the consideration of the last three years of the previous cultural policy period of the Netherlands, when the international strategy focussed more on the instrumental use of culture to support the diplomatic and economic goals of the Netherlands (in Rosenthal & Zijlstra, 2012; see also Asbeek Brusse et al., 2016; Verhoef, 2015), and the first three years of the current cultural policy period of the Netherlands, that actively focusses her international efforts on international cultural cooperation (in Koenders & Bussemaker, 2016). The Moroccan cultural strategy changed at the beginning of this period as well, when starting 2013 an addition was made to their cultural policy to focus more on the support of Moroccan and Amazigh culture, as well as digitalisation and internationalisation (in UNESCO, 2017; see also Van Hamersveld & Vaughan, 2010). These three policy documents will form the basis of the context analysis.

The data on Dutch cultural export is collected in the DutchCulture database.[4] This is a record of all outgoing cultural activities of the Netherlands dating back to the 1990s, six networks, spanning 2014 through 2019, of contemporary cultural exchange between Morocco and the Netherlands were created as follows. With help from the embassies, cultural funds, and artists themselves, the DutchCulture database records cultural export of the Netherlands. Because they are noting not only the final product or artwork, but also the responsible artists, their international partners, the locations it was shown and those who financed or otherwise supported them, it is possible to deduct most of the international professional relations that underlie the international cultural export

---

[4] This database has been made public in 2018 and since then can be accessed through https://dutchculture.nl/en Data before 2017 is messier, but for Morocco an accurate sample was provided by DutchCulture.

and create six networks (Robins, 2015). For convenience, the assumption is made that these relations are going both ways.

The actors in the network are firstly categorised based on their general role in the network. Becker (1986). In his famous work on art worlds, makes the distinction between the *producers of art*, which includes artist and those that for instance build instruments, and *supporters of art*, which are not only those that make art financially possible (e.g.: funders, audiences, etc.), but also those that make it socially possible (e.g.: policymakers and distribution channels). In a more contemporary taxonomy, Holden (2015) sees three roles in his work on cultural ecologies. *Guardians*, who curate and care for the future of art, *connectors*, who move resources in the ecology for art production to become possible, *platforms*, that show cultural content, and *nomads*, who are the consumers of culture (Holden, 2015).

Because this chapter focusses on the interpersonal relations within the cultural ecology and not on the content of what is actually produced or those that consume that, a shape distinction was made between the *producers of art* (circles), individuals and groups that make art or express culture, *supporters of art* (squares), those that make the production of art or expression of culture possible, thus including the connectors and some of the guardians that Holden (2015) talks about, and *platforms of art* (triangles), that show cultural content, thus including the guardians that curate art as well. In the sample, there are 47.6% producers of art, 22.3% supporters of art, and 30.1% platforms of art (N = 166). About half of them have the Netherlands as their country of origin (53.6%). The rest are either Moroccan (34.3%) or from another part of the world (12.1%: N = 166).

Second, a taxonomy is made by using different colours for the actors. A preferred distinction in art research is to look at different disciplines (Holden, 2015). A start can be made with the policy actors, their departments, and their arm's length organisations. A crucial supporter of international cultural exchange is the *cultural institutes*, cultural centres from one country located in another, who are interwoven with colonialism (Brianso, 2010; Paschalidis, 2009). These organisations were once, depending on their country of origin, locations that taught the new citizens of a country that lived in an acquired area the culture of their new motherland (e.g.: the French Institute) or that provided cultural activities for citizens that moved from the country of origin to a new area (e.g.: the Goethe Institute; Paschalidis, 2009). In the twentieth century, this role grew into large organisations that the taught language and culture of their country of origin to all interested (e.g.: the Italian Institute; Paschalidis, 2009) or took on the role of the protection of things that were considered international heritage (e.g.: UNESCO, 2017; Brianso, 2010). With the realisation that "the other", as Saïd (1978) would say, is someone that needs acknowledgement and respect, in the twenty-first century, these institutes are slowly changing their objective, including more and more of the cultural community and the other country in the exchange process (e.g.: the Danish Cultural Institute; Boulil, 2019; Kieft, 2018; Pratt, 2005). The cultural institutes, whether striving for cultural diplomacy or international cultural cooperation, are usually funded by a ministry of culture and/or a ministry of foreign affairs (Boulil, 2019; Kieft, 2018).

Beyond the cultural institute, a ministry of foreign affairs sometimes has a cultural attaché present at their embassy, someone who is responsible for maintaining the international cultural relations with the country the embassy is in. This is also the case in the Moroccan Dutch cultural exchange (Boulil, 2019). The policy on the Dutch side consists of the Dutch cultural institute, an arm's length organisation of the Dutch ministry of culture, the Dutch ministry of foreign affairs and the European Union. The Dutch ministry of culture also finances several art funds to push international activities and the Dutch ministry of foreign affairs also runs an embassy in Morocco (Boulil, 2019). On the Moroccan side, there are the same two ministries (Boulil, 2019; Van Hamersveld & Vaughan, 2010), but only the ministry of culture is responsible for the two cultural institutes of the country (UNESCO, 2017). They developed these organisations, one focussed on Amazigh culture and the other focussed on music export, with the help of a Swedish developmental aid agency (UNESCO, 2017). The Moroccan ministry of foreign affairs has an embassy and several consulates in the Netherlands. Finally, from the DutchCulture database, it became clear that there are some municipalities involved from time to time and the French cultural institute also shares in the support of some of the Moroccan Dutch cultural activities.

Turning to the taxonomy of the arts, a start can be made with the divisions that policy has. The Moroccan ministry of culture is split up in a department of Book, Libraries & Archives, of Cultural Heritage (which includes heritage studies), and of Arts, which is again split it in festivals, fine arts, music & performing arts, and a subdivision of theatre (Van Hamersveld & Vaughan, 2010). In 2013, a department of Film and Digitalisation was added to these divisions (UNESCO, 2017). The Dutch ministry of culture has three departments, which are Education, Culture, and Science. They divide Dutch culture into six disciplines, each supported by their own funds and cultural institutions. According to Dutch law, these disciplines are performing arts, museums, visual arts, film, literary arts, and architecture, design & new media. These are in general also the disciplines that the DutchCulture database uses, although this varies from year to year (Asbeek Brusse et al., 2016). Trying to find a middle ground, the division between the different disciplines of arts and culture is shown in Table 5.1, which includes the percentages of each group in the data of this chapter. Festivals are left out of the specification, because the data showed that they usually fit into either of these disciplines.

Table 5.1 Disciplines, Art Forms and Colouring Scheme in the Networks[5]

Performing Arts	Visual Arts	Literary Arts	Media Arts	Creative Industries	Culture	Policy
Music	Fine Arts	Books	Film	Fashion	Heritage	Cultural institutes
Dance	Photography	Libraries	New Media	Design	Archives	Ministries
Theatre			Digital art	Architecture	Education	Embassies & consulates
					Museums	
27.1%	13.9%	3%	22.3%	10.2%	15.1%	4.8%

Table 5.2 Dutch Cultural Events in Morocco Registered in the DutchCulture Database in the Previous Dutch Policy Period

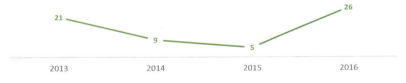

---

[5] N = 166. 3.6% of the actors are not part of the cultural ecology. i.e. restaurants, stadia, etc.

Table 5.3 Dutch Cultural Events in Morocco Registered in the DutchCulture Database in the Current Dutch Policy Period

Results

Networks of Cultural Communities, Part 1

From the start of 2013 until the end of 2016, according to their policy documents, the Dutch government promoted the organisation of cultural activities if they would adhere to several goals, mostly economic and diplomatic (Rosenthal & Zijlstra, 2012). They would take place in a list of countries chosen in advance, mostly countries that had economic or post-colonial relations with the Netherlands (Verhoef, 2015). This does not mean that Dutch cultural activities in Morocco could not be supported by the Dutch public funds, such as those that support economic viable disciplines like media arts or the creative industries, or the Dutch government, through their embassy in Morocco. Rather it means that there was no specific financial or other aid being labelled for this purpose by the Dutch government.

The Moroccans started their new policy in this period as well, trying to professionalise their sector through digitalisation and internationalisation (UNESCO, 2017). In their strategy, they name specifically the African cultural community as the focus of their international efforts, and heritage, literary arts, music & dance, film, and visual arts as the (sub)disciplines they would like to focus their international efforts on (UNESCO, 2017). Looking at the DutchCulture database in this period, it becomes clear that there is some Dutch culture being imported by the Moroccans, despite both of the cultural policies not focussing on this exchange (Table 5.2).

From the additional information behind this data, consisting of actors and their professional partners, three whole networks were deduced: MA NL 2014 ($n = 21$; Fig. 5.1), MA NL 2015 ($n = 9$; Fig. 5.2), and MA NL 2016 ($n = 41$; Fig. 5.3). In this period, little is happening. In 2014, the

Dutch cultural institute (Actor 56) chooses to support a media platform and four of their producers to visit a Dutch support organisation at their Moroccan location (on the left), to help a visual arts support organisation to send six artists to a Moroccan festival (on the right), and to aid a Dutch producer and a Moroccan platform to connect (on the bottom; Fig. 5.1). Then one of the Dutch funds (Actor 46) sends one of their producers to Morocco, but not to any specific Moroccan partner (bottom left) and a Dutch media arts producer visits a Moroccan support organisation (on the top of Fig. 5.1).

In 2015, it is even less. A Brazilian producer of media art, who was supported by two Dutch media art organisations, performs in Morocco (left), two Dutch producers of art, in visual arts (Actor 243) and in performance arts (Actor 18) visit two Moroccan platforms, and a Dutch platform located in Morocco shows pieces of another Dutch platform (middle; Fig. 5.2).

In 2016, when it is already known that the new Dutch cultural policy will start to include Morocco as a target country, more starts to happen. The Dutch embassy in Morocco (Actor 55) starts to support several Dutch producers of art and supporters of art to connect to Moroccan platforms and supporters of art, one of which is the Dutch support organisation with a Moroccan location that was also present in 2014 (Actor 175). The festival from 2014, Actor 142, also reoccurs, but this time invites two producers from the creative industries and one producer of performing arts from the Netherlands. On the top left of Fig. 5.4, it also becomes clear that both the Dutch embassy and the Dutch cultural institute help a Dutch producer of art (Actor 77) with a cooperation with two other international artists to showcase at a Moroccan platform outside of the cultural ecology and at a Moroccan supporter of arts. One of the Dutch funds (Actor 193) in the network of the Dutch cultural institute supports two producers of visual arts to visit one Moroccan platform, one of which is also supported by the Dutch embassy (bottom left). Finally, the Dutch cultural institute connects a Dutch producer of visual arts (Actor 130) to a Moroccan heritage platform (Actor 35).

What is mainly interesting about the cultural export of the Netherlands to Morocco in this policy period is that it mostly reflects the diplomatic goals that the governments of the two countries set out to achieve. They do not actively seek to exchange culture with each other, so this is not happening a lot. When it does happen, the conditions set by the Dutch and Moroccan governments are both met. The Dutch want to see

82 D. BOULIL

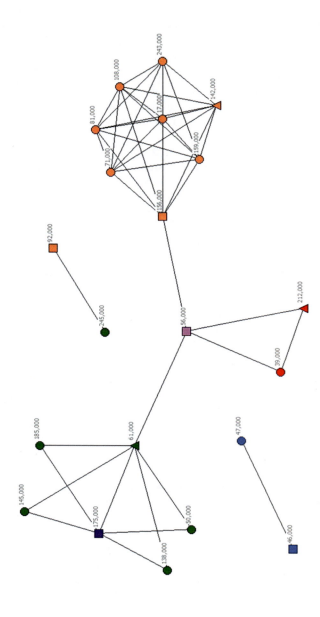

Fig. 5.1 MA NL 2014

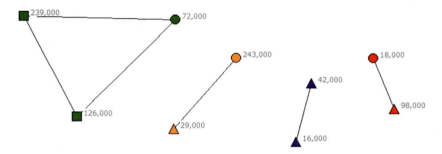

Fig. 5.2 MA NL 2015

economic benefit for their country (and their cultural sector; Rosenthal & Zijlstra, 2012) and the Moroccans want to import those cultural activities that support their local heritage and visual arts and parts of their performance arts and media arts (UNESCO, 2017). The only actors that would be expected to occur more in the three networks are those active in the literary arts, especially with the large Moroccan diaspora in the Netherlands. However, this would then mean Morocco exporting books and other written art forms to the Netherlands, and this is simply not their style (Boulil, 2019).

Networks of Cultural Communities, Part 2

When a policy period ends, a new one also begins. Although the Moroccan strategy remains the same until at least 2020 (and some even until 2030; UNESCO, 2017), the Dutch introduced a new cultural policy in 2017 which will last until the end of 2020 (Koenders & Bussemaker, 2016). In this new cultural policy, the Netherlands state that they aim to cooperate with Morocco "[to make] more room for a cultural contribution to a safe, just and sustainable world" (Koenders & Bussemaker, 2016, p. 7). By this they mean that the Dutch government will only support the cultural exchange with Morocco if it contributes to the stabilisation of the area around Europe (Boulil, 2019). Specifically the Dutch, according to their international cultural policy, are currently supporting activities in Morocco that empowers the local cultural sector to support societal change (towards social cohesion and cultural acceptance), stimulates the participation of youths in cultural activities, creates safe and

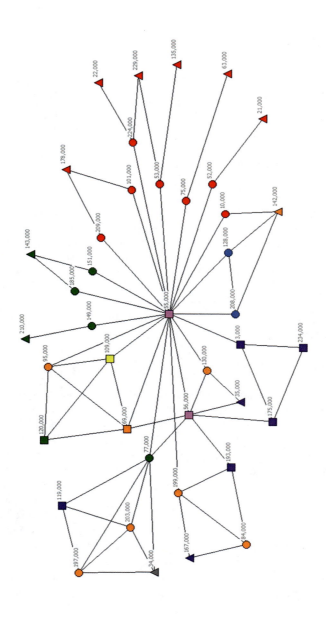

Fig. 5.3 MA NL 2016

5 DUTCH-MOROCCAN CULTURAL COOPERATION? ... 85

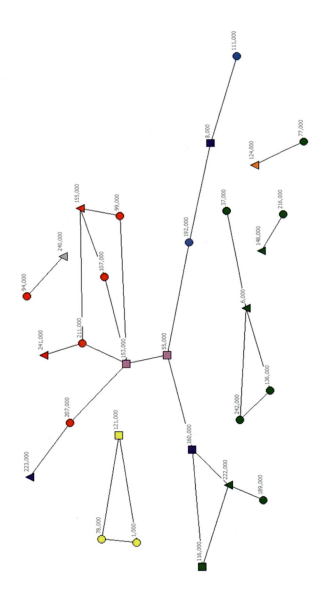

Fig. 5.4 MA NL 2017

sustainable living spaces in cities and contributes to the sustainable care of local cultural heritage (Koenders & Bussemaker, 2016). In this policy period, up until the outbreak of COVID-19, there was some increase in cultural activities between the two countries coming up (Table 5.3).

From this data again three networks were deduced by the same methods as mentioned before: MA NL 2017 (n = 29; Fig. 5.4), MA NL 2018 (n = 52; Fig. 5.5), and MA NL 2019 (n = 35; Fig. 5.6). What first jumps out in Fig. 5.5 is that the literary activities that have been missing are starting to occur (middle left). On the bottom five producers of media visit two festivals in their industry and one visual arts platform, three of which go to the same platform, a festival (Actor 6). In these clusters at the bottom of Fig. 5.5 there is also one familiar actor, Actor 77 also occurred the year before in the exchange network. Beyond this, the Dutch embassy in Morocco, Actor 55, remains the connector of several different groups of relations. Together with their parent organisation, the Dutch ministry of foreign affairs (Actor 153), the four producers of performance art visited three Moroccan platforms (top of Fig. 5.5). They also help one supporter of culture in the broader definition cooperate with a Moroccan supporter and a Moroccan platform of media arts and a Dutch producer in the same discipline (bottom left). They also help a Dutch producer in the creative industries meet a Moroccan producer in the same discipline at a cultural platform in Belgium. Finally, a Dutch producer of performance art plays at a venue that falls outside of the cultural ecology (top centre; Fig. 5.4).

In 2018, the Dutch embassy seem to be doubling their efforts, perhaps inspired by the hiring of a Moroccan expert at the Dutch cultural institute (Personal correspondence, 2020a). Rather than supporting mostly producers of art, in Fig. 5.6 Actor 55 also connects to an equal number of platforms of art and some supporters of art. Coming from the visual arts, media arts, performing arts, and creative industries in the Netherlands, these actors are visiting mainly cultural and media art actors in Morocco (Fig. 5.5). Actor 6, the festival that was visited in 2017 is visited again, but this time only by one Dutch artist (bottom left). The same goes for the festivals Actor 98, from the 2015 network, and Actor 63, from the 2016 network (right). Another interesting cluster forms around Actor 55, the French cultural institute, who connects to a Dutch fund, Actor 186, who supports some activities her discipline, and another festival, Actor 230, who in turn works with a producer of art that is also supported by a Dutch fund, Actor 46. This last supporter of art was active before, in

5 DUTCH-MOROCCAN CULTURAL COOPERATION? ... 87

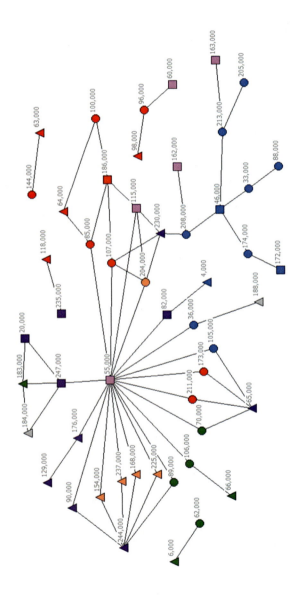

Fig. 5.5 MA NL 2018

88   D. BOULIL

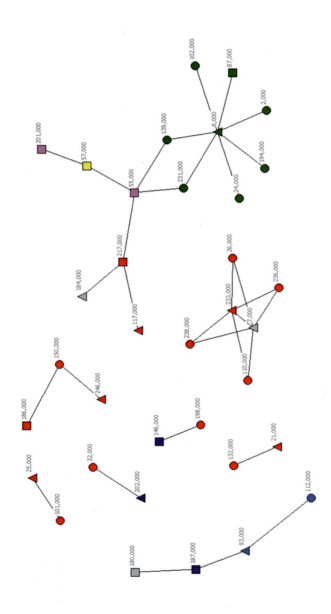

Fig. 5.6   MA NL 2019

the network of 2014, while the producer of art, Actor 208, was active in the 2016 network. Two more producers of art reoccur, both in the performing arts and both from the 2017 network. Actor 107 is on the right of the network visiting the festival Actor 230, and Actor 211 is one of the producers of art supported by the Dutch embassy in Morocco (Fig. 5.5).

In 2019, the heavy activities mellow down again. Figure 5.7 shows the Dutch embassy in Morocco, Actor 55, supporting two producers of media art going to the reoccurring festival Actor 6, and helping two fellow supporters of art connect to one of the Moroccan cultural institutes, Actor 201, and two platforms of art op the top left of that cluster in Fig. 5.7. Below this group of actors, there is another cluster of Dutch producers of arts visiting the same Moroccan platforms, one of which, Actor 184, was visited the year before as well. On the left of this Actor 21 is another festival from 2016 that is being revisited by a Dutch producer of performing arts. Above that two Dutch producers of performing art visit a platform and a supporter of culture. The Dutch fund (Actor 186) that was quite active in 2018, now sends just one producer of performing arts to Morocco, while yet another reoccurrence from the 2016 network (Actor 101) visits another Moroccan platform of performing arts next to that. To end the description of the 2019 network, on the far bottom left of Fig. 5.7, an African born Dutch producer in the creative industries visits a Moroccan location in the same discipline, that is part of a more general supporter of culture, that is again a department of an organisation that falls outside of the cultural ecology.

The international cultural relations between the two countries in this period seem to be increasing through the attention of Dutch policy that is given. Where the network would fall apart in 2015, now the Dutch embassy in Morocco seems to actively aid the Dutch cultural community in their efforts to export culture to Morocco. In total, the number of active actors has almost doubled, with 66 actors in the networks from 2014 through 2016 and 108 actors in the networks from 2017 through 2019. Most of these actors are Dutch, but that number is slowly decreasing in the second period. In 2014, 81% of the actors are engaging in the exchange are representing the Netherlands, while in 2019 this

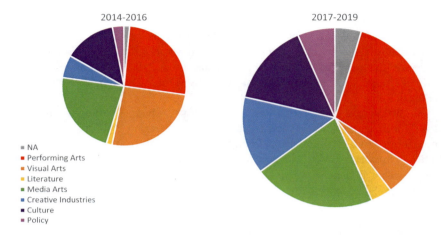

Fig. 5.7 The Distribution of the Disciplines in 2014–2016 and 2017–2019

number is down to 57.1%.[6] This could suggest that rather than the export and import of Dutch culture, which was central in the previous period, is slowly being replaced by a more equal exchange tradition (cooperation; see also Boulil, 2019). Perhaps because the Dutch are now putting the local cultural sector first (Koenders & Bussemaker, 2016), like the Moroccans were already doing in 2013 (UNESCO, 2017).

Beyond Soft Power

Important topics that are addressed throughout this book are soft power and sustainability. To start with the second, of the 166 actors in the dataset, only 18 reoccur throughout the sample. They are mostly the Dutch performance artists and Moroccan festivals in the performance arts, but the other disciplines have almost only new actors every year. By comparing the distribution of the disciplines throughout the whole sample in Fig. 5.7, other things become clear. Although the overall number of actors involved increased, the distribution of disciplines did

---

[6] The average of the two policy periods shows that this change is a little bit smaller when put into perspective, with an average of 62.1% Dutch nationals in the network from 2014 through 2016 and an average of 56.5% from 2017 through 2019.

not increase accordingly. Between the two periods is a large reduction in actors from the visual arts. On the other hand, both the actors from the creative industries, policy field, and those that fall outside of the cultural ecology have about doubled in size. And in this lack of sustainability, hints of soft power can be found.

Nye (1990, p. 167) defines *soft power* as the combination of "co-optive power—getting others to want what you want—and soft power resources—cultural attraction, ideology, and international institutions". In the 2017–2020 Dutch international cultural policy, it becomes apparent that the Netherlands is trying to influence the situation in Morocco, which they identified as part of the unstable ring of countries around Europe, through exporting culture there and supporting the local cultural sector (Koenders & Bussemaker, 2016). Similar strategies are not uncommon for countries from the geographical North and are named neo-colonial by some scholars in the field (Brianso, 2010; Paschalidis, 2009). On the other side, the Moroccan international cultural strategy, and those of other countries from the geographical south (Hampel, 2017), are playing into these attempts to influence their society and use them to support their cultural sector (UNESCO, 2017). This leaves one wondering which of the two countries in the exchange studied above has the co-optive power.

Taking a closer look at the subdisciplines of the actors, it becomes clear that those increases correspond with some of the policy goals of the Netherlands, rather than those of the Moroccans or their shared policy goals. In the creative industries, there is a main increase in the number of architecture related actors, from 4.5% to 7.4% (N = 166), corresponding with the Dutch goal to make more sustainable living spaces in Moroccan cities (Koenders & Bussemaker, 2016). There is also an increase in the actors that lean towards the more social side of culture, from 1.5% in the first policy period that is looked at to 8.3% in the second (N = 166). This is connecting to the attempt to support societal change (Koenders & Bussemaker, 2016). But rather than increasing the support for the only goals that both the Dutch and Moroccan governments wanted to achieve, helping local youths and heritage in Morocco (Koenders & Bussemaker, 2016; UNESCO, 2017), it led to a decrease in the educational actors, from 4.5% to 1.9%, and the heritage related actors, from 7.6% to 2.8% (N = 166).

Rather than speaking of international cultural cooperation, which requires some form of equal exchange and internal drive of the artists

(Cummings, 2003; Gienow-Hecht & Donfried, 2010; Hampel, 2017), what is found is the Dutch attempting to use cultural relations to influence Moroccan society (Koenders & Bussemaker, 2016). The response to this cultural policy from the creative and cultural sector in the Netherlands was, not surprisingly, less than favourable (Raad voor Cultuur, 2019; IOB, 2019). On top of that, the Moroccan parliament told Dutch delegates in early 2020 that they were not pleased with the constant attempts to mingle in their state affairs (Kasraoui, 2020). Luckily, the Dutch policymakers heard the complaints from both their community and their Moroccan counterparts, and the new international cultural policy of the Dutch finally let go of cultural diplomacy. Artists now are free to choose their cooperation partners based on artistic inspiration, rather than diplomatic goals (Van Engelshoven & Blok, 2019).

Conclusion

Where the Kingdom of Morocco and the Kingdom of the Netherlands historically showed little interest in each other both politically and culturally (Benali & Obdeijn, 2005), since 2017 the Dutch changed their cultural policy to include Morocco as a possible partner (Koenders & Bussemaker, 2016). Morocco was already open to international cultural cooperation with preferably African countries (UNESCO, 2017), but seemed to happily welcome the Dutch into their cultural field. When the diplomatic missions pertaining to the culture of both countries started to match, the international export of the Netherlands to Morocco almost doubled in size. Both countries claim to want what is best for their cultural sector (Koenders & Bussemaker, 2016; UNESCO, 2017), but this is the first thing that seems to be forgotten when strategies are put into practice. Even though the possibility of the cultural sector blossoming from cultural diplomacy was well augmented by Carter (2015), comparing the six networks in this chapter it becomes clear that growth happens in the disciplines that are more in line with the diplomatic goals of the Netherlands. Some hope for the future is given, as the Dutch are actively letting go of their instrumental use of culture and diplomatic goals starting 2021 (Van Engelshoven & Blok, 2019).

Acknowledgements A special thanks go out to DutchCulture, the Dutch cultural institute, for providing this data on international cultural export used in this chapter.

REFERENCES

Albro, R. (2015). The disjunction of image and word in US and Chinese soft power projection. *International Journal of Cultural Policy*, 21(4), 382–399.
Ang, I., Isar, Y. R., & Mar, P. (2015). Cultural diplomacy: Beyond the national interest? *International Journal of Cultural Policy*, 21(4), 365–381.
Asbeek Brusse, W. (2016). Cultuur als Kans: Beleidsdoorlichting van het Internationaal Cultuurbeleid 2009–2014. Den Haag, NL: Dutch Ministry of Foreign Affairs. IOB Beleidsevaluatie no. 411.
Becker, H. S. (1986). *Art worlds: Updated and expanded.* University of California Press.
Belhaj, S. (2019, January 19). Van Afropopster tot Dansers: Deze Artiesten Zijn Niet Welkom in Nederland. *Nederlandse Omroep Stichting.*
Benali, A., & Obdeijn, H. (2005). *Marokko door Nederlandse Ogen, 1605–2005.* Arbeiderspers.
Boulil, D. Z. (2019). *All in this together: A social network study into international cultural exchange.* Master thesis, Faculty of Arts, University of Groningen.
Brianso, I. (2010). Valorization of world cultural heritage in time of globalization: Bridges between nations and cultural power. In J. P. Singh (Ed.), *International cultural policies and power* (pp. 166–180). Palgrave Macmillan.
Carter, D. (2015). Living with instrumentalism: The academic commitment to cultural diplomacy. *International Journal of Cultural Policy*, 21(4), 478–493.
Caubet, D. (2006). *Shouf Shouf Hollanda: Succesvol en Marokkaan.* Breda.
CBS (2020, October 13). *Bevolking: Kerncijfers.* https://opendata.cbs.nl/statline/#/CBS/nl/dataset/37296ned/table?ts=1606226898446, accessed 1 April 2021.
Chang, E. (2020, September 10). *Open Call DutchCulture Database 2020 – COVID-19 Adaption.* https://dutchculture.nl/en/news/open-call-dutchculture-database-2020-covid19-adaption, accessed 15 April 2021.
Cummings, M., (2003). *Cultural diplomacy and the United States government: A survey.* Center for Arts and Culture.
D'Ancona, H. (1992). *Nota Cultuurbeleid.* Handelingen van de Tweede Kamer der StatenGeneraal. Investeren in Cultuur, 22 602, nr. 1, 1991–1992.
Fisher, R. (2007). *A cultural dimension to the EU's external policies. From policy statements to practice and potential.* Boekmanstudies and European Cultural Foundation.
Gienow-Hecht, J. C. E., & Donfried, M. (2010). *Searching for a cultural diplomacy.* Berghahn Books.
Hadley, S., & Gray, C. (2017). Hyperinstrumentalism and cultural policy: Means to an end or an end to meaning? *Cultural Trends*, 26(2), 95–106.
Hampel, A. (2017). *Fair Cooperation A New Paradigm for Cultural Diplomacy and Arts Management in Cultural Policy and Cultural Management.* Peter Lang.

Holden, J. (2015). *The Ecology of Culture*. London, UK: Arts and Humanities Research Council. Cultural Value Project Rapport.

Internationaal Onderzoek en Beleidsevaluatie (IOB; 2019). *Diversiteit en Samenhang*. Den Haag, NL: Dutch Ministery of Education, Culture & Science. Kamerbrief.

Iwabuchi, K. (2015). Pop-culture diplomacy in Japan: Soft power, nation branding and the question of 'International cultural exchange.' *International Journal of CulturalPolicy, 21*(4), 419–432.

Jurková, J. (2015). Still searching for a cultural diplomacy. *International Journal of Cultural Policy, 21*(4), 509–511.

Kang, H. (2015). Contemporary cultural diplomacy in South Korea: Explicit and implicit approaches. *International Journal of Cultural Policy, 21*(4), 433–447.

Kasraoui, S. (2020, February 20). *Morocco rejects Netherlands' interference in domestic affairs*. Morocco World News.

Kieft, R. (2018). *From Danish poldermodel to French decentralisation*. DutchCulture.

Koenders, A. G., &, Bussemaker, M. (2016). *International Cultural Policy 2017–2020*. Dutch Ministery of Education, Culture & Science. Kamerbrief.

Lowe, D. (2015). Australia's Colombo plans, old and new: International students as foreign relations. *International Journal of Cultural Policy, 21*(4), 448–462.

Minnaert, T. (2014). Footprint or fingerprint: International cultural policy as identity policy. *International Journal of Cultural Policy, 20*(1), 99–113.

Mulcahy, K. V. (2010). Coloniality, identity and cultural policy. In J. P. Singh (Ed.), *International cultural policies and power* (pp. 155–165). Palgrave Macmillan.

Nye, J. S. (1990). *Bound to lead: The changing nature of American power*. Basic Books.

Paschalidis, G. (2009). Exporting national culture: Histories of cultural institutes abroad. *The International Journal of Cultural Policy, 15*(3), 275–289.

Personal Correspondence. (2020a, October 6). *Conversation with Myriam Sahraoui (DutchCulture)*.

Personal Correspondence. (2020b, October 13). *Conversation with Rachid Seghrouchni (Moroccan Embassy in the Netherlands)*.

Pratt, A. C. (2005). Cultural Industries and Public Policy. *International Journal of Cultural Policy, 11*(1), 31–44.

Raad voor Cultuur. (2019). *Cultuur Dichtbij, Dicht Bij Cultuur*. Raad voor Cultuur. Advies Cultuurbestel 2021–2024.

Robins, G. (2015). *Doing social network research: Network-based research design for social scientists*. SAGE Publications Ltd.

Rosenthal, U., &, Zijlstra, H. (2012). *International Cultural Policy 2013–2016*. Dutch Ministery of Education, Culture & Science. Kamerbrief.

Rösler, B. (2015). The case of Asialink's arts residency program: Towards a critical cosmopolitan approach to cultural diplomacy. *International Journal of Cultural Policy, 21*(4), 463–477.

Said, E. (1978). *Orientalism.* Pantheon.

Sennett, R. (2012). *Together: The rituals, pleasures and politics of cooperation.* Yale University Press.

Singh, J. P. (2010). *International cultural policies and power.* Palgrave Macmillan.

Sun, W. (2015). Slow boat from China: Public discourses behind the 'Going global' media policy. *International Journal of Cultural Policy, 21*(4), 400–418.

UNESCO. (2017). *Maroc 2017 report.* UNESCO. Periodic Reports.

van Engelshoven, I., & Blok, S. (2019). *Beleidskader International Cultuurbeleid 2021–2024.* Dutch Ministery of Education, Culture & Science. Kamerbrief.

van Hamersveld, I., & Vaughan, J. (Eds.) (2010). *Cultural policies in Algeria, Egypt, Jordan, Lebanon, Morocco, Palestine, Syria and Tunisia: An introduction.* Boekmanstichting.

Verhoef, J. (2015). *Grenzeloos Gelegitimeerd: De Geschiedenis van het Nederlands Internationaal Cultuurbeleid als Ideologisch Proces.* Faculty of Arts, University of Utrecht.

Wallis, B. (1994). Selling nations: International exhibitions and cultural diplomacy. In D. J. Sherman & I. Rogoff (Eds.), *Museum culture: Histories* (pp. 265–269). Routledge.

Wyszomirski, M. J., Burgess, C., & Peila, C. (2003). *International cultural relations: A multi-country comparison.* Americans for the Arts.

CHAPTER 6

Promoting Cultural Diplomacy: Nigeria's National Theatre and the National Troupe in Perspective

Sunday Enessi Ododo

Introduction

Scholars of international relations and diplomacy are increasingly giving attention to Cultural Diplomacy because of the roles and significant impacts non state actors have come to play in shaping the relationships between states in the global system. The proliferation of technology and the concomitant ease in cross territorial communications has opened up what was exclusively the purview of career diplomats to embrace creatives who trade in the exchange of arts and culture as a means of relating with people from other countries for mutual understanding and building relationships across borderlines. The gamut of interactions either sanctioned or not by state actors is what is conveniently perceived as cultural diplomacy or soft power diplomacy. It is a programme of exchange that

S. E. Ododo (✉)
National Theatre, Iganmu, Lagos, Nigeria

© The Author(s), under exclusive license to Springer Nature Singapore Pte Ltd. 2022
T. Afolabi et al. (eds.), *Re-centering Cultural Performance and Orange Economy in Post-colonial Africa*,
https://doi.org/10.1007/978-981-19-0641-1_6

includes art, education and ideas, but also incorporates health care and community and economic development, activities beyond the cultural realm (Arts Industries Policy Forum, 2006, p. 5). This form of diplomacy has witnessed an upsurge since the end of the Cold War and the symbolic fall of the Berlin wall in 1991. It is seen as a democratization of the international relations which has replaced the strong arm military might and terror which characterized the Cold War relations days. Cultural Diplomacy more than military might is credited with the defeat of Communism and fall of Soviet Union. By constantly projecting what life was like in capitalist States against the lack being suffered in communist States, America was able to influence defectors who sought means and ways of escaping the miserable existence they were living under Communism. This was an example of how soft power prevails where might failed.

Conceptual Overview

The relationship between nations of the world is in the context of each nation's culture as the international system is made up of many countries with different and diverse cultural practices. Hence, culture is a crucial component in inter-state relations (Sheriff et al., 2019). This is why due diligence is important so as to avoid faux pas when relating with other nations. After all, a nation seeking better understanding with another would not what to unwittingly offend the nation it is making friendly overtures to. What is permissible during bilateral meetings as gifts takes into consideration the culture of the host or visiting nation. Viewed from this premise, culture has played a very powerful but subtle role in exchanges between nations in the past, the present and will continue to have relevance in the future. Contextualizing the foregoing, Bound, Briggs, Holden and Jones assert that "from the reciprocal gifts of Arts and manufactures between the Doge of Venice and the Kublai Khan, to the Great Exhibition of 1851, to the present day, people have used culture to display themselves, assert their power, and to understand others" (Bound et al., 2007, p. 15). From the days of the European explorers who first made contacts with Benin Kingdom and the ensuing exchange of artefacts from Benin for European manufactured goods like umbrellas, the geographical location that later became Nigeria has had a long history of cultural exchange with the world. This shows that the exchange of ideas, symbols and material aspects of cultural heritage between countries of the world is a sine-qua-non for mutual understanding.

Culture despite its various definitions is generally accepted as the total way of life of a people and to this end it encompasses all areas of daily life and living; food, shelter, clothing, music, dance, folklores and history re-enacted in musical and dramatic expressions or text as well as greetings to mention a few. Diplomacy succinctly stated is the relations between countries often on official basis but also through informal means which can include cultural relations or exchange referred to as Cultural Diplomacy. Pajinta conceived of cultural diplomacy as a set of activities, undertaken directly by or in collaboration with diplomatic authorities of a state, which are aimed at the promotion of foreign policy of this state in the realm of cultural policy primarily by means of fostering its cultural exchange with other (foreign) state… (Pajinta, 2014). For the "set of activities undertaken directly or indirectly" certain collaborators are germane, and for the present discourse, the National Theatre and the National Troupe of Nigeria are apropos.

With over 250 ethnics, sub-ethnic and tribal groups and the parallel cultural representations within its borders, Nigeria has so much material of cultural expressions to gift the world. And with its position as the most populous black nation on earth, it is no wonder that Nigeria staged the biggest cultural festival on the continent in 1977 merely 17 years after the country attained self-rule in 1960. The 2nd World and Black Festival of Arts and Culture otherwise known as FESTAC'77 was a fiesta that had over 54 countries of the world in attendance—African countries and Africans in the diaspora were well represented. For the purpose of this cultural jamboree, Nigeria built a National Theatre in Lagos which was the Capital of the Country at the time. FESTAC'77 was so gigantic and colossal that events of FESTAC'77 held in National Stadium, Tafawa Balewa Square—all in Lagos and also the Durbar in Kaduna. Hence, the National Theatre is the legacy of FESTAC'77. The close to one-month event created a platform for cultural exchanges between and amongst the over 54 countries that had representations at the fiesta.

Following the success of FESTAC'77, the National Theatre continued to host and stage national and international events but it was not until 1991 that the National Theatre became a legal entity through the instrumentation of Decree 47 which made it a government agency with the National Troupe of Nigeria created by the same Decree under one Governing Board. This Decree provides for the appointment of a General Manager/Chief Executive Officer for the National Theatre and an Artistic Director for the National Troupe of Nigeria. In summary, the GM/CEO of the National Theatre is expected to be the facility manager while also preserving, promoting and presenting the Cultural heritage of Nigeria to the world. On the other hand, Artistic Director of the National Troupe under the guidance of the Board shall achieve high artistic productions specifically designed for national and international tours and ensures that the productions of the Troupe are geared towards national aspirations, operate and artistically develop the Troupe as a performing body whose repertoire shall embrace drama, dance and music, etc. By mandating the Troupe to create productions specifically designed for national and international tours as well as productions geared towards national aspirations, the Act setting it up gave it very important and crucial roles in Cultural Diplomacy. This is because "Genuine Cultural Diplomacy is …a two-way communication process that includes both efforts to project a nation's image and values to other countries and peoples as well as to receive information and try to understand the culture, values and images of other countries and their peoples" (Jora, 2013). It must have elements of understanding and mutuality.

Though formal establishment of the National Troupe of Nigeria can be traced to Decree 47 of 1991, the Troupe had an existence that predates that Decree. It is on record that the Troupe first auditioned in 1986 in Osasa under the leadership of Hubert Ogunde. It must also be noted that although 1986 was the first national audition, the need for a creating a National Troupe of Nigeria had emerged in the 1970s as Nigeria needed performing Troupe to represent and project its cultural heritage at the FESTAC'77 it hosted. Chris Olude, with a group of dancers and musicians, formed the first National Troupe of Nigeria (Guardian Arts, 2020). Furthermore, invitations for Nigeria to participate abroad in different festivals, trade fairs and cultural exchanges also brought about the awareness of the need for a collection of different dances from the states for the purpose of honouring these invitations (op. cit). These invitations were avenues for cultural exchanges to take place.

Conventionally, Diplomacy is the exclusive preserve of state actors who have the legal backing to represent the interests and aspirations of their states in other states called hosts. This crop of legally sanctioned national representatives on the international scene includes ambassadors, consulate officials, diplomats and attachés in foreign missions. They help to strategically further the achievement and attainment of national interests of their states on the international scene, after all, foreign policy is nothing but the internationalization of national interests. These national interests pursued internationally are called Foreign Policies or Foreign Policy Objectives. It can be in the areas of security, economy, sports or culture. Cultural Diplomacy falls within the category of Public Diplomacy (Cull, 2007, p. 1). The nature of Cultural Diplomacy is such that exchanges are sometimes spontaneous and often times happen without official sanctions.

Cultural Diplomacy is the preferred alternative to the conventional Diplomacy with emphasis on military might, political leverage and economic power. This is so because it encourages dialogue and value sharing. It is multi-dimensional, comprising public diplomacy, information management and relationship building (Hagher, 2011, p. 1). It can be a strategic and well-coordinated course of action that a State sets out to achieve internationally through mutual exchange and transfer of cultural practices. For the furtherance of its cultural diplomacy objectives states often employ national travelling Troupes it takes on foreign missions or host visiting Troupes and performers in its National Theatre.

The National Theatre and the National Troupe of Nigeria have both played telling and significant roles in the area of cultural diplomacy over the years. Since the establishments of the two bodies as enunciated above in 1991, both agencies of Government have shared the National Theatre complex as offices and venue for their performances. It serves as a veritable platform for rehearsals of the Troupe before taking the performances out of Nigeria or staging them within the country. The National Theatre Complex also serves as the "home" of the National Troupe when visiting international troupes come calling.

Roles of the National Theatre in Cultural Diplomacy

The National Theatre over the years has provided a befitting setting and stage for national and international events including FESTAC'77, the hosting of which birthed the National Theatre. Such events have served as profitable vehicles of cultural exchange between Nigeria and many of the countries that have participated in the events. Through them, the visiting countries get to see better, aspects of the Nigerian cultures which must have enhanced mutual understanding and forged better cooperation.

Foreign artists and creatives desirous of seeing what the cultural landscape in Nigeria looks like gravitate towards the National Theatre to feel the cultural pulse of the nation. By studying what is staged, the themes and lessons inherent in such productions that make it to the National

Theatre, they can gauge what the social bearing, triumphs and challenges of the nation and what the local creatives are making out of the happenings around them.

As the host of the National Troupe of Nigeria, the National Theatre continues to help in the preservation of the cultural endowments and heritage of Nigeria which are very important in cultural exchanges when the Troupe travels within or outside the country on tours and performances where aspects of the nation's culture are re-enacted and sometimes reinterpreted on stage for contemporary relevance.

Few buildings in Africa evoke the kind of aesthetic and functional compulsion that the National Theatre edifice elicits in the whole of the African continent. The National Theatre is called the most iconic cultural building, the headquarters of culture and the oyster of culture in Nigeria. All these make the National Theatre more than just a building but an expression of the "can do" spirit of Nigeria; the epicentre of cultural entertainment and renaissance. It has come to represent a cultural heritage of the country, widely used as a synecdoche for Lagos and indeed the nation in artistic and creative works.

Such is the pull factor that the National Theatre has become that foreign dignitaries, mission staff, international societies when in Nigeria always want to visit this most historic venue and home of FESTAC'77. Through such visits, they experience Nigeria in its cultural form devoid of all the pejorative connotations that some international tabloids promote as the only things obtainable in Nigeria. Through such visits, cultural exchange or diplomacy occurs. The continuing existence of the National Theatre is a soft power that helps to project Nigeria as a destination of choice for tourists visiting Africa. With all the cultural agencies domiciled within the National Theatre complex, diverse aspects of the Nigerian culture are always on display. From visual arts to sculptures and dressmaking, the National Theatre with its rich cultural adornment per time presents an eloquent ambience as a microcosm of the nation.

In its early days, the National Theatre was the venue most befitting for official receptions of visiting foreign heads of states. On completion in 1975, the National Theatre was an artistic and cultural splendour that inspired Africa as a whole to increase their cultural consciousness and activities. It was a statement of cultural renaissance for Africans home and abroad. Little wonder that many of the Presidents and Heads of States that came to Nigeria at that period were received at the National Theatre with performances staged for their delights. This connotes that within its walls many of the early bilateral cultural agreements Nigeria entered into were signed.

The National Theatre has played a key role as host venue for cultural exchanges to take place officially and unofficially over the years. Unfortunately, its roles in cultural diplomacy have been largely hampered by the separation between it and the National Troupe of Nigeria. Going by international best practices the two agencies should exist as one entity. Hence, the performing troupe would have served as the core transmitter of Nigeria's intangible cultural assets, while the National Theatre commands tangible cultural presence. Such a synergized existence of the two, in my opinion, would better help the cultural diplomacy of the country.

Roles of the National Troupe in Cultural Diplomacy

Between 1991 when it was established and 2022, a 31-year period and under the direction of 6 Artistic Directors, to wit: Mr. Bayo Oduneye MON, Professor Ahmed Yerima, Mr. Martins Adaji, Mr. Akin Adejumo, Comrade Tar Ukoh and the incumbent, Alhaji Ahmed Mohammed Ahmed, the National Troupe of Nigeria toured over 40 countries and performed dances, dramas, dance/music dramas, musicals and a collection of dances. The import of such performances for cultural diplomacy cannot be overemphasized.

Through the efforts of the National Troupe, many aspects of the cultures that enrich Nigeria had international expressions in Egypt (1991), neigbouring Benin Republic (2002) and Ghana (2003), Egypt (2005), Ghana (2007), Zambia (2008), Gambia (2008), Ethiopia (2013), DRC Congo (2013), Egypt (2014, 2015 and 2016), MASA in Cote D'Ivoire (2022) on the African Continent. In Asia, the National Troupe toured and performed in Japan (1993), North Korea (1994), South Korea (1996), China (1999), Aichi, Japan (2005) and Japan again in (2006) as well as India (2009). In the Americas, USA (1992), San Francisco, USA (1993, 1994, 1995, 2006), Venezuela (2000), Mexico (2001), Brazil (2008) and Cuba (2012) all got a taste of the troupe's repertoire. Furthermore, UEA Dubai (2009 and 2021) and Israel (2011) also had a taste. Aside from the countries and continents aforementioned, the National Troupe of Nigeria performed in the following European Countries: Switzerland (1996), Lisbon, Portugal (1997), Hannover, Germany (2000 and 2010) and Greece (2014).

Some of the specific performances of the National Troupe used as vehicles for cultural diplomacy include; Collection of dances in Egypt, USA, Switzerland, North Korea, South Korea, Lisbon Portugal, China, Venezuela, Dance Drama "Nigeriana" in Germany, Dance Drama "Yemoja" in Mexico, Musical performances at the Pyongyang Spring Festival in North Korea, Dance Drama "Song of the gods" in Japan and Drum Ensemble in Egypt.

The National Troupe was also able to help project the cultural heritage of Nigeria far and indeed wide through these creations. The performances that the Troupe took abroad were geared at national aspirations, and through the tours the National Troupe ably represented Nigeria at international cultural events. Some of these performances were staged when the troupe accompanied government officials on international missions in order to showcase the rich culture of Nigeria. It is worthy of note that between 2006 and 2009, the National Theatre and the National Troupe came under the leadership of Prof. Ahmed Yerima, hence the National Theatre actively participated in the cultural diplomacy embarked upon during this three year period.

Often times, the performances of the National Troupe are so well received that foreign Troupes show interest in becoming collaborators or part of the Troupe while touring the country and practising for further cultural exchanges and mutual benefits. The re-enacting of the cultural heritage of the country in drama, music and dance helps in the preservation of these cultures, while performing them abroad help to imprint them on the minds of the audience wherever they are performed thereby changing the negative perceptions they might previously have had about Nigeria and Nigerians.

Not only history is performed but also contemporary issues to entertain and instruct Nigerians both locally and internationally. By organizing performances for Nigerians in the diaspora during the celebration of National days and holidays of Nigeria and that of their host countries, the National Troupe helps to give pride to the Nigerians living abroad, thereby reconciling them with the cultural vitality of their home zones.

The roles of the National Theatre and National Troupe of Nigeria in the soft power exchange called Cultural Diplomacy have been enunciated above. The challenges of the National Theatre were also mentioned. However, measures are under way under the new leadership of the both the National Theatre and the National Troupe to work more closely together for greater impact on the Nigerian society and the culture and tourism industries. The new thinking in the National Theatre is a Theatre that does not wait to host events but creates events and programmes for both local and international audiences. To play a crucial role in cultural diplomacy, the National Theatre must be a mobile Theatre or an outreach Theatre without boundaries. This connotes a Theatre that can instigate and promote performances within and outside of the edifice and stage it anywhere within Nigeria or abroad. In this way, it can engage in a more robust cultural diplomacy to attract performers and international troupes to its own events. This new thinking also foresees a robust collaboration and partnership with industry players and corporate bodies, while also very open to meaningful sponsorships.

Already, the first step towards this laudable move has already been taken with the staging of the first ever National Theatre Festival of Unity in December of 2020. The determination, organization and planning that went into the three-day event despite the pandemic that disrupted daily life and living in Nigeria as well as all over the world, is testimony to what can be achieved with the right determination. This was the first time that the National Theatre was staging its own show and not just providing a venue for others to have events. This is in recognition of the roles the National Theatre is expected to play in cultural diplomacy as the existence of the National Theatre and National Troupe as two different entities (a state policy) continues to be a major hindrance in the former playing a more assertive role in cultural diplomacy.

Since the glorious days of FESTAC'77, which though a Festival led by the Federal Government of Nigeria, there have been no such concerted efforts to assert Nigeria's cultural heritage on the global stage. When the huge success of FESTAC' 77 is compared with the clear lack of major international gatherings in the National Theatre, the import and impact of State actors in driving cultural diplomacy objectives become glaring. After all, cultural diplomacy is a domain of diplomacy concerned with establishing, developing and sustaining relations with foreign states by way of culture, art and education. It is also a proactive process of external projection in which a nation's institutions, value system and unique cultural personality are promoted at a bilateral and multilateral level (Arts Industries Policy Forum, 2006, p. 5). When the objectives are strategically formulated and well-articulated, the different actors to help in the attainment of these set objectives know the roles expected of them and this helps cultural diplomacy to run like a well-tuned orchestra producing harmonious symphonies. Conversely, the lack of clear cut foreign policy in culture as objectives results in what we have today in the National Theatre i.e. lack of political will to drive cultural diplomacy through the instrumentality of the National Theatre and the National Troupe.

It is no coincidence that the active years of the National Troupe of Nigeria followed the 1988 launching of the Cultural Policy for Nigeria, the National Troupe of Nigeria was formally included in the policy as a formal arm of Government. It was under the Sole Administration of Col. Tunde Akogun (Rtd.). By 1991 the National Troupe was touring the world with Nigerian cultures as currency of exchange in many countries, helping to project a Nigeria of people rich in culture and creativity. This shows the pivotal role agenda setting plays in a cultural diplomacy of a nation. A well-articulated and rigorously pursued policy is necessary at all times. Culture plays a key role in the enhancement of the image of a country by directing the perception of its recipients to areas that will enable a better understanding of its values (Stelowska, 2015, p. 61) in (Sheriff, 2019).

Even though the National Theatre has not occupied the space expected of it in cultural diplomacy, individual creatives have filled the vacuum. The Nollywood, music industry and even sport performers are playing key roles in this regard. The only problem with their efforts is that such efforts are largely uncoordinated and profit driven with no any national interests underpinning them. So instead of cultural diplomacy for advancement of Nigeria what obtains is a distortion of the cultural heritage of the country for gainful returns and due to the wide proliferation of such ungoverned and unsanctioned productions, Nigeria's image in the world is now so skewed that resources are periodically earmarked for national image laundering.

The focus of most of the productions in music and some in Nollywood portrays Nigeria and Nigerians as a country of weak social bearing, get-rich-quick syndrome and ostentatious live style. Syllogistically, such materials from the country's creatives buttress the notion that Nigeria is a country of youths who only engage in advance fee fraud as if it is legal and societally accepted. All these things being glorified in music and film are vices which our innate culture as a people discourages. Hence, if the National Theatre and the National Troupe were to be playing their roles as actors in cultural diplomacy then the narrative will be different and well-coordinated in well thought out and articulated foreign policy objectives. After all, "culture has become a key product in the international tourism market, both from the demand and supply sides" (Sheriff et al., 2019, p. 17).

Conclusion

In speaking with and listening to the experiences of some National Troupe artists who have been on tours within and outside of the country, it becomes glaring that serious contingent plan to earn huge economic returns from their tours is not yet in place. The opportunities inherent in displaying and selling cultural and branded wares on such foreign tours are obvious enough, yet they are not harnessed. On such cultural tours, the artists are on "display" from the moment they land at the airport of the host country to the time they depart. Everything they wear, do or say is taken as projections of the country and such impressions created become the prism through which Nigeria is seen. In the early 2000s, Nigeria made incursion into Asia with the National Troupe of Nigeria having toured Japan, India, North and South Korea and China at different times. It might not be too farfetched to see a connection between those cultural forays and the increasing economic bilateral relationships between Nigerian and some of the so-called Asian Tigers. Of necessity, the National Theatre and the National Troupe should be consistently be a critical part of Presidential team on any bilateral mission abroad because showcasing our rich cultural endowment is surely our unique selling point.

Finally, cultural diplomacy is too important an aspect of foreign policy to be left without clear cut objectives like Nigeria has witnessed since the glorious days of the cultural policy of the 1988 which birthed the National Theatre and the National Troupe came to an end. For these two agencies of Government to have the impact expected of them, a clearly stated cultural policy of the Government that is adequately funded and supported is needed. There might also be a need to merge the two parastatals (National Theatre and the National Troupe) to become one entity as found in other countries. However, the new thinking in the National Theatre of creating its own productions, programmes and events might have finally solved the problem that the separation of the two bodies had posed for the National Theatre in playing a more assertive role in cultural diplomacy heretofore. A merger or not, a well enunciated national cultural policy is pertinent. This will be what the agencies key into while making other artistic decisions that will help in actualizing the stated cultural diplomacy objectives of the country.

REFERENCES

Arts Industries Policy Forum. (2006). *Cultural diplomacy and the national Interest: In search of a 21st-century perspective*. Washington, DC: The Curb Center for Art, Enterprise, and Public Policy.

Bound, K., Briggs, R., Holden, J., & Jones, S. (2007). *Cultural diplomacy*. Demos.

Cull, N. (2007). *The national theatre of Scotland's Black Watch: Theatre as cultural diplomacy*. Los Angeles: British Council.

Guardian Newspaper. (2020, January 19). National Truope of Nigeria, It's sunset at Dawn.

Hagher, I. (2011, July 14). The importance of cultural development to national development. *Institute for Cultural Diplomacy*. Berlin.

Jora, L. (2013). New practices and trends in cultural diplomacy. *Romanian Academy, Institute of Political Sciences and International Relations*, p. 1.

Pajinta, E. (2014). Cultural diplomacy in theory and practice of contemporary international relations. *Politicke vedy/ Studies*, 95.

Sheriff Ghali Ibrahim, Adie Edward, & Nwokedi Lawretta Obiagelli. (2019). Nigeria-China cultural relations: Harnessing the potentials for tourism and national development. *Nile Journal of Political Science*, 16.

Stelowska, D. (2015). Defining cultural diplomacy. *Polish Journal of Political Science*, (3), 50–72.

PART II

Creative Practice, Soft Power and Diplomacy

CHAPTER 7

Rewriting Africa's Single-Story Narrative: Lessons from the Darmasiswa Indonesia Scholarship Program

Silas O. Emovwodo, Maybe Zengenene, and Laurent Andriamalala

S. O. Emovwodo (✉)
Professional Communication and the Media Department, Universiti Brunei Darussalam, Bandar Seri Begawan, Brunei Darussalam
e-mail: popesilasmaro@gmail.com

Theatre Emissary International (TEMi), Lagos, Nigeria

M. Zengenene
Department of Sociology, Airlangga University, Surabaya, Indonesia

L. Andriamalala
Media and Communication Department, Airlangga University, Surabaya, Indonesia

© The Author(s), under exclusive license to Springer Nature Singapore Pte Ltd. 2022
T. Afolabi et al. (eds.), *Re-centering Cultural Performance and Orange Economy in Post-colonial Africa*,
https://doi.org/10.1007/978-981-19-0641-1_7

Introduction

The Darmasiswa scholarship, established in 1974, was initially only granted to students from the Association of South-East Asia Nations (ASEAN) but was extended to students of European and other Asian countries such as Australia, Canada, Hungary, Germany, Poland, France, Japan, and Mexico, among others, in 1976. By the 1990s, it was further extended to all countries with a diplomatic relationship with Indonesia, numbering more than 135 (Ministry of Education and Culture, MoEC, 2016).

The program, which since its inception has seen more than 9,000 students from 135 nations study at 72 colleges across Indonesia, aims to promote the Indonesian language (Bahasa Indonesia), arts, and culture among the youth of other countries and to strengthen cultural and bilateral ties among participating countries (MoEC, 2016). As of 2019, 72 Indonesian universities participated, with more than 500 students from over 100 countries (MoEC, 2016). The program falls under the Ministry of Education and Culture (MoEC), Republic of Indonesia (MoEC, 2016).

The yearlong scholarship program requires that prospective participants are residents in their home countries at the time of application. The scholarship includes a monthly stipend of 2,950,000 IDR (about 200 USD for recipients who get posted to a city where the cost of living is higher such as Jakarta, Surabaya, Bali, Bandung, Batam, Monado, Makassar, Samarinda, and Ambon) or 2,550,000 IDR (about 180 USD in cities such as Surakarta, Malang, Semarang, Aceh, Bogor, Medan, Yogjakarta, Padang, Palembang, Lampung, Bogor, and Purwokerto) (MoEC, 2016). Local health insurance is available, while the organising committee bears the cost of transportation and accommodation from the orientation site to the awardee's assigned institution and visa and immigration fees, which the organising committee bears. However, awardees have to cover the cost of their return flight from their home countries to Indonesia (MoEC, 2016).

In order to be considered for the Darmasiswa scholarship, applicants must have completed secondary education or its equivalent, be between the ages of 18 and 27, be able to communicate in English and demonstrate an interest in learning the Indonesian language, art, and culture (MoEC, 2016).

For the program to achieve its objectives, awardees are attached to an educational institution where they get immersed in their community's day-to-day life and culture by taking classes alongside local students and living in their rented apartments among the locals. The courses on offer depend on the institution, but range from Indonesian language (Bahasa Indonesia), to arts (*karawitan*, traditional dance, handicraft), art/culture (Indonesian culinary and tourism), Islamic studies and art (batik, *degung*, *kecapi suli*, traditional dance, painting), art/culture (Indonesian traditional herbal medicine/culinary), and fine arts (sculptor, graphics, painting) (MoEC, 2016). During the one-year program, the Indonesian government and various institutions organise events at national and regional levels, such as the Indonesian language competition that includes poems, monologues, singing, storytelling, and cooking competitions. These provide an opportunity for international students to showcase their language skills and their own culture to members of their immediate environment.

We contend that art and culture exchange programs, which play a vital role in the mobility of ideas and knowledge exchange among participants while also strengthening diplomatic ties between nations, would help erase negative stereotypes about Africa. Africa is a culture-rich continent; however, inadequate promotion of its culture, political instability, insecurity, and socio-economic challenges have resulted in a negative single story about Africa. The single-story narrative is a phrase coined by Nigerian author Chimamanda Ngozie Adichie. "The single-story narrative creates stereotypes. The problem with stereotypes is not that they are untrue but that they are incomplete, make one story become the only story…" (Adichie, 2009).

Scholars believe that while it is natural human behaviour to categorise the people and things we come in contact with, this results in single stories that are incomplete and an oversimplification of others' identities (Facing History & Ourselves, 2021). Tannen (1990) notes that, in order to make sense of the world, people view it in patterns. However, "this natural and useful ability to see patterns of similarity has unfortunate consequences. It is offensive to reduce an individual to a category, and it is also misleading" (Tannen, 1990:16).

Buttressing the single-story narrative are the authors' experiences as recipients of the Darmasiswa scholarship in Indonesia from 2017 to 2018. On many occasions and in different settings, the authors got questions about the African skin tone and colour; the African way of life; living with animals; religion; weather; food and language (many of those we encountered conceived of Africa as a country). The program offered an avenue for many African students to tell their stories from diverse sociopolitical and economic backgrounds, educating those they encountered that Africa is not a country but a continent with diverse ways of life.

Adichie (2009) draws an essential connection between stories and power. She notes that "it is impossible to talk about the single story without talking about power...Like our economic and political worlds, stories too are defined by the principle of *nkali*: How they are told, who tells them, when they are told, how many stories are told, are really dependent on power" (Adichie, 2009). Adichie (ibid) adds that, in this context, power "is the ability not just to tell the story of another person, but to make it the definitive story of that person" (Tschida et al., 2014: 30). We agree with Adichie that stories matter and hence call for the use of soft power in post-colonial Africa in the form of cultural exchange programs. This will help to demystify and avoid the danger of an African single-story narrative. According to Adichie (ibid), it robs people of their dignity. It makes it difficult for others to recognise our equal humanity by emphasising our differences rather than what we have in common.

Literature Review

Post-colonial Theory

Post-colonial theory is a subfield of literary and cultural studies which crystallised in the 1980s (Omar, 2012). It investigates the intimate relationship between culture and politics, highlighting the interrelations between certain cultural forms and particular political and historical practices (Omar, 2008). In particular, it focuses on how the colonising culture's literature distorts the colonised's experience and realities. It also ascribes inferior status to the literature by colonised peoples, which attempts to articulate their identity and reclaim their past. Post-colonial perspectives critique the cultural hegemony of European knowledge in a quest to reassert the epistemological value of the non-European world (Gandhi, 1998) and its knowledge, which has been denigrated and silenced by colonial canonical systems.

A key defining characteristic of post-colonial theory is its emphasis on revealing the interests behind knowledge production. It also introduces an oppositional criticism that draws attention to and thereby attempts to retrieve the wide range of illegitimate, disqualified, or "subjugated knowledges" (Foucault, 1980: 82) of the decolonised peoples. It investigates the structural relations of domination and discrimination expressed, manifested, constituted, and legitimised in and by discourses.

In investigating the role of cultural exchange programs in mobilising ideas, the emphasis is thus on problematising and calling into question Africans themselves in valuing their history and heritage and promoting it as a way to dismantle the African single story. It involves critically reviewing our habits and ways of thinking and acting about its tangible and non-tangible cultural traditions. This chapter thus aims to open new possibilities for remedial alternatives and innovative ways of thinking about and transforming the African single-story narrative. African writers such as Nwakanma (2008), Adichie (2008), Edward Said, Chinua Achebe, Homi Bhabha, Frantz Fanon, and Tsitsi Dangarembwa, among others, championed the desire to liberate Africa and Africans from colonial bondage and legacies.

Soft Power

The concept of soft power was popularised in 1990 by American political scientist Joseph S. Nye Jr. (Shah, 2018). He was the first to separate the "hard" dimensions of power from a "soft power" approach. Coining this term, Nye projected the principles, values, and culture in a time when military force did not solely define power (Shah, 2018). We argue that this notion of soft power is an overlooked diplomacy tool in post-colonial Africa. For Nye (2008), a country's soft power rests upon:

1. Its culture (making it attractive to others);
2. Its political values (living up to them at home and abroad); and
3. Its foreign policies (seen and understood as legitimate and having moral authority).

All in all, Nye referred to it as the "power of seduction".

From a post-colonial perspective, African nationals and states can harness soft power to make the world the way they want it, i.e. changing and demystifying the African single-story narrative as a continent infested with diseases, wars, hunger, and poverty. According to Shah (2018), competition in the soft power sphere has spilt over into the realm of hard power. Regional bodies like the European Union (EU) and ASEAN also harness the collective assets of their member states as soft power (Ferguson, 2009). For instance, Indonesia has been granting scholarships to nationals of different countries with bilateral and diplomatic relationships for many years. Darmasiswa is an Indonesian program aimed at teaching Bahasa Indonesia and culture. In this case, Indonesia harnessed the soft power in culture and language to extend its influence among other states. Cultural relations have traditionally been close to diplomacy (Melissen, 2005). From a post-colonial point of view, soft power provides an opportunity for Africa's single-story transformation and diplomacy.

For Nye (2008: 95), soft power is not simply influenced through persuasion but "the ability to entice and attract". If soft power is "attractive power", then "soft power resources are the assets that produce such attraction". From a post-colonial point of view, Africa has tangible and non-tangible attractive resources that its countries should deploy as diplomatic and soft power. The continent's rich cultural appeal and abundant, diverse natural resources are critical soft power attractions. Offering cultural exchange programs and scholarships would enable Africa to wield its soft power effectively. Every African state should establish community and national heritage centres, museums, and community libraries. These are the benefits that can accrue from the use of "attractive" power rooted in culture, ideals, and values (Melissen, 2005).

The exercise of soft power is not only about communicating a country's cultural traditions. However, it includes communicating its political values and how fair and credible they are (van Ham, 2005: 48 cited in Shah, 2018). This begs the question of what exactly comprises Africa's single-story narrative and whether this identity influences its foreign policy and soft power strategies. From a post-colonial perspective, Africa as a continent has a long way to go, and it is Africa herself that can change this single-story narrative.

Methodology

The chapter benefitted from a focus group discussion (FGD) with seven Africans from Madagascar, Nigeria, Zimbabwe, and Zambia who participated in the Indonesian Darmasiswa Scholarship Program between 2014 and 2019.

Codes are assigned to the respondents to maintain confidentiality. The FGD was conducted online on 27 March 2021, and lasted approximately two hours using Google Meet video conferencing.

Further details about key informants are as follows:

IA, female, 25-year-old, Madagascar, 2014/2015 (participation year)
JE, male, 24-year-old, Nigeria, 2015/2016 (participation year).
LA, male, 25-year-old, Madagascar, 2016/2017 (participation year)
PS, male, 27-year-old, Zambia, 2017/2018 (participation year)
SE, male, 27-year-old, Nigeria, 2017/2018 (participation year)
MZ, female, 28-year-old, Zimbabwe, 2017/2018 (participation year)
RM, male, 18-year-old, Madagascar, 2019/2020 (participation year).

The FGD aimed to gather data on the respondents' experiences of language learning, educational tours, art festivals, and volunteer and community-based programs during the Darmasiswa program and their impact on their single stories of Indonesia. A further objective was to solicit their views on the viability of projecting tangible and intangible aspects of the African culture through language learning, educational tours, art festivals, and volunteer and community-based programs as a soft power tool to rewrite the African single-story narrative.

Analysis and Discussion

1. Student Exchange Programs Are a Vital Instrument of Soft Power.

Asked if they thought Indonesia was a powerful country, all the respondents were of the view that it is somewhat powerful compared to some African countries. They linked Indonesia's ability to consistently award scholarships to nationals of more than 100 countries, which costs the government much money, to power. However, they decried that there is no program similar to the Darmasiswa that enables Indonesians to visit and learn in their home countries. According to the respondents, this reflects a lack of power.

Most respondents claimed to have had no prior knowledge of Indonesia before receiving the scholarship. SE and PS, however, noted that, for them, the country was synonymous with natural disasters, especially earthquakes and volcanic eruptions, thus making the "ring of fire" sobriquet all the more real. For MZ, Indonesia was an Islamic country since it has the largest Muslim population in the world. These were their single-story narratives of Indonesia. However, the cultural program allowed them to engage with all the stories of Indonesians as they saw them respond creatively and rebuild their lives following such disasters.

Corroborating this, Mette Lending in Melissen (2005) observes that, "Cultural exchange is not only 'art' and 'culture' but also communicating a country's thinking, research, journalism and national debate". From this perspective, the traditional areas of cultural exchange become part of a new type of international communication. The growth of 'public diplomacy' becomes a reaction to the close connection between culture, media, and information activities due to new social, economic, and political realities.

From a post-colonial perspective, the argument is that African countries should utilise their diverse and rich cultural heritage as soft power to enhance their diplomacy. A vivid example is how China deploys soft power to enhance its diplomacy in Africa. Critically assessing this from a post-colonial perspective is more political than social. According to Jennifer G. Cooke (2009), China has made concerted efforts to broaden cultural exchanges with almost every country in Africa. As part of this initiative, the first Confucius Institute kicked off in Nairobi, Kenya, in 2005. Language (Mandarin) also acts as a source of soft power offered in conjunction with cultural programs. China has founded other educational institutions and has granted several undergraduate and post-graduate scholarships to African nationals.

Based on this analysis, we argue that there is a need for more support for cultural exchange programs within Africa to enhance diplomacy and change African single-story narratives. Of late, many African entrepreneurs have settled in China, with signs of African diaspora communities springing up in several Chinese cities. That should be the case in China and every country with diplomatic relations with African countries.

2. Language

Language features prominently as a core aspect of cultural identity. It is difficult for a colonised country to reclaim its identity by expressing it through the official language imposed by the colonists, which reduces its native language to a secondary role. It is crucial to distinguish between the semblance and similitude of the symbols across diverse cultural experiences—literature, art, music, ritual, life, death—and the social specificity of each of these productions of meaning as they circulate as signs within specific contextual locations and social systems of value (Bhabha 172).

The FGD supported this notion, as the respondents noted that Indonesian is the only medium of communication: "Since most participants study Bahasa Indonesia during the course of the program, it is only expected that we speak Bahasa even though we are learning it for the first time" (Malagasy respondent).

"I did not take Bahasa. I was in performing arts and because my institution was an art institute, no one studied Bahasa but handcrafts, paintings, dance and the likes, even though we had only a one-week introductory Bahasa class, we had to take classes in Bahasa, oftentimes the lecturers would even speak in *Bahasa Jawa* [Javanese language]. Initially, we didn't get it, but we had no choice, we started picking words until we were able to engage in conversations" (Zimbabwean respondent).

The respondents from Madagascar noted that the Indonesian embassy in their capital usually organises a three-month pre-departure language course. However, only awardees who reside in the capital can attend. RN pointed out that his government high school in Madagascar teaches Indonesian based on a partnership with the Indonesian embassy. A slot is reserved for a student from the school to participate in the Darmasiswa program each year. So far, three students have emerged as recipients of the scholarship, which has stirred interest among students in learning the Indonesian language. RN and other respondents agreed that this represents soft power at work.

3. Educational Tours and Excursions

The general notion of Africa is that it is a place with no agency, without consideration of its geographical or cultural differences. Such oversimplification is a disservice to the continent's identity (Adichie, "African 'Authenticity'"). Cultural exchange programs would give students from all corners of the world the opportunity to be insiders and explore what

Africa is, thus employing its soft power just like Indonesia. While the media depicts Indonesia as prone to various natural disasters, the Darmasiswa exchange program provides a more nuanced understanding of the country.

The African respondents that participated in the program recalled educational tours and excursions, most of which were funded or subsidised, to heritage sites, museums, and repositories. "While studying Bahasa, we would study about historical places, and after the class, we would visit some of the historic places as part of the class. We saw the Heroes Monument, the Bank repository, and other sites with colonial leftovers, such as weapons used during the war. It helped us understand what we read and helped us relate to the people's past. It is intriguing to see how much details and attention goes into preserving their history and the pride with which they share same with us foreigners" (Nigerian respondent). They also embarked on self-funded private excursions. Asked about their experiences during these trips, the respondents noted the relatively affordable transportation and different modes of travel. Worthy of mention also is the proximity of tourist destinations and relative security make it easy to explore the country. The respondents added that, in this way, they became exposed to the many stories of Indonesia.

The Darmasiswa exchange program thus plays a crucial role in Indonesia regaining its place in the world as a beautiful nation rich in natural, human, and cultural resources. The same could go for Africa by harnessing the continent's cultural heritage and establishing and promoting tourist destinations and educational exchange programs. The use of soft power to enhance Africa's diplomatic relations with other continents will help Africa and Africans to regain ownership of their narratives and become protagonists in their own stories.

4. Art Festivals

Novels, drama, poetry, oral literature, and short stories could play similar social roles as soft power to enhance Africa's diplomacy and change the single-story narrative. The post-colonial perspective seeks to assist colonised peoples in regaining ownership of their narratives and becoming protagonists in their own stories and thus transform the African continent. The prejudices imposed on Africa will become a thing of the past by Africans taking pride in their own.

The respondents said they had lost count of how many art festivals they had attended while some had participated. While RN attended only two art festivals before the lockdowns imposed due to the COVID-19 pandemic, the Zambian respondent stated: "I have attended many art festivals, and I have even participated in some. My first experience was when I and some in my Bahasa class presented a short play about an Indonesian legend. We acted alongside Indonesian stage actors, and it was in commemoration of the city's Heroes Day celebration, so it was a serious thing. We all had to memorise the lines and learn to pronounce words. It helped me to appreciate their folktales and legends as I participated in acting and getting to share their culture" (Zambian respondent).

Stories were the medium with which writers and explorers depicted places, peoples, and cultures strange to them. Similarly, they can be a tool for post-colonial African societies to assert their identity and history. Adichie and the third generation of Nigerian writers tend to question the notion of the nation as a single coherent story (Pereira, 2016). Furthermore, Adichie noted that the Western world and other continents hold a single story of what Africa is, based on racist stereotypes. To counter this stereotype, portraying the diverse faces of Africa through art festivals comes in handy.

5. Volunteer and Community-Based Programs

"Universities and other educational institutions usually organise various community based and volunteer programs. In fact, it is included in the university program; undergraduates go for what is called KKN (internships) during the holidays. Some organise programs which focus on teaching in rural areas of the country. We as foreign students are encouraged to participate and, in the process, we can engage in cultural exchange as we get to share about our countries and way of life" (Nigerian respondent).

JE from Nigeria and IA from Madagascar and the authors participated in the *Cerita Afrika* Initiative. The Indonesian term *Cerita Afrika* means African story, and this community-based program engages with the youth and children by visiting schools in their neighbourhood and delivering presentations on Africa. Since they engage with the students in English, they can practice their English-speaking skills. Indonesia is encouraging

English as a second language, and the *Cerita Afrika* Initiative and other volunteer English teaching programs contribute to the realisation of this objective. Africans and other foreigners are also playing their part. Similar programs in Africa would enable foreigners to contribute to ameliorating some of the challenges confronting the continent while exposing them to the many stories of Africans, thus enabling them to acknowledge Africans' humanity and dignity.

As a form of soft power, cultural exchange programs have great potential to counter stereotypes about Africa and its peoples and to bring the continent's issues to the fore. Through programs like Darmasiswa, Africans can draw on their tangible and non-tangible heritage to bolster their relationship with other nations of the world and place the continent firmly on the map.

Conclusion

From a post-colonial perspective, Africa has remained sidelined in a single-story narrative for a long time. Africa and Africans could utilise the continent's soft power embedded in various educational opportunities and cultural exchange programs to address this negative image and do away with hegemony, domination, legitimisation, and discrimination caused by hard power in the form of wars and conflict. It is thus recommended that African governments, in collaboration with the private sector and non-governmental organisations, consider such cultural exchange programs.

References

Adichie, C. (2009). *The danger of a single story*, TED video (filmed July 2009, posted October 2009), 18:49, accessed April 25, 2021.

Cooke, J. G. (2009). China's soft power in Africa. In C. McGiffert (Ed.), *Chinese soft power and its implications for the United States: Competition and cooperation in the developing world (CSIS reports)*.

Facing History and Ourselves. (2021). *Stereotypes and "Single Stories"*. Accessed April 25, 2021 at https://www.facinghistory.org/resource-library/teaching-holocaust-and-human-behavior/stereotypes-and-single-stories#:~:text=Author%20Chimamanda%20Ngozi%20Adichie%20uses,country%20where%20she%20is%20from

Ferguson, N. (2009). Think again: Power. *Foreign Policy, 135*, 18–24.

Foucault, M. (1980). *Power/Knowledge: Selected interviews and other writings 1972–1977.* Harvester Press.
Gandhi, L. (1998). *Postcolonial theory: A critical introduction.* Allen & Unwin.
Melissen, J. (2005). *The new public diplomacy soft power in international relations.* Palgrave Macmillan
Ministry of Education and Culture (MoEC). (2016). *Darmasiswa scholarship program.* Accessed April 20, 2021 at https://darmasiswa.kemdikbud.go.id.
Nye, J. S. (2008). Public diplomacy and soft power. *The Annals of the American Academy of Political and Social Science, 616,* 94–109. http://www.jstor.org/stable/25097996.
Omar, M. S. (2008). *Los estudios post-coloniales: Una introducción crítica.* Castellón: Universitat Jaume I.
Omar, S. M. (2012). Rethinking development from a postcolonial perspective. *Journal of Conflictology, 3*(1).
Pereira. I. C. (2016). Deconstructing the single story of Nigeria: Diasporic identities in Chimamanda Ngozi Adichie's The Thing Around Your Neck. *Blue Gum, 3,* 21–53. Australian Studies Centre.
Shah. A. L. (2018). Political identity as a soft power: India in the 21st century. Advanced Master of Science in International Relations and Diplomacy Faculty of Governance and Global Affairs, Leiden University 2016–2018.
Tannen, D. (1990). *You just don't understand: Men and women in conversation* (p. 16). Morrow.
Tschida, C., Ryan, C. L., & Swenson Ticknor, A. (2014). Building on windows and mirrors: Encouraging the disruption of single stories through children's literature. *Journal of Children's Literature, 40*(1), 28–39. https://www.researchgate.net/publication/268446210

CHAPTER 8

Cultural Diplomacy and the Orange Economy in Africa: A Case Study of Nollywood

Kasim Adoke and Ishaq Saidu

Background

Africa has an image problem in the international community, partly due to the ugly experience of the slave trade and colonialism that left the continent with low self-esteem, disrepute, high levels of poverty, and political instability. These challenges are serious problems for the continent in the comity of nations. Furthermore, Africa is the most vulnerable continent as the world grapples with climate change, heightened insecurity, and technological advances (Gumbi, 2015). Cultural diplomacy and an improved orange economy could be employed to address this situation.

K. Adoke
Department of Political Science, Ahmadu Bello University, Zaria, Nigeria

I. Saidu (✉)
Department of Economics, Baze University, Abuja, Nigeria
e-mail: ishaq.saidu@bazeuniversity.edu.ng

© The Author(s), under exclusive license to Springer Nature Singapore Pte Ltd. 2022
T. Afolabi et al. (eds.), *Re-centering Cultural Performance and Orange Economy in Post-colonial Africa*,
https://doi.org/10.1007/978-981-19-0641-1_8

Its challenges notwithstanding, Africa has a diverse, resilient, and rich cultural and traditional heritage, which to a large extent, is peculiar to the people of the continent. Given the growing importance of the cultural dimension of international relations, its cultural heritage could be an enabling tool to improve its image and repositioning the continent's economy. Recognition of culture's growing importance in international relations is informed by constructivist theorists who introduced ideas, norms, and culture to the study and conceptualization of diplomacy and international relations in order to counter the growing tendency of power politics that lead to conflict Stelowska(2015, p. 51). Moreover, the use of force is now being rejected by many ordinary citizens (Kang, 2013). The use of cultural diplomacy to develop mutual understanding and improve relationships is not entirely new in both cross-border and domestic encounters. It can be used at the local and international level to embrace a culture of peace and diminish that of war (Gumbi, 2015).

Africa has deployed cultural diplomacy since early times. Indeed, the people of the continent are known to be inherently hospitable, making diplomacy essentially an African culture (Sotubo & Chidozie, 2014). Nigeria in particular has always given cultural diplomacy pride of place in her domestic environment and foreign relations. This is evident in the adoption of schemes like the National Youth Service Commission (NYSC), and the country's foreign policy which is hinged on the belief that peace is fundamental for development. Based on this belief, the principles of the legal equality of all states, non-interference in states' internal affairs, multilateralism, and Afrocentrism have been the guiding norms of Nigeria's foreign policy (Anaemene, 2015; Gumbi, 2015).

Within the context of this discourse, cultural diplomacy goes beyond the above principles to emphasize that culture can be transformed into goods and services which can create awareness, entertain, and have commercial value. Cultural awareness among peoples and nations can thus promote international cooperation and commercial success (Kang, 2013). Climate change and rapid advancements in ICT and robotic science are changing the face of the global economy. There is a shift towards a knowledge-based economy with an emphasis on intellectual property rather than on the availability of natural resources. The orange economy with its inputs of talent and creativity can be harnessed to overcome adversity, generate employment, and create prosperity (Gasca & Luzardo, 2018).

In contemporary times, many countries and international organisations are struggling to cope with humanitarian and economic crises caused by conflict, often due to conflicts over natural resources. The consequences of power politics have sparked increased interest in soft power. It is against this background that this chapter examines how cultural diplomacy and the orange economy can enhance soft power in Africa. The choice of Nollywood as the case study is informed by a number of factors. Nigeria, the home of Nollywood, is the most populous country in Africa with 250 ethnic groups, making it the most heterogeneous society in Africa. Furthermore, in comparison to its counterparts across Africa, Nollywood is the largest producer of films and the biggest employer of labour. It has recorded the fastest growth and also attracts the most viewers in the diaspora.

Conceptualization of Cultural Diplomacy, the Orange Economy and Soft Power

It is important to clarify the terms employed in this chapter due to the general lack of consensus among scholars in the social sciences in terms of the definitions of concepts. Since the subject matter of social sciences is not "self-defining in the way that is often the case in the natural sciences" Brown & Ainley (2005, p. 2), this will assist in defining the context within which this contribution is located. Moreover, they are relatively new terms whose definitions continue to evolve.

Cultural Diplomacy

Cultural diplomacy is a term that is often confusing in international relations. It is sometimes used interchangeably with public diplomacy, propaganda, and cultural relations. It is argued that this "confusion arises from the fact that cultural diplomacy is very different from other sorts of diplomatic interactions" Gienow-Hecht & Donfried (2010, p. 13). Scholars whose focus is "state involvement and clear-cut state interest" are more likely to link cultural diplomacy to propaganda-like activities. On the other hand, those who focus less on state involvement in cultural diplomacy tend to base their definitions on "cultural relations and benevolent long term strategy" Gienow-Hecht, (2010, p. 9).

Kang (2013) observes that cultural diplomacy has multi-dimensional aspects; its currencies include cultural relations, cultural cooperation, public diplomacy, and even propaganda. The author adds that cultural diplomacy involves different tools designed to advance the national interest. He thus describes cultural diplomacy as a "multidimensional process of international cultural politics underpinned by varying national objectives and sociopolitical context" Kang (2013, p. 1).

In contrast, Arndt (2006) does not regard cultural relations as one of the currencies of cultural diplomacy. He argues that the former grows naturally and organically without government intervention while the latter can only be said to take place when formal diplomats, serving national governments, try to shape and channel these cultural flows to advance the national interest Arndt, 2006 in Kang (2013, p. 3).

Cummings defines cultural diplomacy as "the exchange of ideas, information, art and other aspects of culture among nations and their peoples to foster mutual understandings" Cummings (2003, p. 1). For Enders, it is the "instrument that serves for political purposes, and although it establishes its own objectives.... these are derived from the general foreign policy objectives" Enders, 2005 in Pajtrika (2014, p. 100).

These definitions lead to the understanding that cultural diplomacy is intended to serve socio-economic and political purposes even though they are not explicitly stated. As the definition of the term continues to evolve it is likely that all of these points would be explicitly captured.

Cultural diplomacy manifests in a number of ways including offering of cultural gifts to visiting dignitaries; display of cultural dances in honour of dignitaries; organisation of cultural events by missions and embassies to honour and celebrate celebrities—who are usually cultural ambassadors; organisation of cultural festivals and events; arrangement of educational exchange programmes between two countries or communities; reaching of cultural agreements between two or more countries; and rendering of assistance to a needy country. It also takes place when a country establishes cultural institutions to teach outsiders its languages and to offer cultural services, e.g. Alliance Francaise, the Goethe Institute, British Council, and the United States Information System. Another important medium through which cultural diplomacy is manifested is through the cinema whereby movies produced in one country are exported to others for the purpose of creating awareness about the ideals of the originating country, and so on (Asobele, 2002; Gumbi, 2015).

Nigeria has made considerable investments in cultural diplomacy. Given the heterogeneous nature of the country, it has always applied cultural values to build unity among its diverse groups.

Nigerian Cultural Policy

In order to maintain an orderly and meaningful socio-political, economic, aesthetic, and religious norms of its people, Nigeria adopted a National Cultural Policy in 1988. The policy seeks to affirm the country's unique peculiarities and promote national unity. It is a "legal document prescribing guidelines, procedure, methods and practices of culture in the country" (Samuel & Chimeziem, 2009) that promotes cultural practices among the 470 ethnic tribes in Nigeria Anyanwu (2019, p. 7).

This policy is codified in a document titled "Cultural Policy for Nigeria" and printed by the Federal Republic of Nigeria in 1988. It is important to highlight the objectives of the policy, which are captured under Sect. 8.3 as enshrined in the policy document and in the following order on page 6 of the document;

> 3.1. The policy shall serve to mobilise and motivate the people by disseminating and propagating ideas which promote national pride, solidarity, and consciousness.
> 3.2. The policy shall serve to evolve from our plurality, a national culture, the stamp of which will be reflected in African and World affairs.
> 3.3. The policy shall promote an educational system that motivates and stimulates creativity and draws largely on our tradition and values, namely: respect for humanity and human dignity, for legitimate authority and the dignity of labour, and respect for positive Nigerian moral and religious values.
> 3.4. The policy shall promote creativity in the fields of arts, science, and technology, ensure the continuity of traditional skills and sports and their progressive updating to serve modern development needs as our contribution to world growth of culture and ideas.
> 3.5. The policy shall establish a code of behaviour compatible with our tradition of humanism and a disciplined moral society.
> 3.6. The policy shall sustain environmental and social conditions which enhance the quality of life, produce responsible citizenship and an ordered society.
> 3.7. The policy shall seek to enhance the efficient management of national resources through the transformation of the indigenous technology, design-resources, and skills.

3.8. The policy shall enhance national self-reliance and self-sufficiency and reflect our cultural heritage and national aspiration in the process of industrialization.

Following the above objectives the policy document, under Sect. 8.4 captioned "Method of Implementation" declared that the cultural policy shall be expressed in four broad categories of state action, which include; Preservation of culture; Promotion of culture; Presentation of culture; and the establishment of administrative structure and provision of funds for its implementation.

With regard to the preservation of culture, the document states that this refers to "the promotion of cultural property whether of a concrete or non-concrete nature, past or present, written or oral, or relating to values or facts of history" Federal Republic of Nigeria (1988, p. 6). Promotion of culture is concerned with creation of enabling environment for cultural education, consciousness and development by encouraging the integration of traditional values in people's daily lives. As for the presentation of culture, it refers to the question of culture dissemination by which means access to art and culture through theatre, films, exhibitions, seminars, workshops, and publications or mass media is facilitated. Finally, administrative structures and institutions are established by the state to promote the objectives of the cultural policy. The state shall also make arrangement for these structures and institutions to generate funds including through private sources.

The Ministry of Culture and Social Welfare was charged with responsibility for implementing the Cultural Policy. Its name was later changed to the Ministry of Culture, Tourism and National Orientation and today, the Ministry of Information has been merged with that of culture. Several agencies have been created to perform various functions in relation to cultural activities and diplomacy, including the National Council for Arts and Culture; National Commission for Museums and Monuments; National Gallery of Arts; National Institute for Cultural Orientation; National Orientation Agency; National Theatre; Center for Black African Arts and Culture; Nigerian Copyright Commission; National Library of Nigeria; Federal Radio Corporation of Nigeria; Nigerian Television Authority; Film Corporation of Nigeria; and the National Troupe of Nigeria, among others Anyanwu (2019, p. 726; Official Website of Federal Ministry of Information and Culture, 2020).

In recognition of the role played by culture in Nigeria's socio-economic and political wellbeing, Chapter II, Sect. 21 of the Constitution of the Federal Republic of Nigeria provides that Nigerian State shall:

(a) Protect, preserve, and promote the Nigerian cultures which enhance human dignity and are consistent with the fundamental objectives as provided in this chapter, and
(b) Encourage development of science and scientific studies which enhance cultural values.

Nigeria has thus invested in cultural diplomacy for the purpose of both domestic unity and international cooperation. The fact that the country established the National Institute for Cultural Orientation (NICO), a cultural training institute, in addition to the National Cultural Policy shows that Nigeria is actively interested in using the cultural resources of its diverse peoples for national development. In a speech read on his behalf by the Permanent Secretary of the Federal Ministry of Culture Tourism and National Orientation, Mrs Nkechi Ejele at the opening ceremony of the 28th Annual International Conference of the Society of Nigeria Theatre Artists (SONTA, 2015) in Abuja in 2015, on the theme "Repositioning Nollywood for the Promotion of Nigeria's Cultural Diplomacy and National Security" President Muhammadu Buhari expressed his support for the call for Nollywood to be repositioned to promote Nigeria's rich cultural heritage.

The Orange Economy

The term orange economy originated in Colombia and it is used interchangeably with creative economy (UNCTAD, 2008). The Inter-America Development Bank (2003) defines the orange economy as "the set of activities that in an interlocking way allow for ideas to be transformed into cultural goods and services". It is that sector of the economy that has "talent and creativity as leading inputs". Gasca & Luzardo (2018, p. 9). In the same vein, the United Nations Conference on Trade and Development (UNCTAD) (2008) refers to the creative economy as those sectors which specialize in the use of talent for commercial purposes.

In a nutshell, the orange economy is an intellectual property driven economy where economic growth is generated from talent and creativity.

The industries that drive this economy are called creative industries. Creative industries are said to be at the crossroad of the arts, culture, business, and technology, and they range from folk art, music, paintings, festivals, and performing arts to more technology-intensive subsectors such as the film industry, broadcasting, digital animation and video games, and more service-oriented fields such as architectural and advertising (UNCTAD, 2008). While the majority of African countries still depend on commodities as their main source of revenue, the world economy has been reshaped by globalization and technological advancements. The high level of interconnectivity among people across the globe in defiance of borders has highlighted the importance of culture and its creative components.

Andreas Durkin describes creative goods and services which are products of talent and creativity as including art that one can hang on one's wall, print newspapers and craft, but also works that are experienced such as gastronomy and live music. Beyond the physical realm, they include gaming apps on phones, advertising on TV, and streamed movies. The infrastructure that supports interaction with creative goods and services is also part of the orange economy, including stadiums, fibre-optic networks, and museums (Durkin, 2020).

It is important to note that apart from economic gain, creative goods and services generate social gains as they foster social cohesion and community interaction. Studies note that, despite Africa's rich and diverse cultural resources, developing countries under which African countries fall, have yet to take advantage of the potential for the development of creative industries. Furthermore, there has been limited commercialization of African cultural products (UNCTAD, 2008) and those that are commercialized face the serious problem of copyright infringement. A typical example is the high level of piracy bedevilling Nollywood.

Soft Power

The failure of the United States of America, despite its superior weaponry, to win its protracted war with Vietnam—a relatively small Asian nation—revealed much about the limitations of hard power. This prompted Joseph Nye to come up with the concept of soft power in 1990. Since he coined this term it has gained currency in the conduct of international affairs.

Nye (1990) defined soft power as the ability to shape what others want by being attractive cited in Wang & Lu, (2008, p. 425). He posited that a country's soft power can emanate from three resources, namely, its culture (in places where it is attractive to others), its political values (where it lives up to them at home and abroad), and its foreign policies (when they are seen as legitimate and having moral authority) (Nye, 2006).

For further explanation, soft power is the ability of a state to use its resources or assets which may be cultural values, political values, goods and services, and even institutions to win friends through attraction in the international arena in order to make them identify with its national interest. In that sense, the behaviour and actions that emanate from the state negate coercion. So, instead of using military might and economic power to intimidate, threaten or coerce they are used to coopt. It then means that emphasis is on love rather than fear (British Council, 2019; Ogunnubi & Isike, 2015). Quite interestingly, the people of a belligerent country can be made, if attracted, to by-pass their government and fall in love with values and ways of the originating soft power. The emphasis on love clearly shows that soft power involves more of a cooperative than a confrontational relationship even with military might or economic power. According to Nye, military resources do not only produce hard power. They can also produce soft power in the same way that "economic strength can be converted into hard or soft power: you can coerce countries with sanctions or woo them with wealth" (Nye, 2006).

Soft power can help to address the international challenges of the twenty-first century such as terrorism, mass migration, climate change, and infectious diseases. Influence of soft power can be harnessed to build the global conditions required to address these challenges and ensure that the rules of the international system are generally respected (British Council, 2019).

Soft power is hinged on cooption as against coercion. If a country is attracted by another country's policies without the latter using a carrot or stick to influence it, soft power is at play and there is a high likelihood of successfully pursuing common goals. Nigeria is a good example of a country that believes in soft power. Its foreign policy has consistently engaged in activities that portray love rather than hate, including its Afrocentric bent that is geared towards supporting other African countries (Gumbi, 2015). Other examples of soft power are the Marshall Plan, which was used to pump billions of dollars into war-ravaged Europe, educational exchange programmes, and disaster assistance programmes. (Jones, 2019).

Brief Overview of Nollywood

The Nigerian film industry dates back to the turn of twentieth century during the colonial era when peephole viewing of motion picture devices was invented and under the control of the colonisers. Improved motion picture devices were introduced when the first set of films was screened in Lagos at the Glover Memorial Hall in 1903. The first feature film was made in 1926, featuring Nigerian actors in speaking roles. In 1957, the first film entirely copyrighted to the Nigerian Film Unit was shot in colour. Soon after independence, the number of Nigerian content theatres increased. In the 1970s, more Nigerians were involved in active roles in cinema and film due to the Indigenization Decree of 1972, which led to the handover of about 300 film theatres by their foreign owners to Nigerians. Due to some factors like the devaluation of naira and lack of production equipment, there was a decline in the Nigerian cinema in the 1980s. It was picked in the 1990s (Essien, 2020).

The Nigerian film industry continued to grow through the 1990s when *direct to video films* were produced and peaked in the mid-2000s to become the second largest film industry in the world after the Indian film industry (Omanufeme, 2016). In 2016, Nollywood contributed 2.3% (NGN239 billion) to Nigeria's Gross Domestic Product (GDP). The revenue from the "box office" (Nollywood) rose by 36% from $17.3 million in 2017 to $23.6 million in 2018 (Pricewaterhousecoopers, 2017).

Nollywood in Perspective

It is argued that film is the most potent weapon by which the identity and character of a nation, its image, culture, aspirations, peculiar sounds, and achievement are impressed on the minds of people throughout the world (Asobele, 2002). Nollywood's films are a staple in many African homes. For many diaspora viewers, Nollywood represents a piece of home and a source of education about their culture from which they learn valuable lessons (Giwa, 2014). In 2009, Mrs Dora Akunyili, the late former Minister of Information and Communication enlisted Nollywood to serve as part of the then rebranding project (Sotubo & Chidozie, 2014). It has also been observed that Nigerian films have been a major diplomatic tool (Anaemene, 2015).

The increase in viewing centres and current media technologies like YouTube and other media outlets, as well as film festivals all over the world and traditional media for watching films, have meant that Nollywood has the capacity to effectively serve as a tool for Nigerian cultural diplomacy. This calls for serious attention from the government as to the image it portrays. Rather than focusing on only the number of jobs it creates, the government should ensure that Nollywood directors and actors are aware of their socio-political role as cultural ambassadors. One way of achieving this would be to involve intellectuals like Political Scientists and Sociologists in training the industry's major players.

Challenges Confronting Nollywood

Despite Nollywood's many successes and opportunities, it faces several challenges, including copyright infringement, unrefined content, inadequate funding and deficient infrastructure.

Copyright Infringement: Copyright infringement refers to the unauthorized act of doing or causing someone to do any of the acts that are expressly reserved for the owner of the right in a creative work. This right is divided into economic and moral rights, and they are covered in the Copyright Act administered by the Nigerian Copyright Commission (NCC), which was inaugurated on 19 August 1989 following the military promulgation of the copyright Decree No. 47 of 1988 (Nwogu, 2014). The Commission has its headquarters in Abuja and offices in 14 states of the Federation. In spite of this presence and the penalties attached to the offence, the Commission seems to be facing herculean tasks finding lasting solution to the menace. A survey work done by the Commission in 2008 suggested that the existing copyright law is not effective enough and so translates to weak enforcement. Anyone found guilty of this offence upon conviction is either fined or serves a prison term or both. Copyright laws exist to motivate creators of creative works and to encourage innovation (Nigerian Copyright Commission, 2008; Copyright Act, 2004).

The NCC has been fighting piracy in Nigeria for more than 30 years. However, it suffers from inadequate funding, hampering its work. Many have been arrested and convicted but the menace remains. In cities, towns, and villages across the country pirates go about their illicit business without much hindrance. It appears that this problem is not being handled in the appropriate manner and some have attributed this to high levels of corruption. Ayakoroma notes that, "Debilitating societal corruption, non-adherence to the law and official collusion in high places have made it virtually impossible to curb barefaced and rampant piracy of the products of the film industry" cited in Abdullahi (2015, p. 5).

Unrefined content: The film industry has been criticized for not protecting Nigeria's image due to uncensored and unrefined content. The content of a film speaks louder than its other aspects because it forms images in the minds of viewers. Ibagere (2015) criticized the film industry for portraying the country in negative ways and Azuah (2008) adduced that, "most Nigerian films present an unsophisticated and inhuman image of Nigeria because they lack literary merit and promote the demonization of women, occultism, homophobia and fundamental Christianity" (Ibagere, 2015).

Euphemia et al. (2015) observes that content that portrays Nigeria in a negative way is contained in epic films that try to relate the cultural practices of the past. Dwelling on the past even when such practices are no longer attractive to people, creates a bad image of the country and indeed,

Africa. Nollywood should thus dwell more on the positive side of Nigerian cultural practices so that the country can be attractive to others.

Inadequate funding: The film industry has lacked adequate funding for a long period of time. Goodluck Jonathan's administration made $200 million and #3 billion available to the industry in 2010 and 2013, respectively to build the capacity of film makers and actors. This stimulus package enabled it to grow from producing low budget movies to a $5 billion movie industry (Ibagere, 2015).

Conclusion

This chapter examined how cultural diplomacy and the orange economy could enhance Africa's soft power using Nollywood as a case study. It showed that Nollywood has the potential to propel cultural diplomacy which enhances the size of the orange economy. This would stimulate economic activity and improve economic growth as well as promote peaceful co-existence between Nigeria and the outside world. However, harnessing the full potential of the orange economy requires a conducive environment where creativity can thrive. The chapter highlighted some of the factors that need to be addressed in order for Nollywood's potential to be realized.

REFERENCES

Abdullahi, D. (2015). *Teaching and old dog a new trick: Reviewing government's interventions in the Nollywood industry*. Being a Paper Presented at the Annual International Conference of the Society of Nigerian Theatre Artists (SONTA), holding from the 3–6 August, 2015, at The Shehu Musa Yar'adua Centre, Abuja.

Anaemene B. U. (2015.) Cultural imperatives in foreign policy: The case of Nigeria. In K. Nwoko & O. Osiki (Eds.), *Dynamics of culture and tourism in Africa: Perspectives on Africa's development in the 21st century*. Babcock University Press.

Anyanwu C. (2019). Nigeria's cultural policy and the needs of the performing arts. *International Review of Humanities Studies*. 4(2), 717–727. https://www.researchgate.net/publicatoin/334778866

Ayakoroma, F. (2014). *Trends in nollywood. A study of selected genres*.

Azuah. U. (2008). *The lenght of light*. VDM verlag book. ISBN 10: 369106245.

Benavente, J. M & Grazzi, M. (2017). *Public policies for creativity and innovation: Promoting the Orange Economy in Latin America and the Caribbean*. Inter-American Development Bank. https://publications.iadb.org/publications/english/document/Public

British Council. (2019). *Developing creative economics in ODA Countries*. Overview Report. Tom Fleming/Creative Consultancy. http//www.britishcouncil.com

Brown, C., & Ainley, K. (2005). *Understanding international relations*. Palgrave Macmillan.

Constitution of the Federal Republic of Nigeria. (1999). Federal Government Press.

Cummings, M. C. (2003). *Cultural Diplomacy and the United States Government: A Survey*. Center for arts and culture.

Cummings, M. C. (2009). *Cultural diplomacy and the United States government: A survey*. http://www.americanforthearts.org

Durkin, A. (2020). *The orange economy: Where creativity is an economic asset*. https://globaltrademag.com

Essien, M. (2020). *Nollywood: A brief history of Nigerian cinema*. www.curiosityshots.com/Nollywood-a-brief-history.

Euphemia, A. C., Ben, O. I., & Unekwu, O. E. (2015). The representation of Nigeria indigenous culture in nollywood. *Journal of Scientific Research and Reports*, 97–107. https://doi.org/10.9734/JSRR/2015/15596

Federal Republic of Nigeria. (1988). *Cultural policy for Nigeria*. Federal Government Printers.

Gasca and Luzardo. (2018). *Launching an orange future*. Inter-American Development Bank Publication. http://www.creativecommons.org/licences/by-nc- nd/3.0/igo/legalcode

Gienow-Hecht & Donfried (Eds.). (2010). *Searching for a cultural diplomacy*. Berghahn Books.

Giwa, E. T. (2014). *Nollywood: A case study of the rising Nigerian film industry—Content & production*. Research Papers. Paper 518. http://opensiuc.lib.siu.edu/gs_rp/518

Gumbi, K. S. (2015). *The role of cultural diplomacy in promoting Nigerians National Image in the Common Wealth*. International Symposium on Cultural Diplomacy Organised by the Institute of Cultural Diplomacy, July 22–24th 2015, London. https://www.academia.edu/19334107

Ibagere, E. (2015). Globalization and nollywood: Carving a niche on the global plane. *International Journal of Africa Society, Cultures and Tradition*. European Centre for Training and Development Cullingham Kent, UK

Jones, S. (2019). *Understanding soft power in US foreign policy*. https://www.thoughtsco.com

Kang, H. (2013). *Reframing cultural diplomacy: International Cultural Politics of Soft Power and the Creative Economy. Culture, Media & Creative Industries*, King's College London. https://www.culturaldiplomacy.org

Nigerian Copyright Commission. (2004). *Copyright Act*. CAP C28, Laws of Federation of Nigeria and Subsidiary Legislations.

Nigerian Copyright Commssion. (2008). *Survey of copyright piracy in Nigeria*. Management Review Limited, Lagos.

Nwogu, M. I. O. (2014). The challenges of the Nigerian copyright commission (NCC) in the fight against copyright piracy in Nigeria. *Global Journal of Politics and Law Research*, 2(5), 22–34.

Nye, J. S. (2006). *Think again: Soft power*. https://www.foriegnpolicy.com

Ogunnubi, O., & Isike, C. (2015). Regional hegemonic contention and the asymmetry of soft power: A Comparative Analysis of South Africa and Nigeria. *Strategic Review for Southern Africa*, 37(1), 152–177.

Omanufeme. S. (2016, June). Nigeria's film industry is taking off. *Finance & Development*, 53(2).

Pajtinka, E. (2014). *Cultural diplomacy in theory and practice of contemporary international relations*. https://www.researchgate.net/publication/269763112/

PWC's Global Entertainment & Media Outlook (2017–2021). https://www.pwc.com

Raimzhanova, A. (2015). Power in IR: *Hard, soft, and smart*. Institute for Cultural Diplomacy and the University of Bucharest https://www.culturaldiplomacy.org

Samuel, E. & Chimeziem, G. (2009). Towards the implementation of the Nigerian cultural policy for the promotion of culture in Nigeria. *African Journal Online*, 3(1). https://www.ajol.info/index.php/cajtms/article/view/76597

Society of Nigeria Theatre Artists (SONTA). (2015). Remark by Nkechi Ejele, Permanent Secretary, Federal Ministry of Culture Tourism and National Oreintation, at Repositioning Nollywood for the promotion of Nigeria's cultural diplomacy & national security: Proceedings of the 28th Annual International Conference of the Society of Nigeria Theatre Artists (SONTA), from 3rd–6th August, 2015, at the Shehu Musa Yar'Adua Centre, Abuja. Available at https://nico.gov.ng/2015/08/07/remarks-by-nkechi-ejele-permanent-secretary-federal-ministry-of-tourism-cultureand-national-orientation-on-the-occasion-of-the-opening-ceremony-of-the-28th-edition-of-the-sonta-internationalconferen/

Sotubo, E. C. U. & Chidozie, F. C. (2014), Cultural diplomacy and national development: A study of the Nigerian entertainment industry. *An International Journal of Arts and Humanities*, 3 (2). https://doi.org/10.4314/ijah.v3i2.5

Stelowska, D. (2015). Culture in international relations. Defining cultural diplomacy. *Polish Journal of Political Science*, 1(3), 50–72.

Timothy-Asobele, S. J. (2002) *Nigerian cultural diplomacy in the 20th Century*. Lagos PromoComms Limited.

UNCTAD. (2008). *Creative economy report*. http://www.unctad.org/creative-economy

Wang and Lu (2008). The conception of soft power and its policy implications: A comparative study of China and Taiwan. *Journal of Contemporary China*, *1750* 425–447. https://doi.org/10.1080/10670560802000191

Official Website of Federal Minisrty of Information and Culture, Nigeria. (2020). www.fmic.gov.ng.

CHAPTER 9

Nollywood, the Orange Economy and the Appropriation of Nigeria's Soft Power

Olusola Ogunnubi and Dare Leke Idowu

INTRODUCTION

Despite possessing enormous natural, human and cultural resources that major powers plundered and exploited to develop Europe and North America from the era of slavery to colonial and neo-colonial times,

O. Ogunnubi
Centre for Gender and African Studies, University of the Free State, Bloemfontein, South Africa
e-mail: OgunnubiOR@ufs.ac.za

D. L. Idowu (✉)
Political Science and International Relations Programmes, Bowen University, Iwo, Nigeria
e-mail: dare.idowu@bowen.edu.ng

O. Ogunnubi
Carleton University, Ottawa, Canada

© The Author(s), under exclusive license to Springer Nature Singapore Pte Ltd. 2022
T. Afolabi et al. (eds.), *Re-centering Cultural Performance and Orange Economy in Post-colonial Africa*,
https://doi.org/10.1007/978-981-19-0641-1_9

Africa has often been historicized and labeled as a backward continent with a cultural orientation, values and worldviews that are anti-developmental (Achebe, 1959; Bunce, 2014; Harrison & Huntington, 2000; Mhango, 2018; Tsikata, 2014). The reason for this disparaging depiction is not hard to find, as the majority of what constitutes the history of Africa was written by white men who made fallacious and distorted claims about the continent and its people. The dearth of authentic stories of Africa told and written by Africans paved the way for the proliferation of what Mhango called the "besmirched, distasteful, miswritten and misrepresented story of the white man on Africa or history that is taken as the history of Africa" Mhango (2018, p. vii).

Unfortunately, state failure, human rights violations and the menace of political corruption on the continent have helped to validate this single story[1] of Africa propagated by the Western media, nationals and influential leaders (*The Economist*, 2000). Western media are famous for capitalizing on these shortcomings to buttress the propagation of disparaging stereotypes about Africa, Africans and Africans in the diaspora (Tsikata, 2014). However, Nigeria and the continent's other 53 states boast of an array of attractive cultural and creative resources that have impressive global appeal, orange economy value and soft power implications. More specifically, Nigeria possesses abundant and globally admired cultural and creative exports in the form of its highly-rated music (hip-hop and highlife), Nollywood movies, dance, arts and crafts, gospel music (Ogunnubi & Idowu, 2022) and digital comedy skits (Idowu & Ogunnubi, 2022) that have significant economic potential, global appeal, and soft power and diplomatic potential.

Despite their enormous economic value and contributions, global adulation and diplomatic prospects, Nigeria and its foreign policy actors have yet to unravel the soft power potential and orange economy of the country's highly esteemed creative and cultural exports to boost its external image and augment its diminishing revenue base. Furthermore, as noted by the British Council (2013), no detailed empirical research has investigated "the character, size and contribution of the cultural industry to the Nigerian economy" British Council (2013, p. 7). Similarly, apart

---

[1] https://www.ted.com/talks/chimamanda_ngozi_adichie_the_danger_of_a_single_story?language=en.

from the data on the formal and informal sectors' contribution to Nigeria's Gross Domestic Product (GDP) and revenue, the Nigerian Bureau of Statistics has yet to produce empirical data on creative industries' annual contribution to the country's GDP. It is against this background that this chapter critically examines the orange economy of Nigeria's highly rated Nollywood and interrogates its contribution to the country's economic development. It also unravels the appropriation of Nollywood's soft power and diplomatic prospects to boost Nigeria's external image and extend its admiration globally.

Nigeria's Cultural and Creative Industries: An Untapped Creative Economy and Soft Power Pivot

Cultural and creative industries (CCI) are contested concepts that lack a generally accepted definition. Scholars, policy experts and government agencies have intensely debated the meaning and criteria to classify what constitute CCI (Daubaraite & Startiene, 2015). This has resulted in a plethora of definitions by scholars that aim to capture the realities of CCI in their respective states. The United Nations Educational, Scientific and Cultural Organization (UNESCO) defines cultural industries as those that "combine the creation, production and commercialisation of contents which are intangible and cultural in nature. The contents are typically protected by copyright and they can take the form of goods or services" Moore (2014, p. 744). The United Nations Conference on Trade and Development (UNCTAD) describes creative industries as activities that "range from folk art, festivals, music, books, paintings and performing arts to more technology-intensive subsectors such as the film industry, broadcasting, digital animation and video games, and more service-oriented fields such as architectural and advertising services" UNCTAD (2008, p. 6).

Nigeria boasts of enormous CCI, resources and talent that produce creative goods and services that have attractive economic appeal and diplomatic prospects. If properly harnessed by means of deliberate public policies, partnerships and funding, they offer a wide array of economic prospects in the form of job creation, income generation, poverty alleviation (Agoralumiere International, 2009) and the diversification of Nigeria's unidirectional economy. The British Council avers that CCI outputs have a more significant potential to spur investment, create wealth and generate employment than other economic sectors (British Council, 2013). Creative industries accounted for N5 trillion (US$16.4 billion) or 5.3% of Nigeria's GDP of N94.14 trillion (US$308.6 billion) in 2015 (Nwankwo, 2018). In 2016, the Arts, Entertainment and Recreation Sector of the Nigerian creative industry contributed NGN239 billion or 2.3% of Nigeria's GDP (PwC, 2017).

While revenue proceeds from the oil sector are susceptible to variations and crashes in the global price of crude, and the turmoil resulting from the Niger Delta conflicts and the COVID-19 pandemic, the products of Nigeria's CCI have demonstrated a reasonable level of immunity to these shocks (Sayne & Hruby, 2016). This underscores the need for the Nigerian government to not only invest in the country's CCI but also formulate viable policies to optimize the productivity and profitability of this major sector of its economy.

Despite its vast potential and economic prospects, Nigeria's creative industry continues to perform at low levels of productivity and efficiency (Nwankwo, 2018). The main reason is that the government has not adopted a comprehensive strategy to map the activities that constitute this industry and revitalize them through deliberate policy measures backed by adequate funding and financial support. Compared with other sectors of the Nigerian economy, there have been a few policies and financial interventions to protect investors from the high risks involved in investing in this viable non-oil sector. This is arguably the result of the government's focus on earnings from the sale of crude oil. Indeed, the British Council bemoans the "lack of verifiable data on the economic contribution, job creation and other macroeconomic indices of the sector" British Council (2013, p. 5).

Given the dearth of information on the resources and activities that constitute Nigeria's creative economy, the British Council used Lagos as a pilot study to undertake preliminary mapping of this sector in 2013 focusing on its "size, employment profile and other trends" British Council (2013, p. 5). Bearing in mind the lack of global consensus on the conceptual meaning and the activities, goods and resources that constitute creative industries, it relied on the analysis of qualitative data sourced from strategic stakeholders in the industry to map these activities, goods and services into ten categories (The British Council, 2013) as follows:

home video/film/television and radio, performing arts (theatre, festival, carnival, dance, drama, stand up comedy), Music, visual art and animation (photography, painting, graphic design, drawing, sculpture etc), Tourism and hospitality (museums and monument, cuisine, nite clubs, events managements etc), Arts and crafts, fashion and design, Publishing (literature, book fairs, e-resources etc), Architecture (interior décor, landscaping etc), Advertising. The British Council (2013, p. 10)

Although this is not a comprehensive representation of all the creative industries in Nigeria, it is a fair one of a sector that is founded on the innate abilities, creative potential and talents of individuals and that has high prospects of generating wealth and creating jobs by exploiting economic resources and digital information, communication and technology (Peris-Ortiz et al., 2019). Based on this delineation, Nollywood, which is the major focus of this article, falls within the category of home video/film/television and radio.

Beyond the CCI's impressive contributions to national GDP and the Nigerian private sector, Nollywood, hip-hop music, stand-up and digital comic skits and other creative commercial goods and services have achieved global fame and ranking and have thus been christened Nigeria's global brand. Nollywood is the second-largest producer of movies worldwide (Igwe, 2015; Liston, 2014; PwC, 2017; Tella, 2019), with widespread viewership across Africa. Apart from winning the hearts and minds of audiences in different African countries and among the diaspora, Nigerian hip-hop musicians received the MTV Europe Music award for Best African Act in 2005 (Two face Idibia), 2007 and 2012 (D'banj), 2016 (Wizkid), 2017 (Davido), 2018 (Tiwa Savage) and 2019 (Burna Boy). The country's hip-hop music and artists' entertainment and celebrity diplomacy status transcend the shores of Africa. Nigerian hip-hop stars, especially Davido, Burna Boy and Wizkid, have received international awards and accolades and have refashioned the image of Nigeria and indeed, Africa.

Profiling Nigeria's Nollywood Brand

The Nigerian film industry was named Nollywood by Norimitsu Onishi in line with the name of the American Film Industry— Hollywood (Igwe, 2015; Onishi, 2002;). Nollywood embodies and portrays to global audiences an ingenious blend of the rich cultures, languages, practices, philosophies, traditions, folklore, music, arts, slang, sayings and adages of the people that make up Nigeria (Igwe, 2015). It also depicts the film making process in Nigeria which, ironically, is characterized by the production of globally valued movies with low-cost budgets and ingenious use of relatively unsophisticated equipment compared with that used in film production in America's Hollywood and India's Bollywood (Igwe, 2015).

Although characterized by low production costs, and poor editing and video quality occasioned by the use of unsophisticated gadgets, Nollywood's output, viewership and global acceptance have increased (Akwagyiram, 2019; Ezepue, 2020;). Rising from 872 films in 2006 to 2000 in 2013, and an annual average of 2500 films (The International Trade Administration US Department of Commerce, 2020; Tolchinsky, 2015), Nollywood is arguably Africa's fastest-growing film industry and one of the leading global players (Chowdhury et al., 2008). In 2009, Nollywood surpassed Hollywood to emerge as the second-largest movie producer globally after Bollywood which it has closed the gap on (Igwe, 2015; Liston, 2014; Tella, 2019). Nollywood also ranked third in terms of global value and revenue prospects (NOI Polls, 2018).

Digital information, communication and technology and the Internet have enabled viewership of Nollywood films to increase across Africa and among Africans in the diaspora (Omanufeme, 2016; *The Economist*, 2020). In 2014, transnational viewership of Nollywood's products was estimated at 30 million across African states and among Africans in the diaspora (Iweka, 2017). This figure is expected to increase annually as digital technology platforms such as Iroko TV, MultiChoice/DStv/GOtv, Netflix, Canal, Star Times and others enable global viewership of Nollywood movies (Bouillon, 2019; Obioha, 2020).

The Orange Economy and Nollywood's Contributions to Nigeria's Economic Development

The creative or orange economy constitutes all the sectors and activities that are founded on the use of socio-cultural, economic and technological resources to produce intellectual property, and creative goods and services with macro and micro-economic value (Howkin in Restrepo & Márquez, 2015). Nollywood has been recognized as a non-oil sector with huge prospects to boast Nigeria's foreign earnings (Lagarde, 2016). In a bid to augment the faltering economy, the Nigerian Federal Government included it as a priority sector in its Economic Recovery and Growth Plan, with the aim of achieving export earnings of $1 billion by 2020 (PwC, 2017). While Nollywood's export earning potential is laudable, it also boosts Nigeria's GDP and contributes to job creation and poverty alleviation.

Although Nollywood's annual contribution to Nigeria's economy has increased, no empirical data is available on the precise figure, or indeed, the industry's contribution to other aspects of the country's economy. The meager data that exist are sourced from the publications of foreign institutions such as PwC, the United States International Trade Commission and Internet posts. Prior to 2013, Nollywood made an insignificant contribution to Nigeria's economy. This changed with the rebasing of the national economy (Saliu & Jun, 2019). In 2013, Nollywood contributed 1.42% to Nigeria's GDP and this increased to 2.3% or 239 billion Naira in 2016 (Andrews, 2020; Saliu & Jun, 2019; Leach, 2019; Omanufeme, 2016). Furthermore, Multichoice, a major investor in the Nigerian movie industry, contributed an estimated $2.1 billion to Nigeria's economy and invested $428 million in the development of local talent in the country between 2015 and 2019 (Salau, 2020). On average, it is estimated that Nollywood contributes no less than $600 million in foreign earnings to the Nigerian economy (Oh, 2014).

Nollywood also contributes to Nigeria's economic development through job creation. It is estimated that "one in every two Nigerians in the country's labour force is either unemployed or underemployed" (Kazeem, 2020). The most recent data from the Nigerian Bureau of Statistics indicates that the country's unemployment rate increased from 23.1% in the third quarter (Q3) of 2018 to 27.1% in the second quarter (Q2) of 2020 (Kazeem, 2020). This suggests that around 21.7 million of Nigeria's 80.2 million-strong labor force that are willing and able to work are unable to secure paid employment (Kazeem, 2020). Nollywood employs more than a million Nigerians (Omanufeme, 2016), with approximately 300,000 directly employed while a million are indirectly employed through its value chain effects from production to distribution (Henry, 2019; Olaoluwa, 2019). The industry has created jobs for camera people, makeup artists, sound engineers, electrical engineers, script editors, actors and actresses, transporters, video recorders and others (Chowdhury, 2008). It is Nigeria's second-largest employer after the agriculture sector (*The Economist*, 2006). Given its potential to address unemployment, it is important that the Nigerian government formulates viable policies and offers financial support to enable this sector to perform at its optimal level of productivity.

Soft Power, Cultural Influence and Nollywood's Celebrity Diplomacy in Africa

As Africa's major cultural export, Nollywood is a significant soft power resource (Haynes, 2007). Popularized by Joseph Nye in 'Bound to Lead' and 'Soft Power' both published in 1990, soft power is conceptualized as attractive or non-coercive power that rests on a state's ability to influence the actions and posture of other states, and achieve its strategic interests and foreign policy objectives through the use of attraction as against recourse to the use of sanctions, threats and punishment (Nye, 1990a, 1990b, 2004). Soft power thus refers to a state's ability to achieve its desired ends by exploiting attractive resources to configure other states' inclination to prefer what it wants without having to employ maneuvers, sanctions or coercion (Nye, 2008, 2017, 2004, 1990a). It rests on a state's ability to deploy its attractive or non-coercive resources such as culture, ideology and its policies and institutions (Nye, 1990a).

Within the African context, Nollywood is Africa's most attractive cultural resource that continues to enjoy widespread global appeal. Apart from being rated as the second-largest movie industry in terms of the volume of annual production, Nollywood has accrued continental hegemonic influence that has overshadowed the movie industries of South Africa, Ghana, Kenya and other African countries (Miller, 2012; Ondego, 2008). *The Economist* asserts that, "Millions of Africans watch Nigerian films every day, many more than see American fare" (*The Economist*, 2010). Indeed, Nollywood has become the template on which Botswana, Cameroun, Ghana and Kenya have established their movie industries (Ezeonu, 2013).

In exporting Nigeria's attractive cultures and narratives, Nollywood has emerged as a phenomenal non-state cultural ambassador, portraying a good image of Nigeria and the African continent as a whole. This was recognized by former Minister of Information and Communication, the late Professor Dora Akunyili, who sought a partnership with Nollywood to promote her ministry's rebranding Nigeria campaign.

Nollywood has endeared Nigeria to nationals of South Africa, Ghana, Kenya and other African states and attracted global audiences to explore the cultures and people of Africa. It has also influenced the movie industries of other African states. This has led some cultural commentators to raise concerns that the "Nigerianisation of Africa" has compelled nationals of other African countries to come to terms with the Nigerian way of doing things (*The Economist*, 2010). For example, *The Economist* (2010) notes that Zambian mothers lament that their children speak with Nigerian accents learnt from Nigerian television. It also notes that Ivorian rebels fighting in the bush cease fire "when a shipment of DVDs arrives from Lagos" (*The Economist*, 2010). Kenyans have exhibited growing taste for traditional Nigerian clothing due to watching Nollywood movies, with the country's former Prime Minister, Raila Odinga, "seen wearing a loosely flowing *agbada* in parliament" (*The Economist*, 2010).

Nollywood movies' cultural influence in francophone countries is evident in continued interest in francophone channels such as Nollywood.TV and Canal Plus. Such is the power of this transnational attraction and influence that the French government raised concerns about Nollywood's cultural hegemonic influence on the nationals of francophone countries (Jedlowski, 2017). An official noted that:

> French officials became concerned in the second half of the 2000s that Nollywood's influence could eventually threaten the perpetuation of the French language in Africa, and thus the future of France's political and economic interests in the region. Jedlowski (2017, p. 686)

In 2009, a published document that was formulated by the French Senate reiterated these concerns and proposed the establishment of a funding program to translate Nollywood movies into French (Jedlowski, 2017). In a bid to make Nollywood movies and its novel television series available to francophone audiences and extend Nollywood's ethos of making interesting movies with low budgets for francophone Africa, Canal Plus acquired ROK, a leading Nollywood production studio (Bright, 2019; Thomson, 2019). Arguably, this underscores the cultural influence of Nollywood in Africa. In line with the thesis that the viability of soft power does not lie in the way the wielder perceives its soft power resources but in the extent to which the state and the people that it targets perceive it, Nollywood's soft power arguably has a far-reaching effect in winning audiences among nationals of states across Africa, Africans in the diaspora and nationals of other countries (Lagarde, 2016; Miller, 2012).

Apart from Francophone African countries, Nollywood is widely viewed in the southern African sub-region. This is more pronounced among South Africans despite diplomatic spats and regional hegemonic contests between the two countries. Isike and Isike's (2012) "sociocultural analysis of African Immigration to South Africa" found that 90% of the 92 respondents representing Botswana, Congo, Cameroon, Mozambique, South Africa, Zambia and Zimbabwe identified positively with Nigeria and Nigerians because of similar cultural practices identified by watching Nigerian movies (Nollywood). Eighty-three percent of the respondents also expressed positive views of Nigerians because they identified similarities between their culture and those of Nigeria and its people. Similarly, 87% of the South African respondents agreed that watching Nigerian movies gave them a positive view of Nigerians in South Africa.

If adequately harnessed by the Nigerian government and its foreign policy experts, Nollywood's cultural exports and the global attraction it confers on Nigeria have the ability to shape the preferences of other states to change the demeaning image of Nigeria. It also has the potential to become a veritable tool for cultural and public diplomacy. The government should thus exploit Nollywood's transnational and cultural communicative functions to communicate and diffuse its national interests and foreign policy stance to global audiences.

More importantly, just as Hollywood is often used to portray the cultural exceptionalism, hegemony, ideological position and geostrategic policy stance of the United States on global issues (Coyne, 2008; Moody, 2017), the Nigerian government could appropriate the communicative functions and global appeal of Ije,[2] Invasion 1879[3] and other Nollywood exports to express the country's policy stance to global audiences, especially those that have to do with Africa's development. To achieve this end, Abuja should use the social capital and themes of Nollywood movies and jingles to redirect, remold and tweak the mindset of transnational viewers on Nigeria and its policy stance on global issues.

Beyond serving as a communicative tool to project Nigeria's foreign policy stance on major global issues, Nollywood also offers significant prospects for celebrity soft power and diplomacy. This aligns with the view that, apart from harnessing their attractive foreign policy posture and

---

[2] https://www.youtube.com/watch?v=oyx5S8Ik1WQ.

[3] https://www.youtube.com/watch?v=WdiQAMh5dyk.

institutions, states should pursue soft power through non-state resources (Ogunnubi & Tella, 2017). Given their soft power of attraction, global acceptance and influence, celebrities in the entertainment industry, sports, science and technology, academia and other sectors are fast becoming relevant non-state actors in the international system. Among others, Angelina Jolie and George Clooney have been appointed as peace ambassadors by international organizations such as the United Nations in recognition of their celebrity soft power.

Likewise, Nollywood actors, actresses and Nigerian movie producers have become celebrities who unintentionally wield significant celebrity soft power spurred by the increasing transnational reach and adulation of Nollywood movies, and their actors and actresses. Nwankwo avers that:

> Nollywood stars sometimes appear to be even more popular outside the country. Whenever I travel to East Africa, I must contend with questions about Nollywood stars. The average person in Ghana, Kenya and Uganda seems to know and admire Nollywood stars Nwankwo, (2018, p. 474)

This is corroborated by the observation that Nollywood movies, and their actors and actresses are renowned in South Africa as well as most countries in Africa especially in "east, central and southern Africa" (Onyenankeya et al., 2017). Interestingly, South African audiences are not only fond of Nigeria's cultural expressions diffused through viewing Nollywood on African Magic; they are also unconsciously appropriating and incorporating some of Nigeria's symbolic cultural expressions into their ways of doing things (Onyenankeya et al., 2017). This adulation of Nollywood within Africa and globally is enshrined in Nollywood's expression of globally valued cultural contents; themes and plots that African audiences can easily relate to because they align with daily experiences in most African states (Onyenankeya et al., 2017).

Nollywood movie stars such as Stephanie Okereke, Genevieve Nnaji, Patience Ozokwor, Mr Ibu, Osita Iheme and Chinedu Ihedieze (Aki and Pawpaw), Pete Edoche, Omotola Jalade-Ekeinde, Mercy Johnson and Richard Mofe Damijo, movie producers such as Gabriel Afolayan, Funke Akindele and Kunle Afolayan, and directors such as Tunde Kelani, Lancelot Idowu and others have become continental idols that are celebrated across Africa for their role in projecting a positive image of Nigeria and its culture and, indeed, Africa (Ogunnubi & Isike, 2018). Similarly, *Jacobs Cross*, *Tinsel* and other notable Nigerian soap operas like *Super*

Story, and comedy series like 'Jennifa's diary', 'Meet the Adebanjos', 'The meeting', and more recently 'Citation' have gained wide viewership across Africa courtesy of MultiChoice/DStv and Netflix (Ernest-Samuel, 2019; Ogunnubi & Isike, 2018, *The Economist*, 2006).

Apart from receiving major awards, global recognition of Nigeria's iconic actors and actresses culminated in the annual invitation to Nigerian Nollywood idols to become members of the Oscar Academy awards (Augoye, 2021; Husseini, 2018; Omanufeme, 2016). In 2018, Omotola Jolade-Ekeinde and Femi Odugbemi were invited to join the voting membership of the Oscar Academy (Husseini, 2018). Ngozi Onwurah, Femi Odugbemi, Omotola Jolade-Ekeinde and Wunmi Mosaku were nominated and involved in the selection of winners of the Oscar Awards in 2019 (Premium Times Agency Report, 2018). The 2019 edition featured the selection of Tunde Kelani (Nollywood movie director), Adewale Akinnuoye-Agbaje and Chinonye Chukwu (Augoye, 2021). Ahead of the 2021 awards, Nigeria's Genevieve Nnaji and Akin Omotosho were selected as voting members (Augoye, 2020). This is a reflection of ongoing global recognition and acceptance of Nigeria's movie industry and by extension, its actors and actresses and movie producers. Most importantly, the soft power value of Nollywood movie idols is enshrined in their ability to convert transnational adulation of their charm, stage personality and global recognition into celebrity diplomacy tools to rebrand Nigeria and advance its strategic cultural interests.

However, despite Nollywood's significant economic and diplomatic prospects, Nigerian policymakers have yet to formulate viable policies and detailed financial commitments to complement the efforts of investors in the Nigerian movie industry to facilitate optimal productivity and improve the quality of Nollywood movies. Similarly, Abuja and its foreign policy experts have yet to come to terms with Nollywood's cultural diplomacy potential to advance the cultural hegemony of Nigeria's culture within the continent and portray a positive image of the country at the global level.

Conclusion

From the colonial era to the present, African states have been historicized and labeled as backward with anti-developmental cultural orientations, values and worldviews (Achebe, 1959; Tsikata, 2014). Western media perpetuate this disparaging stereotypical depiction of the continent and its people by highlighting the decades of governance deficits, intractable conflicts and wars, and corruption-induced underdevelopment that ravage the continent. Nonetheless, African states possess massive cultural and creative resources that have such global economic and soft power appeal that they have been plundered and stolen by those depicting Africa as "the hopeless continent" (*The Economist*, 2000).

This chapter unraveled the orange economy and Nollywood's soft power prospects. It argued that Nollywood offers the Nigerian government the opportunity to address stereotypical imaging of Nigeria, and to rebrand and boost the country's external image. Furthermore, Nollywood is a powerful tool to communicate the beauty of Nigeria's culture and to assert a cultural influence on other countries. Nollywood's regional expansion, transnational acceptance and significant cultural influence have the potential to strengthen Nigeria's leadership credentials and its capability to shape the preference of transnational audiences and assert its regional influence.

REFERENCES

Achebe, C. (1959). *Things fall apart*. Astor-Honor.

Agoralumiere International. (2009). *A research into the impact of arts, culture and creative industries on Africa's economy: Nigeria*. https://www.academia.edu/31230499/RESEARCH_INTO_THE_IMPACT_OF_ARTS_CULTURE_AND_CREATIVE_INDUSTRIES_ON_AFRICAS_ECONOMY, accessed 10 December 2020.

Akwagyiram, A. (2019). *Action! Nigeria's film industry draws global entertainment brands*. Reuters, 10 September. https://www.reuters.com/article/us-nigeria-entertainment-nollywood-idUSKCN1VV0aHQ, accessed 16 November, 2020.

Andrews, S. (2020). Netflix Naija: Creative freedom in Nigeria's emerging digital space? *The Conversation*, 19 March. https://theconversation.com/netflix-naija-creative-freedom-in-nigerias-emerging-digital-space-133252, accessed 20 November, 2020.

Augoye, J. (2020, July 1). Genevieve Nnaji, akin Omotoso get Oscar voting rights, *Premium Times*. https://www.premiumtimesng.com/entertainment/400625-genevieve-nnaji-akin-omotoso-get-oscar-voting-rights.html, accessed November 9, 2020.

Augoye, J. (2021, October 31). Oscars 2022: Nigerian movies fail eligibility rule test - selection committee. 8 July. https://www.premiumtimesng.com/entertainment/nollywood/492610-oscars-2022-nigerian-movies-fail-eligibility-rule-test-selectioncommittee.html, accessed 20 December, 2021.

Bouillon, S. (2019, July 9). Nigeria's Nollywood film industry reels in foreign investors. https://www.thejakartapost.com/life/2019/07/08/nigeriasnollywood-film-industry-reels-in-foreign-investors.html, accessed 10 November, 2020.

Bright, J. (2019, July 15). *Canal+ acquires Nollywood studio ROK from IROKOtv to grow African film TechCrunch.* Tech Crunch. https://techcrunch.com/2019/07/15/canal-acquires-african-film-studio-rok-from-iroko%20tv-to-grow-nollywood/

Bunce, M. (2014). International news and the image of Africa: New storytellers, new narratives? In J. Gallagher (Ed.), *Images of Africa: Creation, negotiation and subversion* (pp. 42–62). Manchester University Press.

British Council. (2013). *Mapping Nigeria creative industries: Report of Lagos pilot study.* British Council. https://www.britishcouncil.sl/sites/default/files/lagospilotmapping%20report2013.pdf, accessed December 1, 2020.

Chowdhury M., Landesz T., Santini M., Tejada L., & Visconti G. (2008). *Nollywood: The Nigerian film industry.* Harvard Business School, 2 May. https://www.isc.hbs.edu/Documents/resources/courses/moc-course-at-harvard/pdf/student-projects/Nigeria_Film_2008.pdf , accessed December 13, 2020.

Coyne, M. (2008). *Hollywood goes to Washington: American politics on screen.* Reaktion Books.

Daubaraite, U., & Startiene, G. (2015). Creative industries impact on national economy in regard to sub-sectors. *Procedia-Social and Behavioral Sciences, 213*, 129–134. https://doi.org/10.1016/j.sbspro.2015.11.415.

Ernest-Samuel, G. C. (2019). Multichoice® corporation's intervention in Nollywood: A case study in glocal partnership expectations, issues, and outcomes, In B. A. Musa (eds.), *Nollywood in glocal perspective.* 209–229. Palgrave Macmillan. https://doi.org/10.1007/978-3-030-30663-2_11

Ezeonu, I. (2013). Nollywood consensus: Modeling a development pathway for Africa. *The Global South, 7*(1), 179–199.

Ezepue, E. M. (2020). The new Nollywood: Professionalization or gentrification of cultural industry. *SAGE Open, 10*(3), 1–10. https://doi.org/10.1177/2158244020940994

Harrison, L. E., & Huntington, S. P. (2000). *Culture matters: How values shape human progress.* Basic Books.

Haynes, J. (2007). Nollywood in Lagos, Lagos in Nollywood films. *Africa Today, 54*(2), 130–150. https://doi.org/10.2979/aft.2007.54.2.130

Henry, N. (2019, October 7). *Here's a fresh perspective on how much revenue Nollywood generates every year*. Wee Tracker. https://weetracker.com/2019/10/07/nollywood-revenue-reach-usd-1-billion-yearly/, accessed 8 December 2020.

Husseini, S. (2018, June 29). Meet voting members of Oscars 2018: Odugbemi, Omotola. *The Guardian*. https://guardian.ng/news/meet-voting-members-of-oscars-2018-odugbemi-omotola/, accessed 15 February 2021.

Idowu, D. L., & Ogunnubi, O. (2022). Soft power in therapeutic comedy: Outlining Nigeria's creative industry through digital comic skits. *Creative Industries Journal*, 1–22. https://doi.org/10.1080/17510694.2022.2025703

Igwe, C. (2015). *How Nollywood became the second largest film industry*. British Council. 6 November. https://www.britishcouncil.org/voices-magazine/nollywood-second-largest-film-industry, accessed 20 February 2021.

Isike, C., & Isike, E. (2012). A socio-cultural Analysis of African immigration to South Africa. *Alternation, 19*(1), 93–116.

Iweka, K. (2017). *Nollywood could be a blockbuster for the Nigerian economy*. ACCA. 1 July. https://www.accaglobal.com/pk/en/member/member/accounting-business/2017/07/in-focus/ik-jul17.html, accessed 15 January 2021.

Jedlowski, A. (2017). African media and the corporate takeover: Video film circulation in the age of neoliberal transformations. *African Affairs, 116*(465), 671–691. https://doi.org/10.1093/afraf/adx017

Kazeem, Y. (2020). *Nigeria's unemployment rate has more than tripled in the last five years—and it will only get worse*. Quartz. 14 August. https://qz.com/africa/1892237/nigerias-unemployment-rate-tripled-in-five-years/, accessed 10 November 2020

Lagarde, C. (2016). *Nigeria—Act with resolve, build resilience, and exercise restraint*. International Monetary Funds. 6 June. https://www.imf.org/en/news/articles/2015/09/28/04/53/sp010616, accessed 11 December 2020.

Leach, K. (2019). *Nollywood is ready to go global thanks to netflix*. Bloomberg. 23 May. https://www.bloomberg.com/news/articles/2019-05-24/nollywood-is-ready-to-go-global-thanks-to-netflix, accessed 14 November 2020.

Liston, E. (2014, April 10). Hello Nollywood: How Nigeria became Africa's biggest economy overnight. *The Guardian*. https://www.theguardian.com/world/2014/apr/10/nigeria-africa-biggest-economy-nollywood, accessed 15, December, 2020.

Mhango, N. (2018). *How Africa developed Europe: Deconstructing the his-story of Africa, excavating untold truth and what ought to be done and known*. Langaa Research & Publishing CIG.

Miller, J. (2012). Global Nollywood: The Nigerian movie industry and alternative global networks in production and distribution. *Global Media and*

Communication, 8(2), 117–133. https://doi.org/10.1177/1742766512444340

Moody, P. (2017). Embassy cinema: What WikiLeaks reveals about US state support for Hollywood. *Media, Culture & Society, 39*(7), 1063–1077. https://doi.org/10.1177/0163443716686673

Moore, I. (2014). Cultural and creative industries concept—A historical perspective. *Procedia—Social and Behavioral Sciences, 110*, 738–746. https://doi.org/10.1016/j.sbspro.2013.12.918

NOIPolls. (2018). *Celebrating the creative industries: The Nollywood phenomenon*. Noi Polls. 11 December. https://noi-polls.com/celebrating-the-creative-industries-the-nollywood-phenomenon/, accessed 13 November, 2021.

Nwankwo, A. O. (2018). Harnessing the potential of Nigeria's creative industries: Issues, prospects and policy implications. *Africa Journal of Management, 4*(4): 469–487. https://doi.org/10.1080/23322373.2018.1522170

Nye J. S. (1990b). *Bound to lead: The changing nature of American power*. Basic Books.

Nye, J. S. (1990a). Soft power. Foreign Policy. No. 80: 153–171, https://doi.org/10.2307/1148580

Nye, J. S. (2004). *Soft power: The means to success in world politics*. Public Affair.

Nye, J. S. (2008). Public diplomacy and soft power. *The Annals of the American Academy, 616*(1), 94–109.

Nye, J. S. (2017). Soft power: The origins and political progress of a concept. *Palgrave Communications, 3*(17008), 1–3. https://doi.org/10.1057/palcomms.2017.8

Obioha, V. (2020). *Nigeria: More people view Nollywood films on Africa magic—Survey*. All Africa. 29 April. https://allafrica.com/stories/202004290068.html

Ogunnubi, O., & Idowu, D. L. (2022). Music diplomacy: The soft power of Nigerian gospel melody, In O. Ogunnubi, & S. F., Folarin. (eds.), *Religion and global politics: Soft power in Nigeria and beyond*. Rowman & Littlefield.

Ogunnubi, O., & Isike, C. (2018). Nigeria's soft power sources: Between potential and illusion? *International Journal of Politics, Culture and Society, 31*(1), 49–67.

Ogunnubi, O., & Tella, O. (2017). Framing South Africa's soft power through non-state sources. *Strategic Analysis, 41*(5), 478–495. https://doi.org/10.1080/09700161.2017.1343228

Olaoluwa, J. (2019). *Nigeria's movie industry, Nollywood generates about $1 billion yearly – Afreximbank*. Nairametrics. 7 October. https://nairametrics.com/2019/10/07/nigerias-movie-industry-nollywood-generates-about-1-billion-yearly-afreximbank/, accessed 10 November 2020.

Omanufeme, S. (2016). Runaway success. *Finance and Development, 53*(2): 30–32.

Ondego, O. (2008). Kenya and Nollywood: A state of dependence Nollywood, In P. Barrot (Ed.), *The video phenomenon in Nigeria*. Indiana University Press.

Onishi, N. (2002). Step aside, L.A. and Bombay, for Nollywood.. *New York Times*. https://www.nytimes.com/2002/09/16/world/step-aside-la-and-bombay-for-nollywood.html?pagewanted=all, accessed 12 December 2020.

Onyenankeya, O. M., Onyenankeya, K. U., & Osunkunle, O. (2017). The persuasive influence of Nollywood film in cultural transmission: Negotiating Nigerian culture in a South African environment. *Journal of Intercultural Communication Research, 46*(4), 297–313. https://doi.org/10.1080/17475759.2017.1329158

Peris-Ortiz, M., Cabrera-Flores, M. R., & Serrano-Santoyo, A. (2019). *Cultural and creative industries: A path to entrepreneurship and innovation.*

Premium Times Agency Report. (2018, June 26), Oscars 2018: Four Nigerians make Academy's 928 members. *Premium Times*. https://www.premiumtimesng.com/entertainment/nollywood/273911-oscars-2018-four-nigerians-make-academys-928-members.html, accessed 15 December 2020

PricewaterhouseCoopers. (2017). *Spotlight —The Nigerian film industry*. PricewaterhouseCoopers. https://www.pwc.com/ng/en/publications/spotlight-the-nigerian-film-industry.html, accessed 14 November 2020.

Restrepo, F. B. & Márquez, I. D. (2015). *Orange economy*. Noura Books.

Salau, S. J. (2020). MultiChoice invests N800bn in Nigerian economy in 5 years—Accenture report. *Business Day*. 24 June. https://businessday.ng/news/article/multichoice-invests-n800bn-in-nigerian-economy-in-5-years-accenture-report/, accessed 15 December 2020.

Saliu, O., & Jun, G. (2019, June 19). Nollywood: Fraught with challenges. 16 June. https://bfmmag.com/international-nollywood-fraught-withchallenges/, accessed 20 November 2020.

Sayne, A. & Hruby, A. (2016). *Nigeria's oil revenue crunch: Falling prices and increased competition strain the economy and stability*. Atlantic Council. http://www.jstor.org/stable/resrep17111, accessed 18 December 2020.

Tella, O. (2019). Nigeria is punching below its weight despite massive soft power capacity. *The Conversation*. 5 February. https://theconversation.com/nigeria-is-punching-below-its-weight-despite-massive-soft-power-capacity-110804, accessed 10 December 2020.

The International Trade Administration, U.S. Department of Commerce. (2020). '*Nigeria - Media and entertainment industry (Nollywood and Nigerian music)*', https://www.trade.gov/country-commercial-guides/nigeria-media-and-entertainment-industry-nollywood-and-nigerian-music

The Economist. (2000, May 11). The heart of the matter. *The Economist*. https://www.economist.com/special/2000/05/11/the-heart-of-the-matter, accessed 12 January 2021.

The Economist. (2006, July 27). Nollywood dreams. *The Economist*. https://www.economist.com/business/2006/07/27/nollywood-dreams, accessed 13 January 2021.

The Economist. (2010, December 16). Nollywood: Lights, camera, Africa. *The Economist*. https://www.economist.com/christmas-specials/2010/12/16/lights-camera-africa, accessed 13 January 2021.

The Economist. (2020, August 27). Nigeria's film industry has taken a viral knock. https://www.economist.com/middle-east-and-africa/2020/08/27/nigerias-film-industry-has-taken-a-viral-knock, accessed 16 January 2021.

Thomson, S. (2019). *Canal+ heads for Nollywood with iROKO channels and production acquisition*. Informa Tech. 15 July. https://www.digitaltveurope.com/2019/07/15/canal-heads-for-nollywood-with-iro, accessed 12 November 2020.

Tolchinsky M. (2015, January 19). Nigeria's Nollywood is putting Hollywood to shame. *Global Risk Insight*. https://globalriskinsights.com/2015/01/nigerias-nollywood-putting-hollywood-shame/, accessed 17 December 2020.

Tsikata, P. Y. (2014). The historical and contemporary representation of Africa in global media flows: Can the continent speak back for itself on its own terms? *Communicatio*, *40*(1), 34–48. https://doi.org/10.1080/02500167.2014.835530

United Nations Conference on Trade and Development. (2008). *Creative Economy Report 2008*. United nations conference on trade and development. https://unctad.org/en/docs/ditc20082ceren.pdf

CHAPTER 10

Pleasure While Flying: Inflight Entertainment as a Medium for Cultural Production and Dissemination

Olusola John

THE EMERGENCE OF INFLIGHT ENTERTAINMENT

Necessity is the mother of invention. Most technological innovations are rooted in cultural practices and people's need to address challenges. The science of arts and the arts of science are thus harnessed to develop innovations that serve society. Inflight entertainment (IFE) emerged about two decades after the Wright Brothers' first flight in the United States. The first documented IFE onboard was in 1921 when the 11 passengers on an aircraft operated by Aeromarine Airways watched a movie titled *Howdy Chicago* during a flight across the city in a "Pageant of Progress." Chicago's highlights were shown on a screen hung in the cabin. The

O. John (✉)
Department of Theatre and Performing Arts, Ahmadu Bello University, Zaria, Nigeria
e-mail: solajohn01@gmail.com

focus was the pictures rather than the audio (White, 1994). White (1994) notes that, in 1925 the 12 passengers on an Imperial Airlines flight from London were treated to the silent movie, *The Lost World*.

Like many other inventions that improve with time, IFE was launched with the public relations' motive of generating interest in the civil aviation industry.

> Inflight entertainment's inspirations came from a range of contexts including theatrical exhibition, the domestic media environment and the business office. Additionally, since the 1920s airlines have used the non-theatrical cinema culture of exhibitions, fairs, social clubs and even models of airplane cabins that resembled the somatic cinema of the earlier, railway-based, Hale's Tours to promote aviation and travel. Inflight entertainment then, may be best understood as a transmedia, as airlines have sought to encourage air travel and keep passengers contented through a range of practices utilizing multiple media forms and technologies. (Groening, 2014a)

Groening's perspective acknowledges theatrical performance's contribution to the emergence of IFE, but also emphasizes the aim of creating a sense of relaxation among passengers to ease anxiety. It can be deduced that IFE's primary objective was not entertainment, but business success. That is, the more passengers are comfortable flying, the more they will fly. After serving many years in the avionics section of the aviation industry, and witnessing the introduction of many inventions and innovations, some of which were successful and others not, Reed (2007) identified five stages in the evolution of IFE prior to its current status.

The "Idea" Phase

This was the phase in which someone conceived of a novel idea, scripted it on paper and weighed the economic gain and how passengers would pay for such a service. The initial intention that passengers would pay per view was later modified as passengers only pay for tickets and enjoy inflight services, although the class of the ticket will determine the services offered.

The "I Got It Too" Phase

In this stage, airlines engaged in a race to offer IFE and begin scrambling for service providers in anticipation of pay per view.

The "I Gotta Have It Too" Phase

In this phase, IFE was incorporated into the system of inflight services at no cost to the passengers since it became a competitive factor in airlines' service provision. Virtually all airlines embraced IFE at this point.

The Peak

The primary goal during this phase was to make sufficient profit through ticket sales to cover provision of IFE.

The "Die Trying" Phase

In this phase, although airlines had invested significantly in experimentation, failures were recorded, either due to flaws in the business concept or the fact that expected levels of revenue did not materialize.

The "Reality" Phase

In this phase, the concept of IFE is fully implemented with a more detailed plan to serve all classes of passengers without necessarily charging for the service. Reed (2007) notes that IFE now includes In-Seat Telephones, Gambling (Games) and Future Connectivity.

It is thus clear that it was not a smooth ride for IFE to reach its current point. Reed's account creates the impression of a well thought out invention with several failures and later success. Similarly, Knittel (1999) noted the glitches in the audio system after several failures and recorded successes:

> Think back to the early days of the worldwide inflight entertainment industry; the successes and failures of the first inflight audio in the mid-sixties and the breakthrough of the first regularly scheduled inflight movie premiering in 1961 on TWA Flight 40 from New York to San Francisco. Starring Lana Turner and Efrem Zimbalist, Jr, 'By Love Possessed' was the

first film to occupy the visual senses of those travelers jetting from America's sea to shining sea. Perhaps it was this lucky group who coined the phrase, 'time flies when you're having fun' after experiencing the ground breaking new inflight entertainment milestone.

However, it should be borne in mind that airlines' primary motive is profit maximization through carrying more passengers. In Groening (2014b)'s view, the emergence of IFE is not unconnected to the shrinking space provided for the passenger as economy class emerged in air travel. "As jet travel moved into a form of mass travel, beginning in 1958, space for the air passenger shrank, particularly in the newly formed economy class. That travelling at unprecedented speed would require bodily stillness and cramped conditions has been a long-time complaint for air travelers…inflight entertainment has allowed airlines to place more passengers in the airplane and keep them content."

THE PRODUCTION OF IFE

Early inflight entertainment included live singers, musicians, fashion shows, etc. All performances were designed to become media events within themselves, not specifically to entertain passengers. The press was invited, flash bulbs popped, and newspapers and magazines throughout the world held their readers in rapt fascination with news of these events in the sky. (White, 1994)

Thus, IFE became an economic platform for inventors, business people, manufacturing companies and entertainment providers, especially Hollywood (White, 1994; Groening, 2014a). Furthermore, "for many airline passengers, inflight entertainment has been involuntary; there has been little agency or choice granted to the passenger." It is driven by airlines' pursuit of sales and patronage (Groening, 2014b). From 1964, IFE incorporated media platforms such as live television broadcasts, magnetic tape, 16 mm film and closed-circuit television "that indicate a more contentious and variegated media environment" (Elsaesser, 2004). Content outsourced to independent producers reflects the airlines' interests. The media include:

Magazines: Glossy, full-color inflight magazines are used to convey cultural messages and promote national carriers' products. These comprise of various sections such as:

> Arts/Life: Usually profiles a prominent artist, writer, filmmaker, singer, actor or scientist, with interviews with the artist and examples of their work. For example, Arik Airlines publishes *Alice* which focus on the arts and culture of the African people. Other airlines focus on business personalities or those that are successful in other spheres of life. Examples include Emirates Airlines' the *Portfolio*.
> Fashion: This section showcases designs, clothing, hairstyles and other fashion related artifacts to educate passengers on the culture of the people of the airline's country of origin. Designers are sometimes profiled and fashion houses advertise their products.
> Culinary: Different cuisines are presented, sometimes accompanied by recipes.
> Movie reviews: These reviews offer insight into the making of certain movies that are on circuit or about to be released. In some cases, the movie has been co-sponsored by the airline. An example is *The CEO*, a movie produced by Kunle Afolayan, a Nigerian film maker, with support from Air France and exclusively available on Air France flights. The movies reflect the culture of a segment of the flying public.
> Tourism: Tourism destinations are often of interest to passengers who may be visiting a country for the first time and may need information on places to visit or accommodation. These tourism sites are highlighted in editorials, adverts or special features and are a common feature of most IFE magazines.

Advertisements: This is a vital feature that generates revenue for publication of the magazine.

Other IFE content includes movies, radio talk shows, TV talk shows, and documentaries often sourced from the distributors. According to Groening (2014a):

> Many of the offerings in-the-air are, in a word, bland. Partly this is because most of the inflight films are recycled from theatrical, pay per view, or cable

release, many are then sanitized to avoid certain types of controversies. But it is precisely their bland and innocuous nature that makes their spectatorial captivation and emotional transportation so remarkable.

Inflight entertainment offerings aim to serve the purpose of light entertainment and thus focus on comedy and melodrama in order to douse the tension that comes with flying. Thus, scenes that contain violence, bloodshed, bombings and accidents are avoided. In most cases, the distributors are responsible for editing movies to suit the needs, even to the extent of changing the ending. The rise of Indie film directors has increased the airlines' pool of suppliers. Nigerian Indie film director, Imoh Umoren, recently announced on Twitter that two of his movies have been accepted by international airlines for their IFE.

Distribution of Contents on Board

The World Airline Entertainment Association (WAEA) was established by a group of vendors and airlines in 1980 (White, 1994). It was renamed the Airline Passenger Experience Association (APEX) in 2010 in consonance with the growing scope of IFE (Groening, 2014b). Movies makers usually depend on distributors to disseminate their movies to cinemas and exhibitions, and to facilitate TV and DVD sales.

> The content used in IFE whether movies, television, news text or music, is subject to the rights granted under copyright legislation throughout the world to the copyright proprietor (i.e., the copyright owner (s) or representative (s)). The terms music royalties, collective management, neighboring rights, and mechanical rights are all related to copyrights, and sometimes mean the same thing. (Avion, 1999)

Thus, no special rights cover IFE aside from those that permit distributors to release movies. The only difference might be the fact that, the laws governing copyright differ from country to country. Thus, while meeting the minimum benchmark protection set by international treaties, in sourcing IFE content, airlines must respect the laws of the country where it was produced.

The Relevance of IFE to Air Passengers

Inflight entertainment aims to promote a smooth journey by distracting passengers from turbulence, annoying cabin mates, dusty, oxygen-depleted air and/or cramped seating arrangements that could make the journey unpleasant (Groening, 2013). Studies have highlighted the importance of passengers' comfort on board and the design of inflight facilities systems. For instance, Liu et al. (2009) monitored passengers' heartbeat in response to the inflight music system. They recommended that airlines conduct research on passengers' preferences in order to offer music that is soothing and relaxing. However, this study did not consider the passengers' culture or the philosophy of the artists, but rather the genres and rhythm. Naseem et al.'s (n.d.) empirical study employed a qualitative method to identify the factors that promote passengers' comfort. Interestingly, IFE was ranked fourth out of five factors, with the factors listed as follows: Flight safety, Flight schedule, Flight management, On-board services and the Airline Company's image in that order. Inflight entertainment has been a companion to travelers for so long that it has become so integrated into their experiences, such that refunds are made when the service is not available. Among other things, it keeps passengers' minds off the stress of a long journey by creating the feel of a living room experience. This is reinforced by the design of seats that offer theater-like comfort coupled with a device to select movies or programs that is similar to a remote control used in the home. Comedy and talk shows, in conjunction with music onboard prevent moodiness and tiredness and reduce jetlag. Indeed, passengers are now so familiar with IFE that to travel without it is unthinkable. According to Liu et al. (2009):

> In-flight music systems play an important role in improving passengers' comfort level during air travels. Today, the current in-flight music systems have made significant progress in providing music service with user friendly interface, interaction mode and ever-increasing music options.

Inflight Entertainment and the Promotion of Culture

The promotion of culture via IFE is an aspect of globalization that needs to be investigated considering the cosmopolitan nature of the passengers on board and the number of international flights on a daily basis.

It can be stated that, globalization and air travel are identical in practice. Inflight entertainment enables a rapid exchange of ideas on board as globalization knit diverse cultures together. While distributors are responsible for sourcing IFE, it is also passenger sensitive, as they conduct research on passengers' preferences. However, airlines are loyal to the culture of their country of origin, and they thus offer content that promotes their culture, with less content from other cultures. Such content is readily available through airlines magazines that showcase local fashion, exhibitions, cuisine and movies, which are national signifiers of the cultures they portray. According to Groening (2013), "Inflight entertainment, then, is the cultural condensation of these contradictory impulses to bring the faraway closer (in place) but still maintain distance (through space)." Therefore, through IFE, airlines contribute to the blurring of borders and the globalization of cultures. Both cinema and aviation reflect significant shifts in global understanding. The apparent mastery of space and time enabled by these technologies allows for a malleable and unsettled understanding of the dimensions so crucial to living in the here and now. Together, cinema and aviation have contributed to the development of the vision of a world without borders that is available to the airline passenger.

The Economic Value of IFE

The global IFE and connectivity market grew to USD5.9 billion as of 2019 and was forecast to increase by 9.5% between 2020 and 2028. It is also expected that, due to the growing passenger demand for onboard Internet connectivity and media streaming and willingness to pay additional costs for these services, these products will provide further opportunities for growth. A study by Research and Markets forecast a growth of 1% in these services between 2020 and 2024 at a cost of $347.17M. The study covered around 25 vendors and analyzed market size and trends, growth drivers and challenges, as well as vendor analysis.

Content producers and vendors that seek to take advantage of this market need to conduct research on audience preferences in order to serve airline passengers, especially with the gradual easing of lockdown restrictions across the world in the post-COVID-19 era.

Conclusion

Inflight entertainment has provided pleasure to air passengers for many decades. However, it also serves the purpose of propagating and transporting cultures across borders, thereby creating fluidity in the process of globalization. It can thus be concluded that IFE is an effective tool to enable nations gain competitive advantage in the globalized world.

References

Avion, M. (1999). Key Publishing Limited.
Elsaesser, T. (2004). The new film history as media archaeology. *Cinemas: Journal of Film Studies, 14*(2–3), 80.
Global in-flight entertainment systems market 2020–2024. https://www.researchandmarkets.com/reports/5130952/global-in-flight-entertainment-systems-market
Groening, S. (2013). Aerial screens. *History and Technology: An International Journal, 29*(3), 284–303. https://doi.org/10.1080/07341512.2013.858523
Groening, S. (2014a). *Cinema beyond territory*. British Film Institute.
Groening, S. (2014b). Crying while flying: The intimacy of inflight entertainment. *Écranosphère* (n° 1).
In-flight entertainment and connectivity market. https://www.globenewswire.com/news-release/2021/01/13/2157840/0/en/In-Flight-Entertainment-Connectivity-Market-Worth-USD-7-68-Billion-by-2027-Backed-by-Presence-of-Established-Companies-in-North-America-Says-Fortune-Business-Insights.html
Knittel, L. B. (1999). *The Odyssey of licensing inflight entertainment*. AVION. PDF retrieved on 20 March 2015.
Liu, H., Hu, J., & Rauterberg, M. (2009). *Bio-feedback based in-flight music system design to promote heart health*. Proceedings of 2009 IEEE International Conference on Machine Learning (pp. 446–450). http://citeseerx.ist.psu.edu/viewdoc/download?doi=10.1.1.174.7078&rep=rep1&type=pdf. Retrieved 3 March 2015.
Naseem, A., Gitte, L., Jean, M. R., & Bernard P. (n.d.). *Defining the experiential aspects of the experiential aspects of passengers' comfort in the aircraft interior—An empirical study*. Retrieved 3 March 2015.
Reed, D. A. (2007). *Theory about IFE*. AVION. PDF retrieved on 20 March 2015.
White, J. N. (1994). *A history of inflight entertainment, design affiliates*. http://apex.aero/LinkClick.aspx?fileticket=sVkDdIbJRzE%3D&tabid=197&gt. Retrieved 28 August 2013.

CHAPTER 11

Fighters, Hunters and Blue-Blood: A Postmodern Reading of African Folk Tales and the Soft Will to Africanize

Diana S. Stoica

INTRODUCTION

The invitation launched by this chapter targets the symbols of soft power, as they are valued in a mystical frame of Sudanese folk stories, the metamorphosis they have been through and their final appearance in actual writings. The proposal to analyse Sudanese folk tales of African genesis, collected by the German anthropologist Leo Frobenius, is not casual in regard to the source and the subject. On the one hand, it reflects the importance and the ways Frobenius was talking about the "primitives", based on the writings of Levy Bruhl (Mudimbe, 1988, p. 88). On the other hand, it includes a series of folks of the genesis comparable to the mythology of lands in Africa. These ones encrypt the beliefs, values

---

D. S. Stoica (✉)
West University of Timisoara, Timisoara, Romania
e-mail: Diana.stoica80@e-uvt.ro

© The Author(s), under exclusive license to Springer Nature Singapore Pte Ltd. 2022
T. Afolabi et al. (eds.), *Re-centering Cultural Performance and Orange Economy in Post-colonial Africa*,
https://doi.org/10.1007/978-981-19-0641-1_11

and culture of an Africa that started to be known to the Western world, differently, but still through the eyes of Western anthropologists.

Africans were generally considered to "live" in a symbolic and ritualized world (Hallen, 2005, p. 100) and folks, tales and myths are the sources of the African Philosophy (Bello, 2004, p. 265). It assumes the profile of a foundation on which the African agency acts and an African Self gets recognition. Moreover, the folk tale is a good mirror of the society (Sone, 2018, p. 147), so a collection of folk tales transcribed by a Western Anthropologist like Frobenius could also risk a moralizing direction, if conclusions on the preference of the Western reader for moralizing tales as a principal narrative mode (West & Donato, 1995, p. 394) would allow or guide instinctively the anthropologist to make even the smallest modifications to the text.

However, considering this risk would be marginal to the potentiality of the folk tales to imagine and express the symbols and social values orally transferred from generation to generation, inherited and interiorized, therefore identifiable in certain African groups at the beginning of the twentieth century, studying these symbols in the African ancient folk tales is of a fundamental necessity in order both to understand African culture as well as be able to answer questions about identity and values (Sone, 2018, p. 158). In the meantime, the critical, comparative and imaginative reading of some symbols in the tales could reflect how the ancient culture bases the authentic viewpoints of one group or nation, for the correct and closer to the real understanding of each other, manifest a power on it, create the premise of a particular universalization such as the Africanization.

In this sense and for the purpose to deepen explorations on power and soft power from an African point of view, as it was preserved in the oral tradition, from the Sudanese folk tales collected by Leo Frobenius, the symbols of *fighters (or warriors) hunters* and *blue-blood* (aristocracy) are preferred for this analysis. These characters appear in Part Two of Frobenius's "African Genesis folk tales" in the folk tales of Soninke, Fulbe, Mande, Nupe and Hausa people from Western Africa and the Sahel. The analysis of folk tales of different ethnic groups would assess the context of diversity, but also the holistic necessary reduction for a reading alternative, cultural relativism being instrumentally employed.

The three mentioned characters have their attached symbology: the political values for the *fighters*, the culture for the *hunters* and the authority for the *blue-blood*. Further on, this symbology is framed in Nye's description of the resources of soft power a country possesses, namely the culture (with a focus on the attractivity to others), the political values and its foreign policies, with a focus on legitimacy and moral authority (Nye, 2004, p. 11). In other words, the primary supposition of this paper is that the three characters in the folk tales may express an ideology on power in the African epistemology, while the second premise is that soft power is the alternative the African agency has in its tendency to capitalize the cliché coming into being or recognition of the African Self.

In a Western logic, as seen through the lens of an African philosopher, the myths themselves are created to justify the power one culture needs to conquer or preserve, or its position at the centre of the world, besides its quality of reason primacy or humanity truth's owner (Mbembe, 2017, p. 11). Therefore, the reading of an impersonation of soft power resources in *fighters, hunters* and *blue-blood* would serve the purpose of the reflection in this chapter.

THE MAKING OF A SOFT POWER DISCOURSE

While criticizing the idea of an invented Africa besides the historical and philosophical discourses on it, Valentin Mundimbe puts emphasis on the idea that history itself would be a legend (Mudimbe, 1988, p. 208), reporting the happenings into an invented present. The discourse of African philosophers and analysts on the links between knowledge and power in the African repository of Africa as a continent, but as a symbol as well, started in the wake of the first anti-colonial ideological movements from 1950 (Franz Fanon) to 1970 (Amilcar Cabral, Walter Rodney). It based its assumptions on the logic of a Western thought Enlightment's discovering of the *savage* and on the assertion of "explicit political power presuming the authority of scientific knowledge" (Mudimbe, 1988, p. 29). It expressed the power coming from "writing about"— referred to Western anthropologists writing about Africa (Mbembe, 2017, p. 42), or "speaking in the name of" those oppressed, as suggested by Gayatri Spivak in 1988 and 1999 (Benyera, 2020, p. 11).

These debates on power included the continuous preoccupation for the forms of domination that undermined the intrinsic liberty of the individual as the French post-structuralist Michel Foucault believed (Hindess, 1996, p. 156), agreeing with his contemporary Gilles Deleuze in ordinating the desire for the power between the act of it (its abstract presence) and the interest to exercise it (Deleuze & Foucault, 1977, p. 215).

The overlinking of power discourses to domination, expressed in a long and exhausting African anti-colonial debate articulated the continuity of colonial mentalities (Ndlovu-Gatsheni, 2013, p. 8), as well as the epistemic dependency suggested by dependency theories developed from 1960 to 1970 (Chant & McIlwaine, 2009, p. 26) and colonization (Benyera, 2020, p. 12). Fanon referred to the elimination of all untruths planted by the oppressor, from the colonized (Fanon, 2004, p. 233) and later Wa Thiong' O insisted on language as an important vehicle of seduction for the imprisoning of the colonized soul (Wa Thiong' O, 1994, p. 9).

Although power was used to express the authority and prerogatives leaders had throughout Africa and how these ones were used in order to accompany destiny and make the history of it, the knowledge-power relations also reflected the universalization of a Eurocentric knowledge that tried to impose itself in regard to the African authoritarian ways and prerogatives (Ndlovu-Gatsheni, 2013, p. 13), as well. Thus, it was highlighted the myth of Africa's independence and the unfulfilment of African aspirations (Ndlovu-Gatsheni, 2013, p. 13). From a Eurocentric point of view, saying Africa means "constructing legends on top of a nothingness" (Mbembe, 2017, p. 52) and evidencing it, from an African point of view, expresses the power of Europe standing in the claims of totality. This would justify a sort of power over all other people with whom considering to have nothing in common (Mbembe, 2017, p. 54).

By extension of this idea, the African realities were and are still reflected upon in this factual frame of relations that necessarily include power in all its definitions. A deeper look at the matrix of power framed on the control over the economy, authority, gender and sexuality, such as subjectivity and knowledge (Ndlovu-Gatsheni, 2013, p. 37) would be necessary. But a careful analysis on the subject's subjectivity and knowledge from the point of view of meanings given by the subject to power would be rather useful in order to assess how African ways of describing power are influencing the coming out of their power relations with Eurocentric based world views, in order to balance relations with Europe from this perspective.

An Exploration of African Soft Power Image Particularities

The Fighters (Warriors)

The first symbol encountered in The Sudanese chapter is from the Soninke legend of Wagadu. Wagadu was the first trading empire, the so-called Ghana Empire (the empire of the warrior king), geographically comprising the south-eastern part of present day's Mauritania, parts of Mali and Senegal. This empire was called for the first time Dierra. But Wagadu was also the Soninke goddess (Lynch & Roberts, 2010, p. 31). This symbol is represented by the fighter, under the mask of Gassire, the son of the last king of Wagadu, Nganamba Fasa (Frobenius & Fox, 1937, p. 98).

Gassire's desire is to inherit his father's sword and shield. But a "wise man" prophesies Gassire will not inherit his father's sword, but he will carry a lute. The same lute that will cause the loss of Wagadu. Gassire did not actually believe this. Notwithstanding, he ordered a lute from a smith, but he could not play the lute since it could not sound. According to the legend, the lute could have only sounded if it had a heart, by absorbing blood, breathe and pain (Lynch & Roberts, 2010, p. 32), and Gassire would be giving up his ambition to rule and the glories of battle (Jablow, 1984, p. 524).

In fact, despite being under siege, Gassire sacrifices all his sons on the battlefield, baring only the youngest one. Gassire will fight until the final moment when the lute starts to sound and Wagadu disappears for the first time, because of Gassire's vanity, letting him wander in the desert (Jablow, 1984, p. 525), with the new *dausi* song that was divined for him and that outlasts him.

Besides literary interpretations on this legend and in regard to the sacrifice of the poet who is desperately targeting the immortality of his art (Jablow, 1984, p. 525), from a philosophic-political perspective, the lute represents the symbol for the more powerful but the double-edged weapon used in the battles to defend the territories and identities. The lute would be the instrument of soft power. The desire of Gassire to have it and play it, despite the prophecy on the imminent end of his empire in that case, could represent the soft will, as a preference to soft power in international relations. The lute serves as bait for the enemy, as "Gassire had thrown the lute over his shoulder" and "The Burdama came closer"

(Frobenius & Fox, 1937, p. 104), being first a bait for the Self, until its negation, as in the renouncing to rule "Gassire said: <Wagadu can go to blazes!>".

Gassire, as a fighter in the cinematics of the legend, does not only correspond to a Romantic Western image of the artist (Jablow, 1984, p. 527), but also to that one of a leader able to make choices, based however on divination, picking out the position of the First in arts, with the self-sacrifice and at the cost of losing the position of the First in politics. The lute is the weapon to manifest a cultural power over the others, not only the enemies. As Gassire used to say to his sons before going on the battlefield: "But the strokes of our swords shall echo no longer in the Sahel alone, but shall retain their ring for the ages" (Frobenius & Fox, 1937, pp. 103–104).

The *Dausi*, as the song the lute of Gassire was supposed to play, is the epic of the Soninke people, which appears all along with the mythological African epic, containing also other musical instruments, besides the lute. One is the drum, considered to be the Voice of God (Lynch & Roberts, 2010, p. 38). In the lyrical stance, the epic of Wagadu signifies a certain openness of African communities or fortresses, while turning their face to the four cardinal points where gates are placed (Frobenius & Fox, 1937, p. 106).

These elements allow for the assumption that an interest in the use of culture in the seduction and dominion of the other is inherently present in the representations of an African leader. He, who, by desiring with vanity to sing the *Dausi* for the first time, as a bard and not as ruler any more, seems to justify the African urge to assert the uniqueness of Africa, which is a moral and a political issue, meaning the power to tell one's story (Mbembe & Rendall, 2002, p. 255).

The dichotomist associations of fighters with bards, swords with instruments, temporary glories of the hero Gassire with the concept of a disappearance that could seem for the eternity (the *Dausi* will survive to Wagadu in the divination of the "wise man" and the knowledge of the smith) and also the bait type methodologies used during the battles, could resume that Soninke people's principles on history and identity are transmitted through art. Art would be servicing the will to power of the artist. Furthermore, the world view in reference to losing a territorial identity with the disappearance of Wagadu and its continuous discovery by another hero, Lagarre (Lynch & Roberts, 2010, p. 38), serves the same idea of soft will and continuity, for the construction of a soft power expressed through art.

Moreover, thinking of the lute as a symbol of power and the seduction it wields on Gassire, the power, and moreover its soft essence premise (conceptualization of it as a core to soft power, namely soft will) reveals an egotistical trait according to which its seductive attribute possesses the possessor (Egudu, 1978, p. 86).

The Soninke legend of Wagadu reveals also the perspective on a sort of capital sins that made the country Wagadu or the Goddess with the same name disappear, specifically the vanity, the falsehood, the greed and the dissension (Frobenius & Fox, 1937, p. 108). Wagadu is for the Soninke people an abstract complex of land and Goddess, in other words, the identity, which is not of stone, wood or earth, but it means the strength in the hearts of Soninke people, their beautiful Goddess disappearing each and every time she becomes overtired by the sins of her people, hence symbolically going to sleep, for in the end to continually get up in more splendour (Frobenius & Fox, 1937, p. 109).

Therefore, Wagadu or the real identity would be at a stake of all fighting that describe the context of the tale, although the characters are not fighters fully outlined by their operations in the war. They are more persuaders. For example, a negotiation with the Bida Dragon (a snake) is described in "The fight with the Bida Dragon" (Frobenius & Fox, 1937, p. 116), concluded with the sacrifice of one maiden for the gold rain three times a year, instead of ten maidens, as from the initial request of the snake. This negotiation reflects how the capacity to persuade others lies in the force of a simple "No". This argument would be per se an instrument to define a behavioural change, in accordance with the methods specific to soft power (Simons, 2017, p. 10), based on the reciprocation, theme that will be further developed in the chapter.

The understanding and the use of soft power resources (cultural values, attractiveness, love, marriage and seduction) are also revealed in the tales of other fighters from Wagadu, such as Mamadi Sefe Dekote and Wagana Sako. Although Wagana Sako is a very jealous man, he does not want to challenge the stranger (actually Mamadi Sefe Dekote, his uncle) who is in the house with his wife but he can only hear them, unobserved, from outside. The reason to not challenge him could be a rule for the manifestations of power between equal players, as he does not want to challenge someone who admitted his weakness and being afraid of him.

This would have been an unchivalrous gesture for a Soninke (Frobenius & Fox, 1937, p. 119).

On the other hand, the legend of Samba Gana brings to light the presumable values of the Soninke people: the joy over wealth and the death over defeat (when Samba Gana fails to bring laughter on the face of Annallija, he kills himself) (Frobenius & Fox, 1937, p. 131). Samba Gana is a great fighter winning a large number of townships, but being not interested to amass territories. After falling in love with Annallija Tu Bari, who lost her father and territories, so felt in the deep sufferance, Samba Gana decides to conquer new territories and grant them to Annalija Tu Bari, in order to make her happy (see her laugh). The values of the Soninke people refer to an inside force of attraction, specific to soft power (Ohnesorge, 2020, p. 124) and are synthesized in the concept of laughter on one side and death on the other. Death is the conclusion of a demonstration of hard power specific to fighting and a turning into a soft power of remembrance and glorification.

THE HUNTERS

Contrary to the fighter, in the folk tales of Nupe people, the hunter appears to be a victim of his weaknesses. In the tale of the talking skull, the hunter is fooled by a talking skull who talks only to him and not also to the king brought by the hunter in the forest to wonder on this happening. The king will punish the hunter with death, the hunter becoming a talking skull himself. In his afterlife as a talking skull, the hunter would conclude that his death was a mere consequence of talking (Frobenius & Fox, 1937, pp. 161–162). The story has a subtle clever pun due to the association of *talking* and *skull* as substantive-adjective, along with the concept-based cause (talking) and effect (becoming a skull) relation, which pictures the hunter in the context of power. This context is justified by the fact of the talking skull's charisma exercised on the hunter. Besides, charisma is recourse to magic or spirituality, as defined by Senghor and making reference to Albert Einstein's "mystical emotion" (Eze, 2001, p. 127).

Moreover, the interpretation of the talking skull's position in the tale, as premise and consequence (point of departure and point to arrive), conveys the trait of an African identity, perduring any influences, related to the worship and cult of the ancestors (Diagne, 2004, p. 378). The conversation between the hunter and the talking skull translates into a self-reflection, an identification through the power of attraction on the own or the divination as confusion of the temporal plans of present and future, like in the colossus imagined by Mbembe in regard to the dead man being the double of the living man (Mbembe, 2017, p. 53).

Just like in other African literature recorded by Evan Maina Mwangi, where the dead survives as narrator, the theme of a talking skull symbolizes the idea that voices are eternal, they are charisma and persuasion, meanwhile no external force might dismantle their messages (Mwangi, 2019, p. 96). Also sustained by Nye, the talking, and in this sense the communication, has a pivotal role in the materializing of soft power (Ohnesorge, 2020, p. 60).

Another type of victim is Kassa Kena Gananina, who is also a hunter, even if not named so, because he finally hunts the big Konoba bird (a kite) which continually threatens his fellows and flies away with the meat from the fire (Frobenius & Fox, 1937, pp. 155–157). The metaphor of the feather fallen on the back of the hunter and its considerable weight, causing him substantial pain and impeding his comrades to lift it up, meanwhile, a woman passing by could actually blow it, could be a formula to call attention to the consequences of the use of power, intended as force, but not as a will. Besides, the peculiarity of the feather might convey the listener to conceive the fluidity and permanent character of soft power (indicated by the verb *to blow*), as well. Over and above, the tale reflects sage teaching on the power which could be translated in the idea of Steven Lukes that having the means for power does not signify to be powerful (Ohnesorge, 2020, p. 32).

In fact, although hunters themselves, the two fellows are not able to free Kassa Kena Gananina from the burden of the feather because they try to lift it up, meanwhile, it would have been sufficient to blow it. It is intuitive to consider that power is a matter of modality and that the symbol of soft power as the feather laying on the back of the hunter expresses the consequence of any action of force on nature or the environment, since "power makes no sense if it is of no consequence" (Gordon, 2000, p. 86).

In line with the conceptualization of consequences that a folk tale could both reflect and form in relation to traditional knowledge production and world views, in the Nupe's tale called "Gratitude", the hunter is both a victim and a *protegée* of the animals. He is in danger of being eaten by a crocodile whom he had saved from the wood and brought to the river, but in the end, he is saved by a civet (Boaji) whom he had escaped from hunger by feeding it with the meat of an antelope he had just hunted. The crocodile did not demonstrate gratitude, meanwhile, the civet did. Besides, the other characters to which the hunter have begged for help, appearing on the river meanwhile the hunter tried to defend himself from the crocodile, namely an old woven, an old dress and an old mare, don't want to save the hunter as he is a man. Their common argument is they all know men very well: men use the others and throw them after they don't need them anymore.

This tale shows how, in the popular beliefs, gratitude means using the means of power, or energy (or cleverness, in the case of civet) one has available, with the purpose to support a cause or thank a person, at the right moment. Enclosed in the final allegory, namely: "There comes a time for every man when he is treated as he has treated others" (Frobenius & Fox, 1937, p. 170), the broader sense of gratitude refers to the paying back, so opposing the same power on the related Other, as the power exercised by the Other on the Self. In the theorization of power as proposed by international relations but also more widely by various social studies fields, the possibility of asymmetries is not excluded and the distribution of power has different forms at different times, being in continuous change, also (Ohnesorge, 2020, p. 31).

In this Nupe folk tale, the Asubi,[1] the dress and the mare are manifesting a kind of negative gratitude, expressing the counteractive part of the norm hidden in the conclusive allegory. They manifest, in such perspective, a soft power over the hunter, since they have, in a certain moment, the possibility to decide over the destiny of it. All three characters, the Asubi (Tradition), the dress (the facets of the Inner Self) and the mare (as a symbol of wealth, material goods pragmatically used) are disappointed about the Man and they turn against him as soon as they have the possibility to do it. Their power, in fact, comes from the experience and ends to be experienced for the first time, but would have no actual definition, nor measurability (Nye, 2004, p. 1).

The real and actual positive power reflected in the tale is that one of the civet Boaji, the only one to manifest gratitude towards its saviour. Due to its positive experience in relation to the hunter, its soft power turns into positive outcomes. The sagacity of the civet marks the pattern for emancipation through reconciliation, expressed in the civet's desire to hear both sides of the story in order to decide whether to help the hunter or not, thus putting the crocodile in the situation to explain but also to remake the story. Of course, this request is part of the trap the civet prepared for the crocodile, to bring things at the initial status, when the crocodile was lost in the forest and before the hunter had appeared to save him.

This return to the source is a sign of power that appeared as a reactionary concept in the discourses of Amilcar Cabral (1973). But it also meant the restitution of truth and fairness, according to the hunter's request. Meanwhile, this return signifies the acceptance of history and the experiment on it, in order to produce the knowledge—as the civet claimed: "First I must know everything" (Frobenius & Fox, 1937, p. 169).

The Blue-Blood

Various symbols of will and power are also deducible from some classical representations of the aristocracy (the blue-blood), especially its weaknesses, like presumptuousness, bold treatment of the poor and the effects of the response to such treatment.

The story of Goroba-Dike is about a Fulbe young man from an aristocratic family Ardo. He has no heritage and strongly demonstrates his dissatisfaction for this situation, by slaughtering, killing and disseminating fear among people from Bammana village. They manage to get rid of Goroba-Dike, by bribing the Mabo bard Ulal to convince him to leave the village. The bard succeeds to do that and accompanies Goroba-Dike towards the Pulu people's village, fooling him that these people would owe him a kingdom. Their first stop is the kingdom of Hamadi Ardo. Notwithstanding him being disguised in a poor Pulu man, sheltered by a smith, Goroba-Dike thrives to marry Kode Ardo, the youngest daughter of Hamadi Ardo, being the only one whose little finger perfectly fits the silver ring of the maiden (Frobenius & Fox, 1937, p. 140). Still disguised, Goroba-Dike fights against the Burdama tribe, reporting repeated victories but posing in the poor coward man that stands outside the battlefield. He will make everyone believe that his brothers-in-law, married with elder daughters of Hamadi Ardo, were the brave ones, meanwhile, he continually rides on a donkey in the opposite direction to the battlefield, each time the others go to war. In the meantime, however, he goes there and convinces the warriors of Hamadi Ardo that he is some evil creature that might help them win the Burdama and only asks for one ear of each brother-in-law, as compensation. After a few battles in which Goroba-Dike fights undercover, attracting much shame, refusal and weep of his wife Kode Ardo, the mockery and hostility of the smith, of his brothers-in-law and also the public disgrace, one day, Kode Ardo discovers who Goroba-Dike actually is and what brave actions he did. It is the time Goroba-Dike decides to reveal the truth on his identity, his actions on the battlefield and proves the story with the ears of the brothers-in-law. To thank him, Hamadi Ardo offers Goroba-Dike his kingdom (Frobenius & Fox, 1937, p. 150).

Beyond the many teachings and motives of this Fulbe legend, the re-integration and restitution of a legacy represent the centre of an emancipation narrative, constructed on the signs and elements of soft power and soft will to possess—obtain an inheritance (Goroba-Dike) by soft means (e.g. the attraction, the surprise effect, the role-playing, the fact of experiencing mockery, poverty and the teaching stance of the hero).

Findings on the Images of Soft Power and the Soft Will to Africanize

The most interesting observation is the maturity of the narratives brought to light by the collection of folk tales, asserting, at least partially, the coming out of Africa from "her childhood", as Hegel named the historical moment of Africa in the perception of the West (Obenga, 1997, p. 34). This coming out from Africa's childhood and marginality is highlighted by easily recognizable symbols in any universal logic or order. Besides meaning an out-turn, this coming out, reflected in universalization, is a process, therefore a manifestation of the will to Africanize, to assess a possible African universality or the African becoming of the world (Mbembe, 2017).

During this process, African agency is an important asset and the concept of soft will is of fundamental significance for its coming into being. For the linking of postcolonial narratives of the South (African, implicitly) with cultural heritage and social archetypes created by, and expressed in folk tales, the agency is seen under the six dimensions discussed by Amitav Acharya: the challenge(resistance), attention to the subjective and intersubjective elements, the agency of materially weaker actors (with interchangeable positions), the context, the levels of discourse and the attention to how and when agency works subsequently (the challenges and redefinitions of it) (Acharya, 2018, pp. 18–23).

For different study fields, the rhetoric analysis of the Sudanese folk tales collected by Frobenius, could bring about many conclusions on representations and images of life, preoccupations, values, teachings, ethics, culture and briefly the world views of ethnic groups in the Central but mostly Western parts of Africa. Actually, Frobenius collected tales from three big groups named by him, the Berbers, the Sudanese and the Southern Rodhesians, including many subdivisions. Calling them Sudanese folk tales, Frobenius referred, probably, to other divisions correspondent to that day's knowledge of westerners on the African continent, as it did not correspond to the classification of ethnic groups left to us by Seligman since 1966 (Dafalla, 2015, p. 162).

Actually, the three categories of legends or tales to which the reference is made herein belong to Soninke people, an ethnic group having founded the ancient empire of Ghana, being present in Mali, Senegal, Mauritania, Gambia, Burkina-Faso and Guinea-Bissau,[2] to Fulbe (or Fulani), as an indigenous group of Western Sudan Tribes (Dafalla, 2015, p. 163) and Nupe people, from the middle and Northern Nigeria.[3]

There is a possible first instance critique to the division made by Frobenius, however, the subdivision allows a wide spectre of world views and values that could, in the last instance, serve the purpose to consider the large applicability of an analysis focused on representations of soft power in African folk tales. The proposed decoding of symbols and meanings is realized with the focus on the characters of the folk tales, representing groups of labour or classes (the fighters, the hunters and the nobles—blue-blood), which do not have to be in an unresolved contradiction this time (Bhabha, 1986, p. xxii). They all carry the personal values, teachings and definitions of the soft power, expressed by charisma, contextuality, positionality and own experiences. In these four expressions or qualities of the characters, their soft will, as core element and method for the soft power, is represented and sustained by the creative force of art (the lute of Gassire, the cleverness in communication with the Bida Dragon or of the civet saving the hunter from the crocodile, the role-playing of Goroba-Dike, the contemplative will of Samba Gana to hearing the laughter of Annallija Tu Bari, the correspondence of parallel worlds in the talking skull's legend, etc.) and life.

These characters enter in various contextual relationships with others, humans, post-humans (intended as ancestors), animals or objects and experience the systematic and individual influence that stands for soft power (Simons, 2017, p. 461). Being a compound of hard and soft elements (Simons, 2017, p. 11) power is, as appears also in the analysed tales, a temporary status of one Self, the character, being inherent and energetic. The negative power of Gassire expecting his father's death for the inheritance, the sins threatening Wagadu as well as the killing of Konoba, are such examples of energies of the evil, counterbalanced by the soft power of happenings (the context) or other characters (the progress or becoming of the Self), reported to history most of the times. For example, in the short tale of Lagarre reconquering Wagadu, the disappeared land and Goddess, through negotiation with the Bida Dragon, the so-called snake could be a reference to Etsu Nupe (Bida) which was from the Fula tribe,[4] but ruled the Nupe people.

Expanding the conceptualization of power, the individual influence, or the charisma on the others and on the Self of a leader (whether brave fighters as Gassire, Samba Gana and Goroba-Dike, or a good negotiator as Lagarre) exceeds in the concept-supporting role the notions of space, freedom or sovereignty, as land in pre-colonial Africa was plentiful, but it was the power over the people that was more important (Herbst, 2014, p. 38). The mentioned leaders manifest, as typical for a folk tale's semiotics, the interest for non-patrimonial goods such as the power in a sword (the possibility to reign) and continuity for Gassire, the recognition for Goroba-Dike, or the happiness (also laughter) and splendour of a woman, with a potential symbol of home, for Samba Gana and Lagarre.

One common behaviour for Gassire, Samba Gana and Lagarre, as fighters, Kassa Kena Gananina and the other hunters from the Soninke legends collected by Frobenius, or the noble man Goroba-Dike, is the effort to create a reality to be proposed, and finally imposed: for Gassire is the will to have the lute sound, for Samba Gana is the will to hear Annallija Tu Bari's laughter, for the hunter Kassa Kena Gananina the will to exaggerations, or in the legend of the hunter saved by the crocodile, the will to re-create the reality (by the civet); finally, the will to create an unpleasant false reality in order for the surprise of a better reality to assure and amplify the charisma of Goroba-Dike in relation to the others. This effort is translated in the will and power to define the reality and receive responses from others to said definitions, as if it was theirs, like in the axiom recorded by Ajamu (1997, p. 185).

In fact, there is a symmetrical route from the reality depicted by one character and the real image resulted and subjected to understanding. For example, Gassire's prophecy is to carry a lute, he will carry it. Samba Gana will fight for the vital force and life, pursuing the aim of seeing Annallija Tu Bari laugh, but this will not happen as Annallija Tu Bari's loss (of her father and lands) will end up in loss (of her husband), so memory will generate memory. As a matter of fact, both the missionary Placide Temples and the anthropologist Marcel Griaule observed that the vital force's role was not only to animate the person but also to individuate him or her (Wiredu, 2004, p. 55). The two actions of animating (the advancement of the being) and individuating (the Self-recognition/differentiation) do refer to memory, on one side: the memory of the history (the experience) and the knowledge of one's self (Thompson, 1997, p. 9).

On the other hand, laughter is symbolizing life, irony, game, but also an alternative to death, the cynicism of power seen with oriental lens, in disillusionment (Asad, 1975, p. 106). Laughter is internal and external to the legends, it is preserved as a symbol in the narrative and as a tool for the listener. In the tale of the talking skull, laughter is external. It shows in the more eloquent way how both the spirit of life and death, mirrored in the symbiosis of memory and laughter, intend to pass on African Philosophical ideas about the another world as a part of this world (Wiredu & Gyekye, 1992, p. 140), in defence of a struggle to continuity (laughter- the force of joy and life) and consciousness (memory). This struggle refers to what Theophile Obenga calls "the two fundamental problems of African historiography" (Obenga, 1997, p. 31) through which the definition of the African Self and its promotion to Africanization takes place.

The hypothesis of laughter and memory might also be applied to the other symbols in the folk tales, even, with great significance, to the story of the hunter Kessa Gaganina, who got burdened under the feather (the memory that in certain circumstances becomes heavier than it could actually be). But, the fact that it could be also blown away, leaving the hunters, as artefacts of Africanity, in a rather ridiculous position, shows, with intent to external incentivization of laughter, that, however, the preoccupations to avoid the identity's loss or Africanity's deconstruction, should be central. And every step towards regaining the history as reflected in African discourses is an act of soft will of the African on the estranged African (Eze, 2001, p. 199).

The symbols of soft power are frequent and common in the picture of the leader's profile, whether he is a fighter, the son of a king or a blue-blood. He has charisma, diplomacy skills, the capability to collect and support the critics from others, drawn by divination or the guidance of one counsellor, with an appetite for gaming, punishment and the exercising of hard powers (e.g. the chastising of the smith who blamed him, in the case of Goroba-Dike). Along with these characteristics, the tales schematize a strategy before any actions (in the teachings of the smith, the wise man, the old woman, etc.), which is yet an important resource of soft power (Nye, 2004, p. 3), besides the attraction component (Nye, 2004, p. 5).

While charisma and leadership in the context of an individualistic approach to the symbol of the fighters in the folk tales could contain elements of a possible representation on the soft power in an African precolonial ancient orally transmitted culture, when analysing the symbol of the hunter, it was suggested that in relation to power, the hunter has a secondary role. He is a victim, the Other which experiences the attraction towards the Self, in an equation where the Self is using means of soft power in order to persuade, or more, the Other.

In fact, hunters are under the exercise of attraction ran by animals or things, as tokens of nature (outside the culture of the Self). The soft power idea connected to them is not normative, in the sense that rules seem to lack, being difficult to form or predict behaviours as focused on experience, specificity and historical course. Moreover, it can be "wielded with both noble and reprehensible intentions" (Ohnesorge, 2020, p. 64). It is the case of the Asubi, or the dress, or the mare, who all refuse to help the hunter due to the prejudice of their previous experience. A tale's teaching is constructed, not necessarily on power, but for sure on elements of will that go along the social relations and communication between subjects.

In the same tale, the crocodile is a user of soft power, due to its openness to consult four other subjects on his decision to eat the hunter that just saved him. The democratic approach of the crocodile in the context of this paper's aim, to bring closer images in a time–space fluid ideology on soft power, suggests what Nye appreciated on the non-democratic countries forced to recognize the importance of this soft power's feature for the economic objectives (Nye, 2004, p. 20). The crocodile would have the interest to have a good lunch, but the notion of fairness invoked by the hunter, that makes the crocodile accept the popular voice on this, expresses, finally, the contextuality, thus, the relativism of power redemption.

The main significance of the dress would recall to the reader of the twentieth century, the idea of layer or mask, which would be, in line with

Fanon's symbology, the encumbrance of the Self to be revealed due to being trapped in a game of dichotomies (e.g. black and white) (Bhabha, 1986, p. xxxiv). In the same game would find himself the hunter talking to the talking skull, case in which his own mask is the skull, as time plots are being changed and confused. In the Africanization narrative frame, the talking skull could be the mask as symbol used by Fanon, in his analysis of the Negro—or the African, implicitly, if we consider Mbembe's more recent critique on Africans as Blacks (Mbembe, 2017, p. 91)— seeking admittance to the white sanctuary, based on which he concludes that "attitude derives from the intention" (Fanon, 2008, p. 36). And the action (to be admitted as a talking skull) derives from the will and belief in the existence of another world as possibility (the magic world of talking skulls). Actually, the hunter's attraction for the skull would have been linked to much curiosity on the part of the hunter, who ends up wanting and acting accordingly in order to become a talking skull himself. This situation was theorized by Nye through the concept of the "second face of power" (Nye, 2004, p. 6) and could be compared with the final image of the two talking skulls in the forest. This tale was valued in actual cultural discourse by changing the essence of "simple talking" of the hunter to the "telling a lie", while this seems not to be a lie, in the repository of the tale.[5] The problematization of this version is whether to choose power over truth. The need to separate power from truth would underline the falsehood as means of power, envisaged also in the less explained idea of Wagadu's disappearance cause, from the Soninke legend.

Besides a strange and problematic individualistic approach, the elements of charisma or attractiveness, contextuality, experience, democratic and even time-sensitive particularities of soft power's image in the analysed tales, there is also a strong propensity to a profound logic of numbers, which, along with the culture, play a central role in the shaping of soft power. Numbers connect these elements, contributing to the re-composition of the tales on the rhythm of a poem, with repetitions sometimes attractive, but otherwise, redundant and exhausting: the negotiation with the Bida Dragon for the number of maidens to be sacrificed for it, or the stories of battles carried by Gasirre, are some of the latter ones.

As for repetitions, they place the focus on a reiterated, maybe unique, maybe Ubuntu-istic discourse on the African Self, which is discovered or only reckoned in the supposed fidelity to the real tales, as the wilful contribution of Leo Frobenius to the epistemology of African Philosophy (Mudimbe, 1988, p. 94).

In the process of Africanization, seen as restitution and reparation by Mbembe (2017, p. 54), the symbols of vital force (the laughter and life, as well as memory) and the soft will (as Nietzschean will to power) are load-bearing columns. Many elements of the legends are linked to these symbols, especially in reference to reparation, that for Mbembe means reciprocation—the repositioning in a relationship (Mbembe, 2017, p. 182). Reciprocation is met in regard to Gassire whose karmic possibility is to carry a lute that cannot sound on a level of reality, reciprocating with a virtual level of wander, with a lute that can sound. It is also present in the folk tales of negotiation with the snake Bida Dragon, the reciprocation of gratitude, the reciprocation between father-in-law and Samba Gana, in relation to them being honoured by Annalija Tu Bari; or, the moral representation of aristocratic weaknesses between Goroda Dike and his wife.

The repositioning in relationship is conditioned by a will for the particular order of elements. And this order is given by an ontology whose existence was also sustained by the habits, norms and ethical African precepts (Diagne, 2004, p. 23). It is in regard to this order that the cultural functions of the folk tales show their effects in a more visible way. Acting on the order of priorities is manifesting a soft power on the other, whose priorities are already there and defined. Instead, putting priorities in relation means manifesting the will to consider and reconsider the subject and the vital force of power.

This distinction could be regarded as inherited in the African ontology from ancient reasons, as elements of establishing an order of priorities. Naming the priorities that are present in the Wagadu legend in reference to Gassire, who puts in relation the desire to inherit the power from his father (suggested in the symbols of wealth and war) with the desire for immortality (through the song of the lute determining the loss of his land) (wealth), is practically impossible, due to antagonisms difficult to resolve. However, the carrying of battles and the sacrifices of Gassire's sons reveals the establishment of order to the named priorities, due to the contextuality of the soft will to preserve both priorities, even with no success. And maybe in this context, the deepest moral precept of the legends stand.

Conclusion

This chapter is a tiny taste of what African folk tales could signify for the discourse of Africanization. Selected symbols were regarded from the point of view of the power and the will they or their contexts express. The power and the will to power were integrated into the idea of order, as principal to the definition of the reality as life, death or a game and from other two perspectives: the laughter and the remembrance (memory). These could be regarded as non-power over universality, since laughter and memory are important elements of any folk tale comprising values of a certain universality. Their use in a discourse of soft power, starting with the soft will and in the context of the ideals and aims to Africanize, is necessary in order to simplify and support the African Agency and all discourses for the present and future of African identity.

There are several ways to consider and view the metaphors and significates used in the folk tales of Frobenius, but beyond any suspicion of fake and Europeanization, they contain the ethics that were found in later Afrocentric narratives, concentrating on the power, the will and the force, recalling the vitality of the laughter and the potentialities and stances of the memory. All these meant to pursue ideals of becoming what one already is (e.g. Gassire, Goroba-Dike) or conquer what is or only seems to be one's land, the right, the joy or the freedom (Goroba-Dike, Kassa Kena Gananina, Samba Gana—the joy of his wife), meanwhile experiencing the soft will and power to see things from above, from the position where one can see without being seen (like in the case of Goroba-Dike's role-playing, the talking skull).

Getting to discover elements of a soft power discourse, definition and even teachings in folk tales represent the confirmation of the fact that world views did not change much, they were defined and particular, having nothing to do with any colonial heritage, they contributed to the continuity of a philosophical and sage social comprehension, they guided throughout centuries the biases of Self-Identification, Self-Recognition and the Reconciliation, proving to readers informed on actual realities that the time to awake the soft power to a natural positive Africanization in the further balancing of the world could justify its intrinsic existence, being a pure and natural act of the African being.

Notes

1. Described as a "coloured oval mat woven by the Benue in the Kutigi region" (Frobenius, 1937, p. 167).
2. National African Language Resource Center, Soninke—brochure, Bloomington, IN 47406 USA. https://nalrc.indiana.edu/doc/brochures/soninke.pdf.
3. National African Language Resource Center, Nupe—brochure, Bloomington, IN 47406 USA. https://nalrc.indiana.edu/doc/brochures/nupe.pdf.
4. This idea comes from the coincidence on the name Bida, as in the brief description of the National African Language Resource Center, Bloomington, IN 47406 USA in the Nupe—brochure. https://nalrc.indiana.edu/doc/brochures/nupe.pdf.
5. The story is collected and shared on the platform of the multimedia peacebuilding project *Na'eesh Mabadh/Living Together*, under the title of "The Story of the young man and the Skull" available on http://www.southsudanesefolktales.org/?project=the-story-of-the-young-man-and-the-skull.

References

Ajamu, A. A. (1997). From Tef Tef to Medew Nefer: The Importance of Utilizing African Terminologies and Concepts in the Rescue Restoration Reconstruction and Reconnection of African Ancestral Memory in Carruthers, J. H., & Harris, L. C. (Eds.), *African world history project: The preliminary challenge*. Association for the Study of Classical African Civilizations.

Asad, T. (Ed.) (1975 Reprint). *Anthropology & the colonial encounter*. (Vol. 6). Ithaca Press.

Bello, A. G. A. (2005). Some methodological controversies in African philosophy. In *A companion to African philosophy* (pp. 261–273). Blackwell.

Benyera, E. (2020). *Reimagining justice, human rights and leadership in Africa*. Springer.

Bhabha, H. (1986). Introduction. In F. Fanon, *Black skin, white mask*. Taylor and Francis.

Cabral, A. (1973). *Return to the source*. African Information Service.

Chant, S. H., & McIlwaine, C. (2009). *Geographies of development in the 21st century: An introduction to the global South*. Edward Elgar Publishing.

Dafalla, M. M. (2015). Interpretations of a Sudanese folktale. *American International Journal of Contemporary Research*, 5(5). http://www.aijcrnet.com/journals/Vol_5_No_5_October_2015/20.pdf

Deleuze, G., & Foucault, M. (1977). Intellectuals and power. In *Language, counter-memory, practice* (pp. 205–217). Cornell University Press.

Diagne, B. S. (2004). Islam in Africa: Examining the notion of an African identity within the Islamic world. In K. Wiredu et al. (Eds.), *A companion to African philosophy* (pp. 374–384). Blackwell.

Egudu, R. N. (1978). *Modern African poetry and the African predicament.* Springer.

Eze, E. C. (2001). *Achieving our humanity: The idea of the postracial future.* Psychology Press.

Fanon, F. (2004). *The wretched of the earth. 1961* (R. Philcox, Trans., Vol. 6). Grove Press.

Fanon, F. (2008). *Black skin, white masks.* Pluto Press.

Frobenius, L., & Fox, D. C. (1937). *African genesis: Folk tales and myths of Africa.* Dover Publications.

Gordon, L. R. (2000). *Existentia Africana: Understanding Africana existential thought.* Psychology Press.

Hallen, B. (2005). Contemporary anglophone African philosophy: A survey. In *A companion to African philosophy* (pp. 99–148). Blackwell.

Herbst, J. (2014). *States and power in Africa: Comparative lessons in authority and control* (Vol. 149). Princeton University Press.

Hindess, B. (1996). *Discourses of power from Hobbes to Foucault.* Wiley.

Jablow, A. (1984). Gassire's Lute: A reconstruction of Soninke bardic art. *Research in African Literatures, 15*(4), 519–529.

Lynch, P. A., & Roberts, J. (2010). *African mythology: A to Z.* Infobase Publishing.

Mbembe, J.-A. (2017). *Critique of black reason.* Duke University Press.

Mbembe, J.-A., & Rendall, S. (2002). African modes of self-writing. *Public Culture, 14*(1), 239–273.

Mudimbe, V. Y. (1988). The invention of Africa: Gnosis. *Philosophy, and the Order of Knowledge, 27,* 191–192.

Mwangi, E. (2019). *The postcolonial animal: African literature and posthuman ethics.* African Perspectives.

Ndlovu-Gatsheni, S. J. (2013). *Coloniality of power in postcolonial Africa.* African Books Collective.

Nye, J. S., Jr. (2004). *Soft power: The means to success in world politics.* Public Affairs.

Obenga, T. (1997). Who am I? In J. H. Carruthers & L. C. Harris (Eds.), *African world history project. The preliminary challenge* (pp. 31–46). Association for the Study of Classical African Civilizations.

Ohnesorge, H. W. (2020). *Soft power: The forces of attraction in international relations.* Springer Nature.

Simons, J. (2017). The Routledge handbook of soft power. In N. Chitty, L. Ji, G. D. Rawnsley, & C. Hayden (Eds.), Routledge.

Sone, E. M. (2018). The folktale and social values in traditional Africa. *Eastern African Literary and Cultural Studies, 4*(2), 142–159.

Thompson, A. (1997). Developing an African historiography. In J. H. Carruthers & L. C. Harris (Eds.), *African world history project. The preliminary challenge* (pp. 9–30). Association for the Study of Classical African Civilizations.

Wa Thiong'o, N. (1992). *Decolonising the mind: The politics of language in African literature*. East African Publishers.

West, M., & Donato, R. (1995). Stories and stances: Cross-cultured encounters with African folktales. *Foreign Language Annals, 28*(3), 392–406.

Wiredu, K. (2004). *A companion to African philosophy*. Blackwell.

Wiredu, K., & Gyekye, K. (1992). *Person and community. Ghanaian philosophical studies I*. CIPSH/UNESCO.

CHAPTER 12

Beyond Entertainment: Power and Performance in Two Urban Festivals in Niger

Susan Rasmussen

INTRODUCTION

Recently, as Akinola and Ogunnubi (2020) point out, there has been an important focus on cultural resources of resilience. Despite real hardships, vulnerability, and precarity, African cultural resources remain vital and offer interesting case studies to explore how cultural performances and creative practices can be converted into an enabling tool for transformation, in terms of both power and agency. This chapter compares performances at two cultural festivals held to celebrate achievements in Agadez, a town in northern Niger, in terms of the types of power conveyed and their broader significance. Specifically, the focus is on

S. Rasmussen (✉)
Department of Comparative Cultural Studies, University of Houston, Houston, TX, USA
e-mail: srasmussen@uh.edu

© The Author(s), under exclusive license to Springer Nature Singapore Pte Ltd. 2022
T. Afolabi et al. (eds.), *Re-centering Cultural Performance and Orange Economy in Post-colonial Africa*,
https://doi.org/10.1007/978-981-19-0641-1_12

two celebratory events with performances that share a common concern with relationships between youths and older adults, but are otherwise quite different. One celebration marks the end of the Ramadan fasting month, which attracts children seeking the blessing of the Sultan of Air, a traditional leader, and is held in his palace courtyard, where griots (bards) and smith/artisans perform praises and neighborhood leaders pay him homage. The other celebration honors young people's completion of job apprenticeships, sponsored by USAID, an American aid agency, held in a technical school's outdoor stadium, where local guitarists and actors perform, Islamic scholars pray, and civic and national authorities speak. Both events feature praise, but also critical commentaries and debates addressing strained relations between the generations in Agadez, where many elders' powers face challenges from the influxes of refugees, returned labor migrants, surging youth unemployment, political violence, and neoliberal restructuring and de-centralization. How are local performers' traditional powers to persuade and control reputation and policy marshaled and re-directed in each festival? The data, based on this anthropologist's long-term field research residences in Niger between 1983 and 2017, suggest both official and unofficial means by which cultural performances creatively re-invent already-existing structures. I ask, what forms of power do these events' performances, respectively, convey, how do they re-invent and critique existing and intruding structures? My findings challenge the assumption of a mechanical hierarchical connection between cultural, state, and civic powers in several ways, showing that local cultural influence is substantial, and does not always translate into Western European notions of power or of "diplomatic" outcomes, and suggesting not solely hegemony (Gramsci, 1971) and cultural/symbolic capital (Bourdieu, 1977), but also local mediation of more complex powers, including some multiple voices and heterology (Foucault, 2000), and appropriations, even resistances to, the official messages in and beyond these contexts. More broadly, I hope to provide more nuanced frameworks for analyzing the play of structure and agency in performances, by looking inward at local cultural responses disputing hegemonic powers. In other words, we need to also focus on different performers' and audiences' perceptions of and responses to power, as well as processes on the sidelines of performances. Performances, whether invoking "secular" or "sacred" power, are not monological, but rather, dialogical (Herzfeld, 2016; Makley, 2018).

The Events, Their Setting, and the Backdrop: History, Culture, and Politics

A Celebration of the End of Ramadan at the Palace of the Sultan (*amenokal*) of Air: Preliminary Description.

This annual event, a blending of mainstream and popular Islam and local cultural traditions, is widely described as a "festival" (Fr. *fete*) and a "prayer or holy day" (Hausa *salah*, Tamajaq *emud*), marking the end of the Muslim Ramadan fasting month. The celebration takes place in the palace courtyard of the Sultan of Air, also called *amenokal* (Tamajaq), the traditional leader of the region's Tuareg descent groups and of the Agadezian population (the latter, of mixed backgrounds, also including some indigenous residents who have become absorbed into Tamajaq and Hausaphone groups there) (Hamani, 1989; Nicolaisen & Nicolaisen, 1997; Rodd, 1926). Starting around 5 PM, smith/artisans and griots (bards, oral historians) lead praises of the Sultan. Although the audience is diverse, officially this event is held for pre-adolescent school children and town VIP'S, including elderly chiefs of Agadez's approximately twenty neighborhoods at the end of Ramadan.

On the day I attended (informally invited by friends, warmly welcomed by officials, and given permission to record improvised oral performances), uniformed soldiers were few and subdued, though the Sultan's traditional red-clad guards were ubiquitous, controlling the sometimes-rambunctious children, who burst enthusiastically through a door, scampering into the compound when allowed, despite guards' (mock?) threats with camel-hide whips. The children clustered around, laughing raucously, and grabbed the candy and dates tossed by guards—gifts or alms (*takote*) conveying al baraka blessing from the Sultan, a father figure. The notables approached the Sultan, who was seated beneath an awning, and greeted him, bowing slightly. Smith/artisan and griot drummers and singers performed songs praising the Sultan, made announcements, and orchestrated payments of taxes by elderly neighborhood chiefs.

This combination—of musical performance, religious holy day, reciprocal exchange and alms/gifts, is not contradictory in local viewpoint. In pre-colonial Tuareg stratified society, for example, music and gatherings often accompanied smiths' collections of rents and tithes owed to nobles from client and servile subordinates, who gardened on nobles' oases and owed them portions of harvest in return for military protection.

[Later, nobles' gardens were turned over to subordinates upon slaves' manumission and liberation on independence].

The overt, explicitly-stated purpose of this event, however, was explained as a "*barka da Sallah*", held for children and neighborhood chiefs "in order to express their mutual support and respect", symbolized by three large chiefly drums struck by the griots' children. Complementing this event are families' visits, also at the end of Ramadan, to relatives, who also give al *baraka* in gifts. If one does not give food to children, it is widely feared that children will eat only insects in the afterlife.

A Celebration of Apprentices and Graduates of a USAID Job-Training Program at a School Stadium: Preliminary Description.

Programs sponsored by NGO, state, and international organizations, such as USAID, address older youths (culturally defined as those who are biologically mature, but not yet economically independent) (Rasmussen, 1997). These programs' performances and festivals, entertaining but pedagogical, seek to distract youths from problems at home, to discourage them from out-migration and from joining regional fighting, and to integrate them into secular and neoliberal educational and occupational infrastructures. These goals require re-establishing confidence in formal education through rewards.

The event I describe here, (one of several similar USAID-sponsored festivals I attended in 2012 and 2017, at which I also received permission to record oral performances), was a festive spectacle also celebrating the re-patriation of migrants returning from Libya over several years following the 2011 fall of Ghadaffi. This celebration, called "Solidarity With Those Re-Patriated" or "Solidarity with Returnees from Libya", was held at the stadium of EMAIR (l'Ecole des mines de l'Air), a technical school in Agadez, from 9 AM to about noon. There was a large turnout: high officials such as the Prime Minister, the then-US ambassador, US Embassy and Culture Center staff, and traditional leaders, such as the Sultan and his guards, police, army, and an audience of families and friends of those returned migrants who had completed re-patriation workshops and started job-training in specialized trades. A marabout blessed the event at its beginning. There were speeches by the ambassador and local leaders, followed by music, dances, plays by a youth-group acting ensemble, and songs by traditional and modern artists.

The event not only recognized and showcased trainees' achievements, but also conferred scholarships (Fr. *des bourses*) on top achievers to continue studying trades (couture, carpentry, mechanics, welding).

The Town of Agadez in the Saharan Air Region

Agadez, a Saharan town in the Air Mountain region of northern Niger, is predominantly Muslim, culturally and linguistically diverse, and a vibrant crossroads of Islamic scholarship, trade, and art. The Tuareg, who speak Tamajaq, an Amazigh (Berber) language, have become a prominent presence there following a series of droughts and French colonial and Niger independent state pressures to sedentarize. Until approximately the mid-twentieth century, Tuareg were predominantly rural pastoral livestock herders and camel caravanners (Claudot-Hawad, 1993; Nicolaisen & Nicolaisen, 1997). Most, in particular, the aristocratic *imajeghen*, did not usually reside in towns, but visited them only for trading, staying there with clients and subordinates in their ranked society (Bouman, 2003; Rossi, 2018). Despite some intermarriages and more settled life in Agadez, Tamajaq-speakers and Hausaphone groups tend to remain culturally and linguistically distinct. Most Agadez and Air region residents combine Qur'anic and non-Qur'anic spirits in their cosmologies, rituals, and myths. Except in communities with militant reformist Islamists' influence, most Tuareg women enjoy considerable rights and privileges and social and economic independence. Both men and women inherit and own property, and socialize in public (Bernus, 1993; Claudot-Hawad, 1993; Kohl, 2009).

Hausa arrived in Agadez from migrations from what are now northern Nigeria and southern Niger. Agadezians with earlier roots in that town predominate in the Old City, where many (though not all) are artisans, griots, and butchers, in guild-like organizations headed by chiefs, and directly serve the Sultan of Air. The Sultan/amenokal traditionally kept the Sahara peaceful for trade by arbitrating among warring Tuareg descent groups. With his council of elders and Islamic scholar/marabouts, he still adjudicates disputes, conducts some mediating during sporadic Tuareg rebellions, and oversees tax collection.

Also residing in Agadez are civil servants, state government representatives, and soldiers of diverse cultural/linguistic backgrounds, mostly from southern Niger, and a few Europeans working in aid agencies. Until the political violence of armed militant jihadi groups in the Sahara and the recent outbreak of the COVID-19, tourism provided revenue for smith/artisan jewelers (Rasmussen, 2013). Despite these upheavals, many residents still practice hereditary occupations: metalsmiths, leatherworkers, and griots (bards or oral historians). There are also traditional and modern tailors, weavers, singers, and musicians. Most Islamic scholars (popularly called "marabouts"), who adhere to more moderate local cultural interpretations of the Qur'an, possess and conduct *al baraka* blessing power, practice Qur'anic healing and counseling, and bless festivals, performances, and rituals. Others, more influenced by Islamist piety groups, oppose "popular" Islamic practices and mixed-sex sociability, and shun public secular musical performances (Rasmussen, 2019). Migrants from south of the Sahara crossing the desert, seeking to go to Europe or return to their homes, have temporarily settled in camps on the town's outskirts.

Performances, workshops, and festivals re-integrating migrants focus primarily on returning migrants of local origins. Adults lament youths' marginality and potential anti-social conduct. Many (though not all) returning migrants are young Tuareg men who lived and worked in Libya, and returned to their homes in Agadez and rural Air over several years, fleeing the political violence after the fall of Ghadaffi, under- or unemployed, and some, armed with weapons from that regime. Most of them are considered youths, a local category based on neither linear, chronological, nor biological age, but rather on economics: lack of means to marry. Cultural definitions of adulthood are based on economic stability, marriageability or married status, and ritual roles (Rasmussen, 1997, 2018). This definition differs from some states' and NGO's definitions based on chronological age.

Since the World Bank and International Monetary Fund decentralization and privatization policies in the mid-1980's, Tuareg and other youths in Niger have suffered from marginal employment (Masquelier, 2019; Youngstedt & Keough, 2020).

Faced with these challenges, older persons attempt to preserve social, moral, and spiritual ties between the generations. During school holidays, urban parents send children to the countryside to assist relatives with herding and gardening. Elders serve important protective roles; for example, two elderly sisters and an elderly uncle spent the night in a compound of a woman whose relatives were away on travel in order to protect her from dangers (human bandits and/or malevolent spirits). Elderly persons at rituals are spiritual intermediaries between humans and ancestors—indeed, as "pre-ancestral" themselves (Rasmussen, 2018). This is one important aspect of power in the post-Ramadan celebration at the Sultan's palace: there are efforts to convey this value to small children in analogies made between children and Agadez residents, on the one hand, and between the Sultan, fathers, and elders more generally.

Yet these ideal complementary relationships between the generations do not always retain their power. Although parents still negotiate children's first arranged marriages and bride-wealth, some youths now resist. One adolescent girl successfully resisted an arranged marriage by her parents in order to continue her education. Young men who travel on labor migration often skip traditional socialization with elderly relatives presiding on trading expeditions, at rites of passage, and in apprenticeships. Technology also impacts intergenerational relationships: suitors can call each other on cell phones to arrange a meeting, bypassing the girl's father's permission. On the other hand, in cell-phone conversations, rural parents-in-law can more easily ask for money from sons-in-law. Older relatives are becoming more dependent on children's sometimes uncertain monetary support than previously, when elders controlled most wealth (in herds), thereby inverting some economic roles. Elders' ritual actions are all the more important to "remind" youths of mutual obligations when infrastructural changes challenge them.

In the sections that follow, I show how the symbolism of the Air Sultan's end of Ramadan ritual attempts to remind younger youths of elders' spiritual powers in order to counterbalance economic and political pressures, to emphasize the patriarchal but benevolent powers that bridge sacred and secular, state and local, and to preserve this leader's mediating role. The symbolism of the USAID spectacle honoring participants and graduates of the job-training program attempts to establish lost trust in secular education. Historically, many northern residents, in particular, more nomadic Tuareg, were forcibly taken by French and later central state soldiers to so-called nomadic schools where they were forbidden to speak their Tamajaq language or wear their Tuareg clothing (Keenan, 1977). Later, nomads' attitudes toward secular schools became more positive after its benefits (food for children and civil service jobs) were shown. Then, in the early twenty-first century, following IMF and World Bank policies, many found that education did not guarantee jobs, became disillusioned with school's value, and enrollments declined. Hence, the goal of recent NGO and state aid programs' is to emphasize training in more specialized skills, for example, tailoring.

Analysis and Discussion
The Two Events: A Closer Look

Transformations and disruptions, as well as continuities between intergenerational ideals and practices surfaced in the celebration at the palace courtyard of the *amenokal*/Sultan of Air's ceremony at the end of Ramadan. There, when he distributed dates and candy to children and met with different neighborhood leaders as smiths and griots drummed and praised his generosity, performers symbolically compared the Sultan to a father: he should be a father to his subjects, who should be like children to him. Thus here, the ideal spiritual and material care and nurturing by elders, transposed onto political leadership, symbolically conveys the economic obligations, not absolute privileges, from this leader.

In prevalent views of intergenerational mutual dependence, as fathers grow older and transform into grandfathers, giving between children and parents should be mutual and reciprocal. Adults should give alms to small children on Fridays to lessen their own sins, and adults (including leaders) should also give food (or more generally, bring resources) to impoverished persons to preserve protective *al baraka* blessing during dangerous and/or anomalous events. Small children should also bring food to frail elders, maintain their supplies, and relay their messages.

As powerful as the Sultan's feeding of children at the ritual was, there was nonetheless some asymmetry. The Sultan gave to the children, but the children did not give in return, (except in terms of hoped-for future loyalty to and respect for him); only the *chefs de quartier* elderly men did (in tribute/taxes, which were part of a mutuality in which there is confidence in the Sultan's ability to bring in development). The huge crowd of eager children, after gathering up the snacks, ran off. A few guards and other adults there remarked disapprovingly, "These children have no respect/shame (Tam. *takarakit,* Hausa, *kumiya*)." Perhaps on one level this was buffoonery, a carnivalesque, cathartic reversal of roles of youths toward elders, but on another level, the important process was the recognition of the simultaneous ritual spirituality and bringing in of economic and spiritual resources, conducted to the children and Agadez subjects by the Sultan as father figure.

The first day featured singing of improvised praise-songs by smiths and the second and third day, by griots, accompanied by *acanza* (small handheld) and *ganga* drums (larger mortars covered with goatskin, struck with hands) and the *algaita* horn. One song went as follows:

"May God protect the Sultan of Air, We thank God who enables us to review the year
Sultan, we have confidence (trust, *amana*, also tax) in you
This heritage, it is the heritage of benediction
The seat of the Sultan of Air
We thank you, Sultan, again
This year is the year of benediction
Happiness is upon us
My Sultan of Air is capable of speaking and listening (to us)
Confidence (trust, tax), a duty
May God protect the current Sultan, who succeeded his father, (who died in 2011)
The seat of the Sultan needs work
The Sultan needs many hands (i.e., seeks the participation of those he rules)
And in addition, he needs much advice
May God protect the Sultan Oumarou
The Sultan Oumarou has helped us
He gives us food and money
May God increase the celebration (value) of the Sultan
The sultanate it is a heritage that is valuable
May God prolong the life of the Sultan
May God give a benediction (blessing) to the Sultan"

Relevant here are several overlapping powers. Foremost is the sacred power, *al baraka* blessing/benediction, conducted by religious specialists. An interlocutor and transcribing assistant asserted, "the *al baraka* of the Sultan of Air is so strong that, if his clothing becomes stuck on a tree and the tree tears them, that tree will wither and die!" Many healers, especially Islamic scholars of *icherifan* descent from the Prophet, are saturated with special moral qualities. Most important of them is *al baraka*. Derived from God, this power may be transmitted by a prominent holy person or a respected elderly female herbal medicine woman (Rasmussen, 2001, 2006) when conducted through contact with their saliva, clothing, tombs, or alms, which reinforces their medico-ritual treatment. After their death, their power increases. This blessing must be protected by offerings at tombs. Yet truly great holy persons with this power should be modest, not seek glory. Here, sacred ritual and the secular performance and powers are not separate (Comaroff & Comaroff, 1993), and the Sultan embodies both.

Meanwhile, however, not visible from the courtyard and not mentioned by anyone at the Sultan's event was a competing event called Zero, featuring fancy car maneuvers in the sand. This event, held several miles away on the town's outskirts, was attended by many older adolescents, some seated on parked cars' hoods. These car shows have become more frequent than the older camel races in Agadez. Most elders disapprove of, but do not forbid Zero, lamenting that "instead of valuing camels and keeping them in the family, youths nowadays want to sell them for cars."

At the USAID-sponsored "Solidarity with Returned Migrants from Libya" event at EMAIR, griots, smiths, popular musicians and singers, and *animateurs* (hosts) were all present and participated at intervals between speeches by officials, primarily entertaining (with some buffoonery, as at the Sultan's event), to maintain audience interest and attention, but also, much more: welcoming returned migrants, congratulating and honoring graduates of the job-training program, and more generally, conveying messages discouraging out-labor migration, joining of armed groups, and instead encouraging a western, even subtly Protestant work ethic, re-vitalizing local jobs, and following neoliberal free-market policies. Yet some critiques of prevalent stereotypes of youths also occurred.

Although hegemonic power was asserted here (Gramsci, 1977), in cultural domination from the "top-down" in the official speeches and congratulations, there were also critical responses. A local acting ensemble presented the following unwritten, improvised play, entitled simply, Tchikoubas, also the name of their *fada*, an informal social group of friends:

(Seated character):	I am going to set out tea.
	(A person arrives) My friend, you arrive now, you got lost?
(His friend):	Greetings. I have an old motorcycle (i.e., had motor breakdown).
	I am arriving from Libya, I have not been doing anything since my return except the work of guns (i.e., armed activities ambiguously alluded to)
Animateur:	Wait, I am going to speak to you about Libya, where one had all types of

	work, for example, gardening instead of staying in Niger, mainly the same work is here in Niger.
Wife of unemployed character:	What happens in the fada? (alluding to a friendship group)
Animateur (Commentator):	You must listen. The *fada* members are discussing organizing gardens here, of onions, potatoes, in order to make a living (obtain food, nourish selves). (i.e., the man was told to stop complaining, and organize a *fada* with networking toward gainful employment, thereby expressing the performers' resistance to official denigration of all *fadas* as law-breaking gangs).
	What do you think of this initiative?
Participant:	I want to speak to my father so he sells this sheep.
	(Women arrive)
Animateur:	And you, the women (here)? What do you want to do?
(Woman character):	I stopped school in order to go to Libya, now I want to return to school.
Animateur:	Good, I encourage you (to do this)
Gardener:	(displaying his garden products): Good, that is the proof that one can cultivate (here in Niger)

Notable at this celebration are specialists called (Fr.) *animateurs* (denoting approximately "emcees", "masters of ceremonies" or "hosts"), a new profession. Animateurs apprentice, but do not inherit this occupation (in contrast to smith/artisans and griots), and come from varied social backgrounds. But few persons of aristocratic background are *animateurs* since, like smiths and griots, animateurs are widely considered lacking in reserve/respect; they may pronounce what persons of noble descent cannot from the latters' ideal reserve/respect/shame (Rasmussen, 2013). Talented animateurs who display wit in addition to clarity launch successful public careers, making announcements, giving instructions, and explaining official policies (e.g., democratization) during public festivals. Griots and smiths are still important in longstanding verbal arts, but differ in that griots should praise and flatter, and smiths in some Tuareg groups sing ribald songs that tend to mock as well as praise noble patrons.

The mixed messages in the short play/sketch above simultaneously clear up "official" misunderstandings about youths' *fadas*, but also, echoing more official messages, discourage youths from labor migration to Libya, in chaos with political violence and uncertain fortunes. The play underlines that the fada is a positive social group, in opposition to some national newspapers that negatively stereotype them all as "gangs" committing illegal activities, such as selling pilfered gasoline by the side of roads, hiring to settle a grudge, etc. But many are predominantly groups where social esteem is offered to unemployed, marginal youths and information about jobs are circulated (Masquelier, 2019). Those in Agadez gathered at neighborhood homes to chat, smoke, listen to music, and offer mutual support and respect. In Agadez, older persons tend to gather at smiths' forges, whereas younger persons tend to gather socially to chat, listen to music, and discuss job opportunities in *fadas*. In many *fada* conversations, not surprisingly, Libya remains on the minds of many. According to some migrants, during his regime, Ghadaffi welcomed Nigeriens, in particular Tuareg, and provided some migrants with higher salaries, free or low-cost housing, clothing, health care, and job-training. For example, one man was trained as an electrician in Libya and remained there working for fourteen years, but on his return, could not find employment in Agadez, even at the electrical company. Other migrants, by contrast, reported exploitation by dishonest employers in the Libyan countryside, for example, denial of payment and occasionally, even murders of workers after they completed gardening or herding.

The play's animateur/commentator and characters, like officials' speeches, tried to dismantle the more "romantic" perceptions of opportunities in Libya and promote individual agency in neoliberal capitalist terms. On the other hand, the plays also re-defined controversial *fadas*. Despite real challenges in Niger's shrinking civil service and limited private sector jobs since the IMF and World Bank restructuring, as well as ecological crises (climate change, droughts, floods, and locust invasions) and regional violence threatening more traditional occupations, the play exhorted youths to look for work in Niger, not in Libya, and to not complain, but instead, actively do something: for example, return to school, sell remaining livestock, or organize in trading garden products, not resort to armed rebellion or "banditry." Yet even longstanding subsistence practices innovatively organized into co-operatives face challenges from the violence in the Sahara and Sahel: for example, Boko Haram attacks have interrupted a gardening coop's onion trade between Niger's Aïr gardens and Burkina Faso's markets.

In another performance at this USAID-sponsored job festival, the guitarist Bibi and his band performed the following song, entitled "Being Together in this Era":

> Together in this era, one creates respect that is what I say to you, my brothers.
> I beg you, one must be united that is the advantage.
> I would (also) like you to be careful in this era, to love your relatives and friends.
> I want everyone now to know each other (in solidarity), one must not be like the shade of a doum palm, that (he) who is under that tree does not benefit from its shade.
> The person who benefits is the one who is far from that tree (i.e., one must not sit and wait, or do nothing, despite comfort of a shady tree in the heat; instead, one must leave this deceptive comfort and seek to control one's future).
> In this era, one only wants your goodness (i.e., women who do not have money only want a man with property and gainful employment).
> You must think, use your head, help the one who helps you (i.e., mutual aid).
> Whatever the (kind of) assistance.
> What is tiring, is to help one who does not recognize this (assistance).
> Near the closing, the animateur reminded the audience that,
> "The honorable Sultan of Aïr in Agadez, El Ibrahim, passed away. A minute of silence must be observed." Performers, speakers, and audience fell respectfully silent.

Then, at the event's closing, another group of musicians, called Tesko, performed a song entitled, "The Heritage Increases Thanks to God":

> Everyone who abandons their heritage is bad.
> Currently parents much scold their children who forget their heritage.
> I tell you, please, you must protect it.
> If one abandons traditions that is a pity.
> I greet the Sultan of the Aïr.
> May God bless him and pardon those who abandon their traditions.

> Today, he who has heritage will bring armchairs for important chiefs.
> A marriage of love is better than one that one finds on the road (i.e., on travel beyond Niger).
> One cannot teach someone who has already learned.
> It is better to let him reflect.
> The Europeans they are here.
> The sons of Azawad (Tuareg) are here.
> The people of the (aid) projects are here.
> We thank God who allowed us to assemble here, in the historic Air town.
> The region important to tourism.
> Everyone has only to be responsible.
> Today, we are enthusiastic (hopeful), there is no more rebellion.

Neoliberal goals of individual agency and salaried work, rather than relying on the informal economy or civil/state service jobs, dominated the discourse of animateurs and performers, albeit with some sly insertions of critical social commentary and assertions of local cultural mores emphasizing reciprocity and community. Officials' speeches were more congratulatory than didactic, but echoed the overt goals of the program.

This event, well-intentioned though also having a "hidden agenda" of US foreign relations' goal of stemming the influence of militant fighters and staging relations with Libya, offered hope. But even some performers expressed skepticism: for example, another play cautioned that unless one can feed one's family, banditry would not disappear. Indeed, the long-term effects and sustainability beyond the performance have been uncertain. Young women who wish to continue school must still resist impoverished parents' efforts to arrange early marriages to wealthier men. In another Saharan town, a young man, trained in air-conditioning repair, ironically found few residents who could afford air-conditioners and thus a low demand for his services. As of this writing, the Sahara and Sahel have suffered continuing violence from militants and other unknown attackers, and most recently, from the 2020 COVID-19 pandemic. Yet during that day's celebration, praises and advice offered hope for the future.

Along the stadium walls were booths proudly displaying samples of students' skilled work: for example, fabrics for tailoring and tools for welding, Spectators enthusiastically viewed each display. There was generous distribution of supply kits for mechanics, carpenters, tailors, and masons to 100 youths who tested adequately in these skills, and announcements of ten loans and scholarships for youths mostly from Niamey, rather than Agadez—a point critiqued by some participants later.

Despite real admiration for these achievements, some audience members' responses after the USAID event revealed a stark contrast between the official spectacle's hegemonic official power and entertaining distraction and the unofficial local critical commentaries: for example, one person remarked that the town hall "allows some unqualified (persons) in ahead of others on a list of those qualified to receive resources." A retired person commented "We'll wait and see the results—what will this produce, and whom will this benefit?" Someone complained of neglect of rural residents. Persisting problems identified by participants in the USAID program were banditry, drug addiction and trafficking, youths' leaving elders and traditions, and lack of communication between different regions.

Conclusions and Implications

Performance and Power

The performing arts offer a powerful platform for thinking about issues of collective mobilization, power, and critiques of power (Bourgault, 2003; Handelman, 1990; Schechner, 1985; Turner, 1982). The celebrations analyzed here provide illuminating cases for debates regarding the position and potential of performance as both "diplomatic", that is, mobilizing people, but also creatively challenging official power.

In and around these events, heterology (Foucault, 2000), both discourse about the Other and discourse by the Other, became a "way of evaluating in a given space what is perceived to be lacking in another" (Diagne, 2015, 7). Heterology allows an intermediary space, a reversible stage of sorts, where the final word does not necessarily lie with the primary subject of discourse and the speaker is open to critique. A space of experimentation, heterology enables ironic commentaries and practices sometimes occurring outside, nearby or shortly following events, and structural contradictions to events' messages. One event, at the Sultan's palace, was more of a sacred/religious ceremony (though with traditional and civic practices and leaders); while the other, the graduation under the auspices of USAID, a "development" agency, was more secular entertainment on the surface, but also didactic. The USAID event brokered power and performed "diplomacy" through performances staging an understanding of the historically tense relationship and rancor between the United States and Libya to an audience with traditionally strong ties, and until recently, regular travel and migrant labor to Libya, with USAID superimposing a new "message" discouraging migration there. Also conveyed, more subtly and perhaps unconsciously, especially in American officials' speeches, was a "sacred" Protestant work ethic, albeit re-framed as "secular" neoliberal individualist free-market employment. At the Sultan's event, the exchange/dialogue highlighted a spiritual plane, but also included respectful homage from neighborhood chiefs to the Sultan as political mediator, and more recently, also tax-collector for the central state. Its entertainment highlighted the Sultan's generous giving of *al baraka* and sweets to the children. Thus, the USAID event was overtly on a more "secular" neoliberal plane, and the Sultan's event, more overtly on a "sacred" plane, but in each event, were hints of just the opposite, with third-parties also interjecting critiques from the sidelines, thereby suggesting the complexities, contradictions, and paradoxes of artificially separating sacred and secular powers. Powers here were multiplex and creative, in re-inventions of "diplomacy," locally defined as more inclusive mediation. Although the events' performances did relay state and civic agendas, they provided voices for groups marginalized by structures of authority and wealth. Rooted in local cosmologies that official ideologies have not erased, therefore, entertainment events can become instruments of critical commentary by performers, audiences, bystanders, and non-participants.

REFERENCES

Akinola, A., & Ogunnubi, O. (2020). Soft power or wasteful entertainment? Interrogating the Prospect of Big Brother Naija. *The round Table*. https://doi.org/1080/00358533.2020.1717088

Bernus, E. (1993) [1981]. *Touaregs Nigeriens: Unite d'un people Pasteur*. l'ORSTOM.

Bouman, A. (2003). *Benefits of belonging*. Optima.

Bourdieu, P. (1977). *Outline of a theory of practice*. Cambridge University Press.

Bourgault, L. (2003). *Playing for life*. Carolina Academic Press.

Claudot-Hawad, H. (1993). *Touaregs: Portraits en fragments*. Edisud.

Comaroff, J., & Comaroff, J. (1993). *Modernity and its malcontents*. University of Chicago Press.

Diagne, A. (2015). 'A performance in the contemporary art world', *Performance and the diaspora, Africa acts July 5–12*. La Sorbonne.

Foucault, M. (2000). *Essential works of Foucault, 1954–1984*. In J. Faubion (Ed.), R. Hurley, (Trans.). The New Press.

Gramsci, A. (1999) [1971]. *Selections from the prison notebooks of Antonio Gransci*. In Q. Hoare & G.N. Smith (Eds.), ElecBook.

Hamani, D. (1989). *Au Carrefour de Soudan et de la Berberie: Le Sultanat Touareg de l''Ayr*, Niamey. Institut de Recherches en Sciences Humaines Etudes Nigeriennes numero 55.

Handelman, D. (1990). *Models and mirrors*. Berghahn.

Herzfeld, M. (2016). *Siege of the spirits*. University of Chicago Press.

Keenan, J. (1977). *Tuareg: People of ahaggar*. St. Martins Press.

Kohl, I. (2009). *Beautiful modern nomads*. Reimer/Verlag.

Makley, C. (2018). *The battle for fortune*. Cornell University Press.

Masquelier, A. (2019). *Fada: Boredom and belonging in niger*. University of Chicago Press.

Nicolaisen, I., & Nicolaisen, J. (1997). *The pastoral tuareg*. Rhodos.

Rasmussen, S. (1997). *The poetics and politics of tuareg aging*. Northern Illinois University Press.

Rasmussen, S. (2001). *Healing in community*. Bergin & Garvey/Greenwood.

Rasmussen, S. (2006). *Those who touch*. Northern Illinois University Press.

Rasmussen, S. (2013). *Neighbors, strangers, witches, and culture-heroes*. Rowman & Littlefield.

Rasmussen, S. (2018). Intergenerational relationships and emergent notions of reciprocity, dependency, caregiving, and aging in tuareg migration. In A. Hromadzic & M. Palmberger (Eds.), *Care across distance* (pp. 55–75). Berghahn.

Rasmussen, S. (2019). *Persons of Courage and Renown: Tuareg Actors, Acting, Plays, and Cultural Memory in Northern Mali*. Rowman & Littlefield.

Rodd, L., & of Rennell. (1926). *The People of the Veil*. MacMillan.

Rossi, B. (2018). *From Slavery to Aid*. Cambridge University Press.

Schechner, R. (1985). *Between Theater and Anthropology*. University of Pennsylvania Press.

Turner, V. (1982). *From Ritual to Theater*. Performing Arts Journal Publications.

Youngstedt, S., & Keough, S. (2020). *Water, Life, and Profit*. Berghahn.

CHAPTER 13

The National Troupe of Nigeria Post-Ogunde: A Cultural Diplomacy Fad or Farce?

Joseph Kunnuji

INTRODUCTION

Following the Nigerian civil war (1967–1970), the Federal Government, under the military dictatorship of General Yakubu Gowon, began initiating policies aimed, on the one hand, to emphasise unity (in the culturally diverse nation) and, on the other hand, create a national cultural identity. While the National Youth Service Corps (NYSC)[1] scheme was

---

[1] The NYSC scheme was set up to involve Nigerian youth in nation building and familiarise them with other ethnic groups making up the nation. Through this scheme, university graduates, below the age of 30, are subjected to paramilitary training and posted to various states, other than their own, to work for the federal government for 12-calendar months. NYSC is considered an avenue for national reconciliation following the Nigerian civil war.

J. Kunnuji (✉)
Odeion School of Music, University of the Free State,
Bloemfontein, South Africa
e-mail: kunnujijo@ufs.ac.za

© The Author(s), under exclusive license to Springer Nature Singapore Pte Ltd. 2022
T. Afolabi et al. (eds.), *Re-centering Cultural Performance and Orange Economy in Post-colonial Africa*,
https://doi.org/10.1007/978-981-19-0641-1_13

designed to address the former, the National Troupe of Nigeria (hereafter, NTN) was created to meet the latter need. Indeed, such initiatives as the National Troupe of Nigeria are pervasive in postcolonial Africa. Gerhard Kubik (1981, p. 85) documented that many African countries established national dance ensembles on attaining political independence. Examples of such ensembles include the Tanzanian National Dance Troupe and Uganda's Heartbeat of Africa. In such ensembles, Nannyonga-Tamusuza (2012, pp. 207–208) added, 'the creation of a widely encompassing national culture was emphasised, while local and ethnic differences tended to be played down; with time different distinctive ethnic music have been mingled, giving way to hybridised national musics'. Notably, in creating national identities, whether through government-initiated schemes, the mass media, popular bands or individual musicians, regional styles and instruments have often emerged as emblematic of African nations: *mbira* in Zimbabwe and *kora* in The Gambia. In Nigeria, the NTN emerged as an initiative of Dr Hubert Ogunde, who served as its first Artistic Director. While the NTN was still at its nascent stage, Dr. Ogunde died, and the troupe has yet to recover from this irredeemable loss of its pioneer director.

This chapter, drawing on in-depth interviews and secondary sources which record the activities and running of the NTN, first pegs its fundamental problems to the one-man-show model, which is replete in many innovations in Nigeria and further afield within the continent. Given this, the chapter identifies the lack of succession plans as a reason why many innovations wane following their originators' demise. Furthermore, I employ postcolonialism as a framework to argue that the idea of a national cultural troupe is problematic as it reinforces the essentialism replete in the view of Africa as monolithic. Instead, as Nigeria is diverse, the idea of a regionally representative art glosses over many nuanced and vital subtleties, hence a model which focuses on grassroots may be better suited for Nigeria's cultural diplomacy purposes. Therefore, the chapter advocates specificity and the encouragement of grassroots troupes in Nigeria, and while proposing Hunpe Hunga's pedagogical initiative which foreground indigenous systems in contemporary Badagry, Lagos State. Accordingly, the multiplicity and plurality of art forms within Nigeria is potentially a source of attraction to the country. Next is an overview of postcolonialism, which is central to the ensuing discourse.

Theoretical Framework: Postcolonialism

Colonialism became popular in Africa in the late nineteenth century, around the time that philosophers purported the idea of universalism and the equality of humans. One way by which these philosophers defended colonialism was that a period of political dependence and tutelage was necessary for the civilisation of non-Western societies—the civilising mission (Kohn & Reddy, 2017). The pretext of civilising the uncivilised legitimised colonialism both on the minds of the colonial masters and their subjects. However, it aimed to exploit better the colonies for European countries' economic advantage. The control of both the natural resources and trade with the people was within the purview of colonialism.

To be effective, there was the needed to create a status class to mediate between the European colonial masters and the millions they governed. The mediating class 'must be by blood from the governed but by tastes, opinion, words and intellect, English' (Thomas Macaulay, 1835, cited in Mookerjee, 1944). The colonial masters would then achieve the creation of the mediating status class among Africans through Western education. Thus, Western education was designed to advance the superiority of British culture and suppress indigenous knowledge. And its introduction in Africa marked a significant turning point in the history of the peoples, and to this end, echoes of colonial rhetoric are ingrained in current structures in Africa. Put differently, although colonialism is said to have ended in most African countries, its impact continues to be a daily experience. Colonial structures have remained in many cases, while Western tastes have become centralised. Accordingly, indigenous knowledge and arts have emerged peripheral and exoticised in many contexts, being approached as repositories of the past, which have limited use beyond cultural showcases. And this has implications for the global wealth distribution and the perpetuity of European dominance. This chapter's discourse offers an additional explanation of *postcolonialism*, examining how colonialism's legacies and implications affect cultural performance in Nigeria today. In other words, I analyse the functionality of the NTN through the postcolonialism prism throughout this chapter.

Edward Said's (1978) *Orientalism* was the foundation of some of the ideas purported by postcolonialism proponents. Homi Bhabha and Gayatri Spivak have also contributed immensely to postcolonialism (Bhabha, 2004; Spivak, 2010). Their thoughts are summed up in the four primary characteristics proposed by Barry (1995, pp. 193–195) as essential considerations in analysing cultural materials using the lens of postcolonialism:

- An awareness of the representation of the non-European as exotic or immoral 'other' (the centralisation of the West as normal, while the non-West is the 'other').
- An interest in the role of language in supporting or subverting that power dynamic (for education and codification of law. A vital question: 'is the language use in this cultural material supporting or contesting the colonial legacy?'
- An emphasis on identity as double, hybrid or unstable (the mixed identity of the colonised).
- A stress on 'cross-cultural' interaction—who has agency and where is the money flowing?

Although some of the foundational studies that gave rise to postcolonialism focused on Asia, their findings are cross-cutting and broadly applicable in the global south, explaining the world's construction around the imperial forces. Based on this construct, some of the previously-colonised countries' circumstances are beyond their control. For instance, the Western education system has led to the waning of traditional institutions, such as the *hunpameh*—a traditional monastery among West Africa's Ogu people. This traditional monastery ensured the intergenerational transfer of religious and art knowledge and skills among West Africa's Ogu people (I will return to this later).

Accordingly, Basil Davidson (1992) argued that the colonial intrusion prevented African institutions from maturing and reaching their potential. Sequel to Fitzpatrick's (2018) observation that the establishment of colonies helotized the indigenous population, it seems plausible to argue that indigenous systems and structures that ensured the maintenance of the social fabric were undermined by introducing Western ones. The mainstream educational system in postcolonial Africa, for instance, weakened the 'common conscience' (Durheim, 1933 cited in Shizha, 2016) and shared system of belief, upon which traditional African societies thrived. Focusing on Nigeria, Onipede (2010) explains that the human and capital flight, which have continued through neo-colonial canons and the global economic order, undermine the country's development.

Shizha (2016) added that while colonisation conquered the body, mind and land, its aftermaths include the battle to build workable structures in African societies. This chapter spotlights one such area of struggle relating to developing a cultural diplomacy tool in Nigeria vis sustaining a national troupe.

The postcolonial discourse has recently attracted a cross-examination from Albrecht et al. (2020). The book polemically challenges the double standard and the West and non-West binary inherent in postcolonial discourses, which, employing anti-West blinkers, ignores the imperial usurping of the sovereignty of African societies by the Ottoman Empire before the colonial era. The impact of the Ottoman Empire, which made second-class African subjects remain visible in Africa today despite several years of colonial influence. By and large, the proponents of Postcolonialism and their critics agree on the plundering of Africa by external forces at different points in history. This chapter thus identifies a silver lining in a localised pedagogical initiative that bears the potential of a pan-African solution to the cultural diplomacy concerns of Nigeria. The suggestions in this chapter aim at decentring the West through the use of cultural performance as a diplomatic tool to strengthen Nigeria's soft power mechanisms, which create an attraction for the country.[2]

Background to the Discourse: Ogunde and the Establishment of the NTN

Dr. Hubert Adedeji Ogunde, a world-class theatre luminary, was the brain behind the establishment of the National Troupe of Nigeria (as Ogunde christened the group) in 1988, and he was also the founding Consultant and Artistic Director. NTN's pioneer membership of 120 cultural ambassadors reflecting Nigeria's federal character emerged through an intense selection process. They were camped and trained in Ogunde's home town, Ososa, Ijebu Ode Ogun State, under his supervision and at his facility. The coaches and mentors in charge of dancing, singing,

---

[2] My use of the concept of Cultural diplomacy captures a state's exploitation of its cultural products including the performing arts (music, dance, drama), packaged and presented to foreign publics to advance a country economic and foreign policy goals while creating an attraction for itself (Mark, 2010).

acrobatic display and drumming were members of the Ososa Experiment.[3] In essence, the NTN set out on its pioneer's private administrative and artistic structures. Besides, the national troupe was nurtured within Ogunde's facility and benefited primarily from his knowledge, clout and connections. How did Ogunde become central to a national project?

Ogunde (1916–1990) emerged the go-to person in theatre in Nigeria having pioneered 'Nigerian folk opera', and founded the first professional theatrical company in Nigeria, Ogunde Concert Party, in 1945 (Encyclopaedia Britannica, 2020).[4] His early plays were satirical in opposing colonialism. Post-independence, Ogunde continued to offer political commentary through his music and Yoruba dance drama as he deplored interparty strife and corruption. His coverage was countrywide, and in the 1970s he began to export his productions to the other West African countries. His works had a significant impact on politics, and for this, he was arrested a few times and banned both by the colonial and later the independent governments (Oliver Coates, 2017). Nonetheless, Ogunde's theatrical depth stood him out, and he would become an art connoisseur whom the Nigerian government consulted for matters relating to cultural diplomacy in the 1980s.

Through a training programme that lasted only a few months, the NTN was groomed and nurtured to excellence under the tutelage of Ogunde. He aimed to reveal this troupe to the world through a Hollywood movie, *Mr Johnson*, for which he was a co-producer and for which he contracted the troupe members. The set was in Toro, between Jos and Bauchi in central northern Nigeria. Until this stage, the NTN was a fad read in terms of the promises and hopes it bore as a performance hub and

---

[3] The Ososa Experiment was Ogunde's project of 46 performers with whom he toured locally and internationally. Ogunde had established the Ososa Experiment in 1986 to convince the Federal Government of Nigeria that a performing group, drawing members from all the States of the federation, could be created, which would represent Nigeria whenever the need arose. Ogunde's experiment proved successful with its outstanding performance at the 1986 Commonwealth Festival in Edinburg, Scotland.

[4] In fact, the origin of Nollywood can be traced back to the 1960s when the very first set of films were produced by local filmmakers such as Hubert Ogunde, Ola Balogun, Adeyemi Afolayan, Jab Adu and Moses Olaiya among others. Today, these filmmakers are considered the fathers of the Nigerian film industry as they represented the first wave of local film producers. They began with stage performances and gradually migrated to celluloid film production. In particular, Hubert Ogunde stands out as the father of Nigerian theatre thanks to his contribution to the birth of the Nigerian film industry (Endong, 2017).

a means for the members to attain their career goals and become globally renowned. For Ogunde, it was a dream come true. Unlike the preceding governments, which were averse to his productions, the administration at the time was favourably disposed to his expertise, resulting in the traction of his cultural diplomacy ideas. And for the Nigerian government, it seemed the country's cultural diplomacy goals were being realised. Exchanges were in view, and it appeared the diplomacy plans were about to take off. If all turned out as planned, the NTN could well have become resourceful in branding the country and attracting tourists from far and wide. However, this period of hope would not last for long.

While still on the location to produce *Mr Johnson*, Ogunde developed a heart problem, which would lead to his death. It was an unfortunate event, particularly for the national troupe members as it created a significant detour in their career path. The dream of becoming Hollywood movie stars, touring the world and participating in major Arts festivals worldwide became beclouded by a prolonged period of uncertainty. They initially returned to their base in Ososa and Mr Philip Igete, Ogunde's assistant, was appointed as the Artistic Director of the NTN.[5] The appointment of Igete was not a difficult call for the Federal Government as he had worked closely with Ogunde for several years. However, the demise of Ogunde left a significant lacuna that had not been effectively filled as of 2008 (see Oladejo-Anikulapo, 2008) and, until the time of writing this chapter in 2021, remains a central concern. The death of Ogunde leading to a setback in the NTN, and by extension, Nigeria's cultural diplomacy strategy hinged on the NTN, signals the weakness of a model with an overreliance on an iconic individual. Using the case of the NTN, next, I argue that the structure of the NTN is a colonial vestige, which replaced traditional systems but dwindled, thus creating a gap in the intergenerational transfer of indigenous knowledge and skills.

---

[5] The base of the national troupe would then have to be reconsidered. This had happened impromptu, and neither the government nor Ogunde's family was prepared for the sudden change required at this stage. After several consultations and meetings between the representatives of the Federal Government and Ogunde's family, who had become endeared to the national troupe, the National Arts Theatre in Orile Iganmu, Lagos State, became the base of the national troupe, where training and rehearsals continued.

Ẹyẹ ò d`ẹ ké bí ẹyẹ mọ́: Post-Ogunde NTN, its National Unity Goal and Effectiveness as a National Cultural Performance Hub

Ẹyẹ ò d`ẹ ké bí ẹyẹ mọ́, a Yoruba expression which means that the bird is no longer 'singing'/sounding as it should, is deployed in situations of individual and structural waning in which things have changed for the worse. While employing the sensibilities of this expression, this section argues that a lack of a succession plan has undermined the effectiveness of the NTN as a cultural diplomacy tool in Nigeria.

Following Ogunde's demise, the NTN would experience a few issues bothering on the way forward. These include the residence of the troupe; an artistic path for the group, which was dependent on Ogunde's expertise; the administration of the troupe, which had benefitted from Ogunde's clout and the structure of Ososa Experiment; and its staffing methods, considering that selection of personnel must take the federal character into account. Hence, the troupe's administration became replete with nepotism and pan-regional prejudice, which undermined its effectiveness as a national performance hub (interview with Hunpe Hunga on November 9, 2017, Ajara Badagry). Moreover, the casualisation of non-administrative work in the NTN also complicated its efficacy. As performers were contracted for a production per time, some of them committed to the NTN half-heartedly and unenthusiastically, since there was no job security. This, coupled with Nigeria's economic and political instability, made NTN overseas tours seem like opportunities to seek refuge in other countries to some of the troupe members.

At this stage, the NTN was becoming a farce, considering the dwindling dreams of its initial members who had thought it a means of achieving their potential as cultural ambassadors of Nigeria. It is worth noting that this period in the 1990s coincides with a national economic downturn in Nigeria caused by the introduction of the Structural Adjustment Programme (Adeoye, 1991) and political instability following the annulment of the presumed free and fair election of June 1993 (Adedeji, 2012; Tokunbo, 2019).

However, apart from the economic and political climate which complicated the context within which the NTN operated, it is instructive that Ogunde's administration was well-received among the members of the NTN. While Ogunde was exceptional, his successors did not come close to his artistic and administrative expertise, and this could be traced to the lack of a well thought out succession plan, which is a common setback in many contemporary African contexts. Going by Turino's (2008) argument that *nurture* (rather than *nature* and dispositions) is more critical in the intergenerational transfer of skills, it may be argued that the gap (such as the demise of Ogunde created) is more a result of a lack of an efficient system of skill transfer than the paucity of talents in the younger generation. In many traditional African societies, the extended family structure ensured the intergenerational transfer of knowledge and skills, perpetuating family trades and professions (Durojaye, 2019; Kunnuji, 2020, Chapter 2). All the adults within the extended family inadvertently took responsibility for teaching and mentoring each child. Over several decades, individuals gather considerable skills and knowledge that sufficiently prepare them to take over the family trade or profession. The Yoruba Ayan drumming families and the Mande griot families are famous examples of the perpetuity of professions through the family unit in pre-colonial African societies (Panzacchi, 1994).

Since the colonial era gave rise to the current modernist-capitalist system, the extended family form has consistently given way to the much smaller nuclear family set up. Besides, with children spending ample time within formal Western educational institutions, only to return to their parents or nannies with homework daily, the family's educational function has reduced significantly. And while Western music education, for instance, was central in the colonial system, it should be noted that the postcolonial administrations of Nigeria failed to prioritise the arts (Emielu, 2011). In essence, traditional intergenerational transfer methods were replaced by Western education, and postcolonial Western education neglected the arts, thus creating a generational gap in arts in Nigeria. Perhaps this explains the sparseness of art luminaries raised within the Nigerian educational system in the generation following that of Hubert Ogunde, Fela Kuti and Steve Rhodes.[6] The number of musicians from

---

[6] During the colonial era, missionaries ran the schools, taught Western music, and piano playing, for instance, was commonplace; conversely, music education dwindled in postcolonial Nigeria due to the ambivalence associated with its religious affiliations (Emielu, 2011; Lindfors, 1976; Veal, 2000). Also, the demonisation of the popular music scene among middle-class elites, perhaps because it was nested within night life and in the red-light zones, contributed to its ambivalence in postcolonial Nigeria (Dosunmu, 2010). Whereas, I reckon that the colonial musical background was an essential foundation for Ogunde and other maverick artists, many of whom would later travel overseas to further

neighbouring countries (particularly Ghana and Cameroun) who dominated the music scene in Lagos between the 1980s and 2000 gives some credence to this reasoning. Many bands in Lagos, including Fela Kuti's Egypt 80, Christy Essien and Onyeka Onwenu's bands, prominently featured non-Nigerian members (pers. comm. Muyiwa Kunnuji, an erstwhile member of Fela Kuti's 80 and Christi Essien's band, December 31, 2020).[7]

Regarding the intergeneration transfer of knowledge in postcolonial Africa, Isaacs and Friedrich (2011), in an exploratory study examined family businesses where founders were from disadvantaged communities in South Africa and came up with a few reasons why succession has remained a challenge. First, they observed that 33% of African businesses make it to the 2nd generation and only 16%, to the 3rd generation. It is to be noted that a business's survival beyond the 1st generation does not mean that it lives up to the initiator's vision, not to talk of surpassing it. Isaacs and Friedrich (2011) identified destructive conflicts over leadership, which stem from the business initiators' inadequate succession plan as fundamental in destroying family businesses. Where there have not been conflicts, the successors have failed to document a clear path for the business' development.

---

deepen their artistic knowledge, thus making them sufficiently equipped for the postcolonial and cosmopolitan art scenes in Nigeria. Hence, Fela Kuti's skills and expertise, for instance, also remain unmatched among both his biological and musical protegees in Nigeria (Dosunmu, 2010). While Fela Kuti's Egypt 80 band has continued under the leadership of Seun Kuti, it has not been the same as when the band performed weekly and was resident at the African Shrine under Fela Kuti.

[7] The foreigners who were prominent on the Lagos music scene from the 1990s to early 2000s include electric bass player, King Falna; tenor saxophonist, Papa Tino Batagisha (he played in Ras Kimono's band and Ayetoro band. He also recorded the horn lines on Angelique Kidjo's first album); guitarists Oscar Ellimbi (the bandleader of Onyeka Onwenu's band); trumpeter, Mark Makela Makengele (the bandleader of Sonny Okosun's band); Papa Leo (from Togo, was a guitarist and bandleader in Oliver De Coque's band); bass player from DRC, Lumingu Puati (played the bass on the famous Prince Nico Mbarga, Sweet Mother. He played with the legendary DRC musician Tabu Ley Rochereau).; bass player, Bazi Barab (he played in Edna Ogoli's band); Camerounian keyboardist and producer, Telest Nkono; Guinean trombonist, Papa Boligo; Ghanaian trombonist, Raheem Lagos; guitarist from the Republic of Benin, Jeremiah Sossou; Joe Annan, keyboardist from Ghana who played in Sonny Okosun's band; and guitarist, Paul Tao (prominent in Ebenezer Obey's band) (pers. comm. Muyiwa Kunnuji, January 7, 2021; pers. comm. Michael Adefolaju, 21 March, 2021).

Although their study was on family businesses, its findings and conclusions apply to the numerous projects that end with their visioner's demise in various parts of Africa. The ambivalence about an art profession in yesteryears Nigeria also complicates the availability of hands to take over from the iconic individual who emerged through the colonial systems. Perhaps this explains why Ogunde's company was mainly run by his family members, with his wives playing important acting roles and his children drumming or handling the ticketing (Lindfors, 1976). With this model, a national troupe would then have to have a well-structured plan of succession. It is worth noting that where a few visioners, such as Steve Rhodes, have handed over their art projects to their chosen successors, these successors have not been sufficiently prepared for such takeover, both by the Nigerian educational system and the visioners themselves.[8]

The NTN after Ogunde's demise was destined to struggle given lack of individuals with the art expertise, knowledge and skills at the level of Ogunde. And this sparseness of theatre experts may be traced to the inadequacies of the Nigerian educational system, coupled with Ogunde's failure to mentor his successors to step into his 'shoes'. Today, the NTN merely features as a spectacle at national events such as the democracy day celebration on 12 June, 2019, rather than being a hub of regular cultural performances and international exchanges thereby serving as a key cultural diplomacy tool.

As postcolonialism suggests, it is not that Africans are failures without ideas of what to do. Instead, colonialism destroyed specific structures, such as the extended family structure, without adequately replacing them.

---

[8] Having studied overseas and performed in notable big bands and orchestras, including Fela Sowande's orchestra, Steve Rhodes returned to Lagos and established the Steve Rhodes Orchestra (SRO). One of the critical attractions of SRO performances was Rhodes' arrangements of popular songs for the (jazz) big band, creating a conduit through which audiences may enjoy both art and popular musics. The songs of Yinka Davies, Paul Play Dairo, Sunny Nenji, Lagbaja and Peter King, among others, were among SRO's repertory. During a 2005 SRO concert dubbed Metamorphosis, which I witnessed, in a brief ceremony, Steve Rhodes bequeathed his musical dream to Ben Ogbeiwi, Ayo Bankole Jr. and Gloria Rhodes. Despite this rare and impressive gesture aimed at the band's perpetuity, SRO would not survive beyond a few years after Steve Rhodes' demise. Again, suffice it to say that none of the people listed above as Rhodes' successors possessed the jazz arrangement skills of Steve Rhodes, which was the band's essence. Invariably, without an arranger who matched Rhodes' skills set, the waning of the band was inevitable. Perhaps a few years of tutelage and mentorship in jazz arrangement by Steve Rhodes, preceding the band's hand over, would have better equipped the successors.

Apart from the family, another structure, which was an agency to the intergenerational transfer of skills among West Africa's Ogu people, but which has changed irredeemably today is the *hunpameh*, a traditional monastery with a holistic paradigm for training *vothun* (Ogu religion) priests. Hunpe Hunga was raised in *hunpameh*, and he would later become the master drummer of the NTN. Following his exit from the NTN in 2012, Hunga established an institution to transfer art skills to the younger generation using traditional pedagogical methods. The next section examines Hunga's initiative and argues that its model is potentially helpful to both recentre cultural performance and perpetuate them in contemporary African societies.

HUNPE HUNGA MODEL

As demonstrated in numerous works and across various disciplines of the humanities, pre-colonial African societies were not homogeneous, and this is evinced in their varied and nuanced systems of transferring knowledge. Traditional Ogu societies had total institutions within which indigenous and esoteric aspects of *vothun* practice were transferred through several years of tutelage. The imposed Western system of education, among other things, would then undermine the indigenous ones. The aftermath of this intrusion is that African societies, unified with a state structure, have struggled to learn the ropes and master new systems following the disruption in Africa's development paths (Gumbo, 2016; Edward Shizha, 2016). As postcolonialism has paid due attention to this, this section advances the discussion by spotlighting the innovation of Hunpe Hunga, who creatively designed a pedagogical method drawing from indigenous Ogu institutions while remaining adaptable to the contemporary familial and educational structures.

Born Sunday[9] Oluwagbenga Hunga on the 2nd of June in 1970 in Ajara Agamathen Badagry, Hunpe Hunga began his drumming, dancing and acrobats training when he was five, at the *hunpameh* in Posikoh Quarters, Ajara Badagry Lagos State Nigeria. The word '*hunpameh*' is

---

[9] It is a common practice to name boys born on certain days of the week after those days, like Sunday, Monday and Friday. Certain days of the week are deemed more potentially profitable than other days in Ogu and Yorùbá cosmologies hence children are not named after Tuesday, Wednesday and Thursday.

a derivative of three Ogu words—*ohun* (secrete or esoteric), *pa* (an enclosure or compound) and *meh* (inside). Hence its literal meaning is 'inside the esoteric compound'. In *hunpameh*, selected devotees are taught the liturgy of *vothun* worship including religious songs, dances, drumming patterns and socioeconomic skills such as wood carving, weaving and indigenous textile designs.

In 1988, when the Federal Government of Nigeria made a call for performers nationwide, in a bid to establish a national troupe, Hunpe Hunga auditioned in Lagos State, and through an arduous process with numerous stages, he was selected among the 120 members drawn from across the country.[10] Hunga would later rise through the ranks to become the master drummer of the NTN, a post he held for 18 years from (1994–2012). However, the events leading to his exit indicate flaws in the administration of the national troupe. As mentioned earlier, ranging from corruption, nepotism, pan-regional loyalty, to job casualisation, the NTN's numerous challenges index Nigeria's major issues. Among these issues, the marginalisation of ethnic minorities, which stems from the country's multi-ethnic nature, is suitable for our discussion on the need for a reappraisal of NTN's model.

As Senayon (2018) argues, the governmental canonisation of three major ethnic groups in Nigeria excludes and marginalises the minority ones. Accordingly, each performance of the NTN centralises the practices of a few ethnic groups, while glossing the nuances and subtleties of numerous traditions. Discussing the importance of versatility of an NTN master drummer, Hunga mentioned the requirement of studying different drumming traditions in Nigeria. This begs the question of which drumming tradition is included and which is excluded. By and large, the notion of national cultural identity is problematic as it excludes minority groups. And although Arts Councils exist in all 36 states in Nigeria, these do not cater for the integration of the younger generation, neither do they engender grassroots accessibility of cultural performance. Conversely, creating cultural troupes at the grassroots across the country potentially addresses the exclusion of ethnic minorities. Hunpe Hunga's initiative in Badagry Lagos State serves as a model of the grassroots approach.

---

[10] In a Federal system of government such as Nigeria, selection of national functionaries involves a delicate balance between the skill(s) requirements and a quota system; skills are the first considerations but where there are performers with similar levels of proficiency, the quota system comes to the fore in determining who is selected.

Gbenopo Theatre Company: Hunpe Hunga's Tradition-Inspired Initiative

In 2012, Hunpe Hunga commenced a project, the Gbenopo Theatre Company,[11] following his exit from the NTN. He aimed to decentralise cultural performance and ensure the intergenerational transfer of Ogu art skills with this project. The Gbenopo Theatre Company's instructional style would draw primarily on *hunpameh* methods. In his words:

> I established my group after I left the national troupe in 2012, known as Gbenopo Theatre Company. It is well known in Badagry, in Lagos and beyond. It is divided into an adult group and a children's group. The performing group for the kids is known as Gbenopo Theatre Company Children's Creative Station. I created the children's arm to ensure the continuity of this legacy; one must build kids—they are the future of every society. There is also a succession pattern in which the children's creative station feeds the adult group. Some older ones have left to start their own groups or even quit music, and the kids have always replaced such adults. (interview with Hunpe Hunga on 9 November, 2017, Ajara Badagry. The interview was conducted in Yorùbá and translated by author)

In summary, Hunga's art project draws on indigenous knowledge and pedagogical systems while employing formal administrative structures to make cultural performance more accessible at the grassroots and better integrate the younger generations. Next, I examine the traditional pedagogical system central in this localised model.

---

[11] As of 2017, Gbenopo Theatre Company had grown in leaps and bounds, featuring both on the local scene and beyond, and at various festivals including the African Drum Festival in Ogun State, Badagry Festival and Diaspora Badagry Festival. Hunga rides on his connections and experience to expose the troupe, portraying the Ogu musical practices to the rest of Nigeria. The troupe is versatile as it blends drumming and dance with drama and songs, and any of these could be presented exclusively if required—it encompasses all aspects of the performing arts. Hunga is the artistic director of the company, which is currently planning the production of its first drama video recording. He is able to administer the company, having worked with some of the best artistic directors in Nigeria, most of whom are playwrights. He has thus gained enough experience and written drama scripts, which include: *My Badagry; My Nigeria*; *Two Sides of A Coin;* and *Visa Lottery: Modern Slavery*. Hunpe Hunga narrated that this story 'is based on my experience having seen several African immigrants in the US. Visa lottery entices Africans to bring their family to the US, it is to enslave them over there, hence, my title Visa Lottery; Modern Slavery, so that Nigerians will learn from it'.

At a performance of the Gbenopo Theatre Company Children's Creative Station for a TV recording, which I witnessed, I watched as Hunpe Hunga instructed the children on the different patterns through his use of sentences like '*baba se towe*' (literally, it is my father's or it belongs to my father) and '*gboje n gboje n te*' (literally, I am at ease).[12] With the utterance of these lines, the children all knew what to play. I was intrigued by this and set about finding out the method employed in his teaching.

The Hunpe Hunga pedagogical principles leverage traditional strategies that he learned from the *hunpameh* (*vothun* monastery) within the contemporary context of the hegemony of mainstream Western education. The children attend school in the mornings and return to Hunga's school in the evening, where observation and imitation are syncretised with verbal instructions and written documentation. However, the writing mainly serves as a form of documentation rather than a notation for performances.

Hunga opined that using aural methods, the ears are trained so that as they listen, the children can play back what they hear. His teaching methods also include the vocalisation of drums patterns either using sentences or non-lexical syllables, which are memorised and played on the drums. An example of a popular statement used in teaching is:

Baba she ton we	belongs to my father (it's my property)
Baba she ton we	It belongs to my father
D'ejiro mi na hen tho	I will handle it as it pleases me
e so kpe mi na gbo je	If it's too heavy for me, I will put it down (and if like, I will leave it)
Baba she ton we [interpreted by Kushokeho Jawu]	It belongs to my father

Common sets of non-lexical syllables used in memorising and teaching patterns are:

jan-jan jan-jan jan-jan kle-gi,
jan-jan jan-jan kle-gi kle-gi

---

[12] These expressions are time-honoured Ogu adages that have become assimilated into the drumming language (see also Locke & Agbeli, 1980), with lead drummers often improvising with their tonal inflexions.

The following is a common pattern, captured in non-lexical syllables, used to signal a transition in *akoto* dance:

gite-glem gite-glem
jin-jin ta to to glem

As the Gbenopo Children's Creative Station model demonstrates, there are troves of indigenous knowledge that could be harnessed to advance the development of cultural performance in Nigeria in a way that lessens the marginality of ethnic minorities. Hunga's model is reminiscent of the community-based approach of many Western societies, in which orchestras, soccer teams and other sports and art outlets exist at the grassroots. The national performance group may draw on these grassroots performance groups, similar to how national soccer teams are selected. With this model, those who do not get selected into the national troupe would retain their slots at the grassroots, and this would partly solve the seasonal employment of the NTN members. Besides, the model also engenders healthy competition among the grassroots performing groups within each region, which may lead to developing each community's arts.

Perhaps a focus on the grassroots and the early integration of children is responsible for the well-developed soccer leagues in Europe, which attract investors both locally and internationally. However, the model requires sustained government sponsorship at the initial stage and eventually, these art forms will likely generate sufficient funds through corporate sponsorship. And if sustained, it will address the perpetuity of indigenous knowledge and partly solve some other contemporary concerns such as youth unemployment.

Conclusion

This chapter traced the mechanism of the NTN from its inception, juxtaposed its two eras, one with Ogunde as its Artistic Director and the other post-Ogunde and concluded that NTN's modalities are problematic. With its structure centred around the vision and charisma of an iconic individual, its decline was inevitable. It began as a fad which soon became a farce, particularly for the members. Furthermore, the chapter presented the art studies initiative of an erstwhile master drummer of the NTN, Hunpe Hunga, which localises arts education in Badagry Lagos State, Nigeria, while being structured to ensure the intergenerational transfer of

Ogu art heritage. The adoption of this model promises to benefit Nigeria by creating opportunities for more youths while encouraging multiple cultural hubs at the grassroots and an attraction that promotes Nigeria's cultural diplomacy. The overarching assumption which inspired this chapter's discourse is that Nigeria is willing to be more attractive globally and adopt place branding and soft power alongside its traditional use of hard power. Given this, I advocate the reappraisal, restructuring and a decentralised cultural performance to reveal more nuances, subtleties and uniqueness among the Nigerian peoples. The path to sustainable cultural diplomacy plans in Nigeria begins here.

References

Adedeji, F. (2012). Singing and suffering in Africa: a study of selected relevant texts of Nigerian gospel music. *Matatu, 40*(1), 411–425.

Adeoye, A. (1991). Of economic masquerade and vulgar economy: A critique of the structural adjustment program in Nigeria. *Africa Development, 16*(1), 23–44.

Albrecht, M. et al. (2020). *Postcolonialism cross-examined: Multidirectional perspectives on imperial and colonial pasts and the neocolonial present.* Routledge.

Barry, P. (1995). *Beginning theory.* Manchester University Press.

Bhabha, H. (2004). *The location of Culture.* Routledge.

Coates, O. (2017). Hubert Ogunde's strike and hunger and the 1945 general strike in lagos: Labor and reciprocity in the kingdom of Oba Yejide. *Research in African Literatures, 48*(2), 166–184.

Davidson, B. (1992). *The black man's burden. Africa and the curse of the nation-state.* James Currey.

Dosunmu, O. (2010). *Afrobeat, fela and beyond: Scenes, styles and ideology.* Doctoral dissertation submitted to the Faculty of Arts and Sciences, University of Pittsburgh.

Durojaye, C. (2019). *Evoked emotional responses in the performance practices of selected Yorùbá Dundun Ensembles.* Doctoral thesis submitted to the South African College of Music, University of Cape Town.

Emielu, A. (2011). Some issues in formal music education in Nigeria: A case study of Kwara state. *British Journal of Music Education, 28*(3), 353–370.

Endong, F. P. (2017). Nollywood in Cameroon: Transnationalisation and reception of a dynamic cinematic culture. *Cinej Cinema Journal, 6*(2), 130–143.

Fitzpatrick, M. (2018). Colonialism, postcolonialism, and decolonization. *Central European History, 51*, 83–89.

Gumbo, M. (2016). Pedagogical principles in technology education: An indigenous perspective. In Emeagwali & Shizha (Eds.), *African indigenous knowledge and the sciences: Journeys into the past and present* (pp. 13–32). BRILL

Isaacs, E. B. H., & Friedrich, C. (2011). Family business succession: Founders from disadvantaged communities in South Africa. *Industry and Higher Education*, 25(4), 277–287.

Kohn, M., & Reddy, K. (2017). Colonialism. *The stanford encylopedia of philosophy*. https://plato.stanford.edu/entries/co [January 4, 2021].

Kubik, G. (1981). Neo-traditional popular music in East Africa since 1945. *Popular music 1 (Folk or popular? distinctions, influences, continuities)*, 83–104.

Kunnuji, J. (2020). A chronicle of cultural transformation: Ethnography of Badagry Ogu musical practices. Doctoral thesis submitted to the South African College of Music, University of Cape Town.

Lindfors, B. (1976). Ogunde on Ogunde: Two autobiographical statements. *Educational Theatre Journal*, 28(2), 239–246.

Locke, D., & Agbeli, G. (1980). A study of the drum language in Adzogbo. *African Music*, 6(1), 32–51.

Mark, S. L. (2010). Rethinking cultural diplomacy: The cultural diplomacy of New Zealand, The Canadian federation and Quebec. *Political Science*, 62(1), 62–83.

Mookerjee, S. P. (1944). Education in British India. *The Annals of the American Academy of Political and Social Science*, 233, 30–38.

Nannyonga-Tamusuza, S. (2012). What is 'African music'? Conceptualisations of 'African Music' in Bergen (Norway) and Uppsala (Sweden). In Nannyonga-Tamusuza & Solomon (Eds.), *Ethnomusicology in East Africa: Perspectives from Uganda and beyond* (pp. 188–215). Fountain Publishers.

Oladejo-Anikulapo, J. (2008). Ogunde… This month I am feeling the doyen. http://eyinjuodu.blogspot.com/2008/04/ogunde-this-month-i-am-feeling-doyen.html [January 5, 2021]

Onipede, K. J. (2010). Technology development in Nigeria: The Nigerian machine tools industry experience. *Journal of Economics*, 1(2), 85–90.

Panzacchi, C. (1994). The livelihoods of traditional griots in modern Senegal. *Africa: Journal of the International African Institute*, 64(2), 190–210.

Said, E. (1978). *Orientalism*. Pantheon Books.

Senayon, E. (2018). The language provisions of the national policy on education and the endangerment of Ogu in Southwestern Nigeria. *International Journal of Bilingual Education and Bilingualism*, 2018, 1–13.

Shizha, E. (2016). African indigenous perspectives on technology. In Emeagwali & Shizha (Eds.), *African indigenous knowledge and the sciences: Journeys into the past and present* (pp. 47–62). BRILL

Spivak, G. C. (2010). Can the subaltern speak? In R. Morris (Ed.), *Can the subaltern speak? Reflections on the history of an idea*. Columbia University Press.

The Editors of Encyclopaedia Britannica. (2020). Hubert Ogunde. *Encyclopaedia Britannica*, published March 31, 2020, https://www.britannica.com/biography/Hubert-Ogunde [December 27, 2020].

Tokunbo, B. (2019). 'African factors' in the metamorphosis of indigenous pentecostalism in Ekitiland. *Nigeria. Black Theology, 17*(2), 150–162. https://doi.org/10.1080/14769948.2019.1627095

Turino, T. (2008). *Music as social life: The politics of participation*. The University of Chicago Press.

Veal, M. (2000). *Fela: The life and times of an African musical icon*. Temple University Press.

CHAPTER 14

Afrophobia and Cultural Diplomacy in Nigeria-South Africa Relations: The Role of the Creative Industries

Olusola Ogunnubi, Uchenna A. Aja, and Oladotun E. Awosusi

Introduction

Contemporary engagements in international relations has witnessed a "soft-turn" from the traditional usage of hard power current to the soft power means. The shades of globalization, bolstered by technological

---

O. Ogunnubi
Carleton University, Ottawa, ON, Canada
e-mail: OgunnubiOR@ufs.ac.za

Centre for Gender and African Studies, University of the Free State, Bloemfontein, South Africa

U. A. Aja (✉)
Department of Political Science, University of Ilorin, Ilorin, Nigeria
e-mail: ajauchenna27@gmail.com

© The Author(s), under exclusive license to Springer Nature Singapore Pte Ltd. 2022
T. Afolabi et al. (eds.), *Re-centering Cultural Performance and Orange Economy in Post-colonial Africa*,
https://doi.org/10.1007/978-981-19-0641-1_14

advancement, have also greatly affected state's ability to shape the international system with the traditional "carrot and stick" without concomitant consequences. According to the foremost advocate of soft power, Nye (2004), soft power is the ability to affect/influence others to obtain the desired outcomes through attraction rather than force or inducement. To Nye, a state's soft power is anchored on three core resources namely: cultures, values and policies. Soft power is, thus, conceived as the sum total of the values, cultures, behaviors and institutions of a state that can serve as a tool of attraction, and by extension project its good image to the outside world (Nye, 1990; Ogunnubi, 2019; Tella, 2016). States with "soft resources," in essence, wield attractive, persuasive and influential powers through its strategic/diplomatic employment. As an embodiment of state's cultural heritage and practices, creative industry is a vital soft power component which can be engaged to project its prestigious image as well as promote friendly relations with the outside world.

In perspective, however, Nigeria and South Africa are the two African Powers, which have for decades been caught in the web of intermittent Afrophobic/xenophobic prejudice, occasioning strained diplomatic relations between the two counties. The increasing trend of the deeply rooted mistrust and prejudice are not only questioning the putative hegemonic stance of the two African regional powers, but also impairing the project of African Renaissance, and as such, scorning the Black continent in the global scene (Adeoye, 2017; Awosusi & Fatoyinbo, 2019).

To mitigate this generic Afrophobic continental challenge, and specifically, to invigorate the epileptic relations between Abuja and Pretoria. This chapter argues for a cultural diplomatic engagement in terms of the employment of some organs of the creative industry such as film industry, afro-pop music, national festivals and cultural troupes as soft power resources to enhance people-to-people (P_2P) interactions between the two countries. The authors advance that, by engaging mutually esteemed cultural values, heritage and practices between citizens of both states, the shared distrust that enflames xenophobic prejudice and attacks can be significantly cramped.

O. E. Awosusi
Department of International Relations and Strategic Studies, Legacy University, Banjul, The Gambia

On the Theory and Praxis of Culture and Foreign Policy

Culture as an essential ingredient of people-to-people and inter-state interactions predated the Westphalian international structure. It is as old as the history of earliest human relations, trade contacts, migrations and traditional diplomatic practices (Stelowska, 2015). In the pre-Westphalian era, for instance, culture was a major instrument of traditional diplomacy in form of gift exchanges usually between and among ancient empires and kingdoms such as the Greek City-States. Culture serves as means of fomenting mutual confidence and understanding among the peoples. Essentially, culture has been a source of collaborations, interactions and conflicts between and among peoples, kingdoms, and states (see Huntington, 1996; Ryhan, 2015). Aside from its intrinsic thrust to the existential identity of a state, it poses an irrefutable influence on state's internal and external sovereignty. In the global arena, for example, culture serves as a distinguishing phenomenon between and among actors. It is a unique system of contact between actors in the international system. Culture can be said to be the groundwork of a foreign policy, because the cultural elements make up the cultural framework in which the foreign policy is operationalized.

Conceptually, culture transcends the traditional notion of mere human intellectual achievements (the arts) such as opera, classical music, visual arts, and literature. It embraces, but not limited to attitude, behavior, traditions, customs, norms, ideas, literature, arts and crafts, music, sports, festivals, food, socio-political ideas and orientations. Indices of culture are summarized in the words of Tylor (1871, p. 5) "as that complex whole which includes knowledge, belief, art, morals, law, custom and any other capabilities and habits acquired by man as member of society". According to a Polish culture historian, Czarnowski (2005, p. 34), culture is "the shared heritage, the fruit of the creative and processed effort of countless generations". While attempting to proffer an appropriate framework for holistic understanding of the concept of culture, UNESCO (2001) notes that, "Culture should be regarded as the set of distinctive spiritual, material, intellectual and emotional features of society or a social group, and that it encompasses, in addition to art and literature, lifestyles, ways of living together, value systems, traditions and beliefs". In effect, culture is the sum total of people's way of life, embracing material and non-material elements. It is a defining parameter of every society, kingdom, nation, or state.

On the other hand, here, foreign policy simply refers to the overall behavior/policy of a state toward the external world. In practice, however, foreign policy is more than policy formulation and execution toward the external environment. It encompasses the understanding of the prevailing internal and external environmental components, structure, and ingredients (internal and external) (see Frankel, 1963; Morin & Paquin, 2018). Culture is one of those internal assets within the ambit of state, which unswervingly shapes foreign policy direction.

Further still, as man and culture are interlaced, so are culture and state. The latter pair constitutes an entity having interconnected elements. Culture is the core identity of a state, and as such, the internal actions and inactions, and external disposition of any state can be best defined via the prism of its cultural systems and practices. The understanding of the foreign policy behavior of state actors, in effect, is anchored on the apt grasp of the state's cultural disposition and structure. According to Mahe (2012), the process of designing and operationalizing a state's external policies is amply influenced by its cultural system and practices.

Traditionally, however, the global society is viewed as a set of geographical regions and agglomeration of nation-states. According to Vlahos (1991), this framework, obviously, discounts culture as the main source of human reality. To him, thought systems and behavior are influenced by culture; they are not the product of mere nationalism. Given this "traditional framework," the place of culture has over the decades, gained less attention in International Relations discourse. Theoretical and empirical studies in International Relations have over the years, emphasized power in terms of political institutions, economic resources, military capabilities, geographical spread, and population growth among others, as the defining norm and determining indices of state's external relations. Although "pre-Cold War studies" emphasized the importance of culture as part of the foreign policy of a country, given the power-politics of the ideological war era (1945–1989), however, culture as a concept and theory enjoyed diminutive attention. Instead, cultural discourses were limited to the specific disciplines of Anthropology, Sociology, Social Psychology, or Linguistics (Hudson, 1997, p. 2). In fact, for many years, Cultural Studies and Foreign Policy were studied as parallel disciplines.

From the late 1980s, International Relation treatise took a "constructivist/cultural turn." Through his work, entitled "*Social Theory of*

International Politics," Alexander Wendt popularized *Constructivism* as an explanatory framework in International Relations. To the Constructivists, the foreign policy behavior of a state depends on the collective identity of a society, influenced by recognized social norms, including shared values and expectations. To them, these are anchored on two variables: Firstly, their communality-the quantities of actors of a social system who share those norms, and secondly, their specificity—how a particular norm guides/regulates behavior. In effect, through the prisms of norms and ideas (culture), international arrangement aids actors to redefine their identities in the course of synchronization and cooperation. This is to say that, a state's foreign cultural policy reflect the norms and values of that society and guides its external behavior (Wendt, 1999).

Another theoretical explanation which underpins the interlink between culture and international relations was provided in the popular work of Samuel Huntington, entitled "Clash of Civilizations?" in 1993. Huntington analytically demonstrated how culture, has become a core factor impelling and determining the actions and inactions of the people in the contemporary global society. Specifically, he argued that language and tradition (culture) were the first elements through which civilizations (the highest cultural grouping of people), distinguish from one another. In another publication, Huntington buttressed his argument that "the most essential distinction among humankind is no longer ideological, political or economic, but cultural" (Huntington, 1996, p. 21).

Over the last two decades, the entwining of culture, foreign policy, international relations has gained momentary attention. While espousing soft power, American Political Scientist, Joseph Nye in his work entitled *"Soft Power: The Means to Success in World Politics"* draws attention to the indispensability of culture to state's external relations in the contemporary global system. According to him, the three elements of a country's soft power are its culture, foreign policy values, and policies. Nye (1990) argues that culture wields pivotal influence on foreign relations as an ingredient of soft power. In his words, soft power is the ability to affect others to obtain the outcomes one wants through attraction rather than force or inducement. The external behavior of state, in essence, can be influenced through attraction (using culture) rather than the traditional "hard means."

As earlier noted, culture, as a practice, voyages with human history, civilization, and development. Since the earliest human relations and contact, culture has been engaged to promote friendly relations. Aside the relation/diplomacy among the ancient Greece proto-states, the practice of cultural relations in Africa dated back to the pre-colonial era. The old Oyo Empire, as case in point, was distinguished for its cultural diplomatic practices in terms of exchanges of gifts such as "aroko," kolanut, beads, cowries, clothes, salt, etc., with other surrounding kingdoms to foster peaceful coexistence or to declare war on enemies (see Adegbulu, 2011). During the era of the European-led Christian missionary activities in Africa, Asia, and other parts of the world, cultural tools were massively engaged to woo the locals. The employed strategy to propagate religion, especially in Africa was cultural attraction and influence. It was a subtle "cultural mission" which paved the way for the succeeding colonial ventures. That is to say that, Christian missionaries incited and provided the fundamental and ideological basis for the "tactical" replacement of traditional culture with western culture (Awosusi & Ekpo, forthcoming). As seen globally, European imperialism and colonialism were anchored on cultural engagement. Culture was a major "force" employed by the colonial powers to allay the apprehensions of the colonies while advancing the European imperial/colonial aspirations. Colonialism was, in fact, synonymous with "foreign cultural policy" premised on the replacement of the traditional culture, especially languages of the peoples/colonies with Western culture.

In the modern practice of international relations, state actors, through overt and covert means, have engaged culture as instrument of state policies. This cultural engagement has been theorized and termed cultural diplomacy. Cultural diplomacy, as an art, involves the employment of cultural indices of a state to advance its foreign policy objectives. The home of the modern practice of cultural diplomacy has been attributed to France given its foremost effort in 1923 to establish a distinct cultural office in the French Foreign Affairs Ministry, marking the emergence of formal interface between French culture and Foreign policy (Stelowska, 2015). Meanwhile, in 1883, as a subtle tactic to recoup its dwindling relevance and power in the European politics,[1] France established *Alliance Francaise,* primarily to promote French Language (culture) beyond borders. Following the French cultural engagement in foreign relations, and specifically, the experience of the devastating World Wars, other World Powers subscribed to the idea of exploring culture as an element of

---

[1] Given the 1815 Vienna internationalism, and the consequent defeat of France in the Franco-Prussian war of 1870–1871, its (France) relevance in European politics waned.

foreign relations. For instance, in 1934, Britain established the British Council while Germany instituted the Goethe Institute in 1951, aimed at effectively advancing their culture, particularly languages abroad. Similarly, in 1953, the United States created the Fulbright exchange program to promote its cultural assets (Stelowska, 2015). During the interwar years, the1930s specifically, Germany under Adolf Hitler palpably employed culture as instrument of external relations with Latin America. This, however, provoked swift response from the United States of America to favor efforts aimed at promoting inter-American Cultural Relations in 1936 (Wapmuk, 2020a). The Cold War politics and its aftermath, in fact, saw a momentary engagement of cultural ingredients as a soft power tool to pursue states' foreign policy. Drawing from Asia, China has for years "weaponized" culture in their external relations. Chinese contemporary foreign policy is, pivotally hinged on the employment of cultural tools as soft power to advance its national aspirations. In 2004, for example, China established the Confucius Institutes in over 100 countries of the world with its headquarters in Beijing, to teach and promote Chinese culture, specifically language across the world, and as such, advance the Chinese "goodwill" in the host countries.

Evidently, individual states in the global system have unique cultural system, values and elements, which define their identity, domestic public engagements, and by extension attitude in relations with external environment. According to Iriye (1979), since cultural system and values are defining variables of a state, international relations can be inferred as interactions among cultural systems. That is to say, culture is a state's identity, and as such, there exists a thick line of interaction between a state's culture and foreign policy. This aligns with the position of Ninkovich (1981) that, foreign policy is only an expression of powerful cultural forces beyond its comprehension. As would be seen in the latter part of this chapter, Nigeria and South Africa are heterogeneous countries with diverse and rich cultural ingredients such as languages, foods, festivals, film industry, arts, music (Afro-pop and others), literature, and other creative industries. These cultural experiences have certain cross-cultural relations that are not only reflecting on both countries people-to-people interactions domestically, but also their attitude toward one other and the global community at large. Culture, in effect, functions as a key instrument for alliance and cooperation in the international system.

Nigeria-South Africa Relations in Historical Context

Nigeria and South Africa have a lot in common. Apart from having common historical experiences of imperialism, colonialism, racism, and under-development, both countries are adjudged to have abundant resources and strategic partnership potentials to lead the African continent. In view of their enormous potential and importance to Africa, it was, therefore important for Abuja and Pretoria to enter into strategic partnership. While the history of Nigeria-South Africa relations took roots from 1960s, studies show that it was only after the apartheid regime ended in 1994, that both countries fully consummated their relationship (Ogunnubi & Aja, forthcoming; Zabadi & Onuoha, 2012). Following Nigeria's independence in 1960, the Balewa government adopted Africa as the centerpiece of its foreign policy. This involved an anti-colonialism and anti-apartheid policy. From this period, Nigeria took advantage of its position as the most populous Black Country in the world to champion the drive toward eradicating apartheid in South Africa and was instrumental to the international sanctions imposed on the oppressive apartheid regime. This was exemplified in Nigeria's confrontation with South Africa following the Sharpeville massacre of March 21, 1960. Officially, the incident led to the death of 72 Blacks and left about184 persons wounded (Onuoha, 2008). Nigeria also expressed its commitment to the anti-apartheid struggle by spearheading the expulsion of South Africa from various international organizations such as the Commonwealth and International Labor Organization and prohibited South African aircraft from flying over its airspace and using its airport or seaport facilities.

While successive military and civilian governments both played major roles in the anti-apartheid campaign, it is estimated that Nigeria spent over $60 billion in this exercise (Odoh, 2019). Zabadi and Onuoha (2012) contend that, from the time apartheid ended, three broad phases of Nigeria-South African relations can be constructed. The first episode (1994–1998) was characterized by a period of antagonism. The authors argue that the end of the apartheid did not result in the expected rapport and cooperation between Nigeria and South Africa. Owing to accusations of gross human rights abuses and extrajudicial killings by the Abacha regime, the South African democratic government headed by Nelson Mandela demonstrated a level of hostility. Also, the fact that Nigeria was under military rule further complicated this relationship. This antagonistic relation reached its climax with the uneventful execution of environmentalists, Ken Saro-Wiwa and eight of his fellow Ogoni activists in 1995 (Ogunnubi, 2014). This led to Mandela's call for the eventual expulsion of Nigeria from the Commonwealth. Further, President Mandela also threatened to impose additional sanctions on Nigeria.

However, the emergence of Thabo Mbeki as South Africa's President in 1999 and Nigeria's return to democratic rule in the same year created a fertile environment for mutually rewarding bilateral relations. As Zabadi and Onuoha (2012) noted, this second phase lasting between 1999 and 2008, began with a period of cooperation and slight conflict of ideologies. In line with Mbeki and Obasanjo's common vision on improved continental relations, the two governments signed bilateral agreements on trade and investment in 1999. The agreement sought to protect South African companies and investments in Nigeria from future nationalization and double taxation (Zabadi & Onuoha, 2012). Building on their established relations, both governments consolidated this bilateral relation by establishing a Bi-National Commission (BNC) in October 1999, and Nigeria-South Africa Chambers of Commerce (NSACC) in May 2000. These establishments encouraged the growth of trade and investment between both countries. According to Lawal (2007) the number of South African firms doing business in Nigeria increased from just four in 1999 to over 100 by 2007. Trade relations between both countries also rose from $16.5 million in 1999 to $2.1 billion in 2008.

The third phase (2008 to date), is earmarked as the era of peer competition and regional hegemonic rival. However, during this period, Nigeria and South Africa have cooperated toward ensuring the reconstruction and strengthening of the continent's framework for peace and security. They have worked unanimously toward strengthening the African Union in order to effectively address its myriad of security and governance challenges. This is premised on the fact that, bilateral diplomatic cooperation between Nigeria and South Africa can help shape Africa's future. Also, beyond cooperation in trade and investment, during this period, Nigeria and South Africa have engaged in diplomatic rivalry and peer competition. As a result of the recommendation of the UN High Level panel on Threats, Challenges, and Changes for the reform of the United Nations Security Council (UNSC) to add more representation especially from the developing world, Nigeria and South Africa are engaged in competition for the proposed African slot. The prospect of a permanent seat for Africa unites Nigeria and South Africa as much as it divides them. While Abuja and Pretoria are staunchly united on the importance of Africa having a permanent seat in the proposed reformed UNSC, they are sharply divided over who is best qualified to represent the continent when this comes to fruition (Zabadi & Onuoha, 2012). The hegemonic rivalry further exacerbated with South Africa's invitation to the G8 and membership of G20 and BRICS. Nigeria saw this as a move by South Africa to gain international clout and dominance. Beyond the competition for a seat at UNSC, the diplomatic rivalry also extends to the continental level. During the Arab uprising and revolution for governmental change in Libya, the Nigerian government recognized the National Transitional Council (NTC) as the legitimate government, while the South African government supported Muammar Gaddafi. The government of both countries was also at loggerheads as regards the measures to resolve Cote D'Ivoire's electoral crisis in 2010. South Africa supported French and UN intervention, while Nigeria vehemently opposed the idea. Also, in 2012, South Africa deported 125 Nigerians on allegations bordering on the possession of fake yellow fever vaccination cards. In retaliation, Nigeria deported 84 South Africans. Further, during the February 2020 election for the Secretary-General of the African Continental Free Trade agreement (AfCTA) in 2020 both countries presented candidates. However, South Africa's Wamkele Mene emerged victoriously. The multiple instances of intense competition between both countries is evidently a signature of their bilateral relations, which is often to the detriment of Africa's interest. Within the context of this study, it is also clear that Afrophobia represents a social combative space where hegemonic ambitions find expression.

The Facade and Prejudice of Afrophobia in Nigeria-South Africa Relations

Following the emergence of constitutional democracy in 1994, South Africa became a viable alternative for African nationals seeking greener pastures abroad. Due to its favorable political and social environment and a fairly advanced economy coupled with the availability of world-class infrastructure, South Africa was a preferred destination for asylum seekers and refugees alike. Ebegbulem (2013) observed that following the dawn of democracy in South Africa, Nigerian professionals were among the early migrants. Available data estimated that about 2.2 million foreigners are residing in South Africa (Lee, 2015), and 300,000 of them are Nigerians (Kiewit, 2019). However, these figures may not be exact, as many illegal migrants are without official documentation. In effect, Afrophobic prejudice negatively affects the ideals of African Renaissance, thereby making a mockery of the African continent in the international sphere (Awosusi & Fatoyinbo, 2019).

Regrettably, Afrophobic incidences have emerged as a reoccurring feature of Nigeria-South Africa relations. However, recent events from 2015 have reinforced the fact that South Africans are not entirely comfortable with the influx of African migrants. The result is pervasive Afrophobic/xenophobic attacks on these foreign nationals in South Africa, including Nigerians. Thus, these episodic xenophobic reoccurrences put a dent in Nigeria-South Africa relations despite their putative status as African regional powers. As South Africans accuse African nationals of taking over their land, wives and businesses and alleged to be the driving force behind the high rate of crime in the country, the prejudicial undertones of Afrophobia in the country cannot be overemphasized. These Afrophobic stereotypes and prejudices take the form of derogatory names such as "Makwerekwere/ Magrigamba" used to refer to African nationals (Oni & Okunade, 2018).[2] These names might seem harmless but the intent of the user and the manner it is used constitutes mockery against African nationals living in South Africa. Afrophobic sentiments against foreign nationals are sometimes reinforced by governmental officials, the mass media in speeches and policies that specifically discriminate against African nationals or portray them negatively (Tella & Ogunnubi, 2014).

In the same vein, since 2015, violent Afrophobic attacks have consistently occurred against African nationals in South Africa. These attacks have been blamed on issues of poor governance, rising rate of unemployment, inequality, and to a certain extent an after-effect of colonialism and apartheid regime. This is further complemented by fierce competition for limited resources between South Africans and African migrants. The 2018 xenophobic violence that targeted foreigners residing or studying in South Africa resulted in injuries of varying degrees on about 617 migrants, dozens raped, properties worth millions of Rands were either looted or destroyed, with more than 100,000 displaced (Tafira, 2018). Although there was limited evidence to suggest that Nigerians or other Nigerian businesses were directly affected by the attack, Nigeria felt the

---

[2] These are names associated with West Africans migrants who come into South Africa without valuables and later return to their countries wealthy.

need to intervene on behalf of the affected countries (Ogunnubi & Amusan, 2018, p.63). Furthermore, similar attacks were carried out in 2017 and 2019 with devastating effects on Nigerians in South Africa. The recurring wave of xenophobic incidences in South Africa led the Chair of the House Committee on Diaspora matters Hon. Rita Orji to criticize South Africa's attitude and responses toward these events. She noted that between 2014 and 2016, Nigeria lost about 137 citizens in South Africa (Chibuzor et al., 2017). In 2019, amidst the reoccurrence of xenophobic attacks and growing threats of reprisal attacks in Nigeria, the Nigerian government took proactive measures which helped to prevent the looting and vandalization of South African businesses in Nigeria. The Nigerian government also recalled its High Commissioner from South Africa; boycotted the World Economic Forum on Africa hosted in Cape Town and summoned the South African High Commissioner to Nigeria, Bobby Moore to explain the reasons for the xenophobic attacks on Nigerians (Ogunnubi & Aja, forthcoming). Additionally, a Special Envoy was sent to the South African president Cyril Ramaphosa to officially express the displeasure of the Nigerian government.

While these measures were vital in quelling the rising tension in Nigeria-South Africa diplomatic relations, they, however, seems insufficient in visibly reducing the Afrophobic prejudice and attacks. Incidences of Afrophobia have the capacity to derail Nigeria-South African relations with huge implications for the African continent and the Pan-African renaissance project. Over the years, Nigeria and South Africa have been involved in a combative regional hegemonic struggle which have led to unhealthy rivalry between both countries. If unchecked, these Afrophobic attacks will likely fuel the feud thereby, portraying Africa as a disunited continent. In other words, relationship between both countries must necessarily rest on a special cooperation arrangement in the spirit of Ubuntu, African renaissance and to ensure the success of the economic union of the new AfCFTA.

The mutual recognition on the benefits of peaceful coexistence have led the governments of both countries to seek ways to end the menace of xenophobia and improve bilateral ties. One of such measures is the adoption of rhetoric of cultural diplomacy. According to Nigeria's Minister of Information and Culture, Alhaji Lai Mohammed, the option of "soft power of cultural diplomacy" will help Nigeria and South Africa to put an end to the incessant xenophobic attacks (Foreign Service, 2017). This approach aims to improve people-to-people interaction thereby encouraging mutual understanding of the peculiarities of each nation. We argue that through the adoption of cultural diplomacy and engagement of the creative industry, the relations between citizens of both countries will be improved. This is important because Afrophobic attacks is pervasive in the informal people-to-people interaction and across cultural spaces. Therefore, by establishing common grounds for intensified interaction through the deployment of cultural diplomacy sourced from the creative industry, both countries are able to deescalate the mutual mistrust that often results in Afrophobic conflicts, thereby fostering unity and building stronger bonds that ultimately lead to continental advancement.

Fostering Stronger Bonds Through the Creative Industry

According to UNCTAD (2010), creative industries are cycles of creation, production, and distribution of goods and services that use creativity and intellectual capital as primary inputs. This includes sectors such as architecture, arts and antiques, drawings, painting, crafts and sculptures, performing arts (carnivals, dance, drama, festivals), movies, music, dressing, grooming, and tourist attractions. Beyond its accrued economic benefits, the creative industry also serves as a medium of social cohesion. Haynes (2007) avers that, in this contemporary society, it is basically impossible to ignore the influence of the creative industry of films, music, and cultural festivals. For Nigeria nonetheless, creative industry is a major source of its soft power projection in Africa. This owes to the fact that the creative talents of Nigerians are in high demand, not just in Nigeria, but across the globe. Given the global appeal for Nigeria's creative industry, it can be employed as an instrument of peace. To put this in perspective, the proper application and utilization of these creative potentials have the capacity to reduce the incidences of Afrophobic prejudice and attacks in South Africa and cement its relationship with other African states, Nigeria inclusive. For instance, through the projection of Nigeria's culture in its movies, music, festivals among others, South Africans will better understand the Nigerian brand and identity. In essence, harnessing the soft power ingredients of Nigeria's creative industry (Nollywood, Afro-pop music and cultural festivals and troupes) would help to promote and portray the positive aspects of Nigeria and its citizens to the South African audience, and vice versa. Nigeria's creative industry is visible in virtually every public spaces in Africa Specifically, in the music sector, several international music artists including Wizkid and Grammy Award winner Burna Boy have made their mark in their respective genre (Ogunnubi, 2014).

In this regard, scholars have asserted that the popularity and content of Nollywood movies have improved the awareness and appreciation for the Nigerian culture (Isike & Isike, 2016; Onyenankeya et al., 2017). To a great extent, the creative industry has projected the positive dimensions of Nigeria's cultural diversity and heritage to the global community, and this can be leveraged upon as a fence-mending tool to address the pervasive mistrust between Nigeria and South Africa. This chapter focuses on the films industry, Afro music and cultural festivals with the level of global relevance and visibility it has given to Nigeria, and how it can be deployed to cement the cracked walls of Nigeria-South Africa diplomatic relations.

Nollywood

Nigerian films industry popularly known as Nollywood has over the years gained global status and recognition. Nollywood is recognized as the 2nd largest film producer in the world, contributing an estimated 2.3% (NGN 239billion) to Nigeria's Gross Domestic Product (GDP) in 2016 (Spotlight, 2017). It is also acclaimed to be the 3rd highest earning movie industry after the United States' Hollywood and India's Bollywood (Erick, 2014). According to Haynes (2007), Nollywood has helped to popularize Nigerian rich cultural heritage across Africa and beyond). Nollywood stories are rooted in Nigerian cultural traditions and social texts that focus on community life. The stories are told using African idioms, proverbs, costumes, artifacts, cultural displays, and the imagery of Africa (Onuzulike, 2017, p. 233). The African and global appeal of Nollywood is strengthened by its focus on Nigeria's culture and identity that present narratives which capture the attention of the global audience. Nollywood movies are not only enjoyed in most African homes, but the cultural values projected in these movies are also imitated and imbibed (Ogunnubi & Ogbonna, 2020). This also stresses the fact that many African families can relate to most of the movies' storylines.

The popularity of Nollywood movies as a cultural phenomenon has garnered interests not only in Africa, but also throughout the rest of the world (Onuzulike, 2017). Nollywood has increased in global reputation to the extent that it is aired on various digital platforms across the world, and with an ever-growing fans base. For instance, MultiChoice (DSTV) has about 8 channels dedicated to showcasing Nigerian movies. This is proof of the wide appeal of Nollywood in Africa and beyond. Given its rich cultural content, it has enjoyed a huge and loyal fans base in Africa and among over 30million African emigrants around the world (Erick, 2014). Most of the Nollywood actors and actresses alike have amassed huge followers on social media that in many cases surpasses the population of some countries. Nollywood celebrities have been elevated to the status of superstars and demi-idols, as some of their followers tend to imitate their lifestyles, dressing, haircuts, accents, and habits. Some of these Nollywood Veterans who have won the hearts and minds of Africans and beyond include but not limited to KunleAfolayan, Nkem Owoh, Chiwetalu Agu, Pete Edochie, Regina Asika, Patience Ozokwor, Richard Mofe amijo, Olu Jacobs, Genevieve Nnaji, Mercy Johnson, Osita Iheme, Chinedu Ikedieze, Ramsey Noauh, Omotola Jolade, Charles Okafor (Mr Ibu), Desmod Eliot, Funke Akindele, Stephanie Okereke, Yul Edochie, Nkechi Blessing, and Zubby Micheal. Their praises are sung on the streets of most African countries while their names and nicknames are frequently mentioned or their acts reenacted by both children and adults. Nollywood productions such as *Lion heart, King of boys, The Wedding Party, A Trip to Jamaica, Wives on Strike, Half of a Yellow Sun, October 1st, Citation* and Soap Operas such as Tinsel, Flatmates, the Johnsons among others have dominated the African airwaves. It is, therefore, an incontestable fact that Nollywood has gained immense currency in Africa and beyond (Ogunnubi & Ogbonna, 2020; Onyenankeya et al., 2017). On this note, Fayomi (2015, p. 35) argues that "Nollywood films have gained acceptance in Africa because of the socio-cultural and educational values that it projects. As a result, it has become an integral part of Africa's self-reflection and identity construction through cultural representations."

The popularity and acceptance of Nollywood have positioned Nigeria to utilize this soft power potential in the continent and beyond, and specifically, to assuage the pervasive mistrust with South Africa. Studies by Onyenankeya et al. (2017) already show that South Africans appear to be attracted to Nollywood films because it reminds them of their own cultural traditions. Leveraging these affective adulations among South Africans is vital to eradicating Afrophobic tendencies and prejudice among the populace. As a strong component of culture, the Nigerian government needs to support and promote the Nollywood industry. Through the National Institute for Cultural Orientation, National Broadcasting Corporation and other regulatory agencies, the government needs to sponsor and commission the production of movies targeted at the South African audience and that showcase the unique cultural diversity of Nigeria and its various contribution to the emancipation of South African peoples. To this end, Nollywood and the South African movie industries can also enter into a partnership for the production of movies the cultural peculiarities of both countries will be on display. The goal is to make both countries understand that there is "Unity in Diversity." Aside the revenues that will be generated for both governments, a joint-movie project will also help to correct the negative stereotypes that Nigerians and South Africans have for each other. Through an understanding and projection of the common historical ties and identities, South Africans can become more accommodating, thereby assuaging their Afrophobic prejudices.

In addition, the Nigerian government needs to take advantage of the powerful voices in Nollywood celebrities. As role models to a growing fan base of the teeming African youths, these celebrities often use their voices and social media platforms to promote Nigeria's image abroad. According to Wapmuk (2020b), Nollywood movies have succeeded at not only entertaining audiences but have helped to educate, enhance, and sustain relationships, to break stereotypes and transcend borders at a number of levels. However, taking into cognizance the cultural and diplomatic relevance of Nollywood, the Nigerian government should collaborate with other relevant stakeholders in the industry to further promote its national interest, present the country in positive light and initiate cultural mix policies that will improve Nigeria-South Africa relations. While the cultural impact of these Nollywood movies cannot be adequately measured, the influence that Nollywood actors and actresses wield is beyond measure.

National Festivals and Cultural Troupes

The most common attraction of international tourists/adventurers to Nigeria is its diverse festivals. Nigeria possesses a rich and diverse cultural heritage which represents a shared identity that binds its people together. With over 250 ethnic groups, Nigeria has an abundant cultural heritage that include its cherished arts, customs, festivals, sacred or worship sites, norms, values, dressing, traditional monuments, architectures, technology and technological sites, and artifacts which are cherished and conserved for historical, political, educational, recreational and religious importance among others (Wapmuk, 2020b). National festivals such as the Lagos Theatre festivals, Calabar carnival, Lagos carnival, Gidi cultural fest among others constitute part of Nigeria's huge cultural export. During these festivals, tourists travel from all over the world to witness and experience the amazing display of Nigerian cultural affinities. There are also other traditional festivals such as the Eyo Festival[3]; the Osun festival, which is in reverence of the Osun river goddess in Osun state, the Sango festival; the Ojude Oba festival hosted in Ijebu Ode; the Carniriv in Port Harcourt; the Ofala festival (Onitsha); the Argungu Fishing festival (Kebbi); New Yam festival of the Igbo community among others.

UNESCO has encouraged the use of cultural festivals as a means of fostering goodwill between countries through cultural touring which includes dance and musical troupes (Wapmuk, 2020b). For example, in 1977, Nigeria hosted the Second World Festivals of Arts and Culture (FESTAC 77). FESTAC 77 was primarily a Pan-Nigerian and Pan-African project aimed at uniting African descents irrespective of their skin color from all parts of the world (North America, South America, Asia, Middle East, Europe) to share in the African culture and identity. To this end, in the spirit of this cultural renaissance agenda, Nigeria's cultural festivals and troupes can be used to expose the country's cultural aesthetics to African communities, including South Africa. Utilizing this soft power appeal by creating an avenue whereby foreign tourists from Africans can travel to Nigeria yearly on cultural interaction is important for building social cohesion in Africa. This can be done through joint state sponsorship cultural tours, institutional and social exchanges and program. This will afford the opportunity for South Africans to gain firsthand experience of the beauty of Nigeria's culture and festivals. The social aspect of both countries' relationship can be solidified through the engagement of cultural troupes as a diplomatic instrument. Cultural dances convey messages through the music, movement, and the attendant gestures and facial expressions (Lorgurum & Tsevende, 2013). In view of this, cultural festivals and dance help to develop affective feelings, which can be leveraged to reduce the Afrophobic prejudice of South Africans.

---

[3] Also known as Adamu Orisha, the festival is acclaimed to be the fore-runner of the World's biggest carnival, the Rio de Janierro carnival and it attracts thousands of tourists all over the world who come to see costumed dancers or masquerades called "Éyo" perform.

Afro-Pop Music

Nigeria's music industry has grown to become one of its most prized assets in the creative industry. Nigerian music and musicians are making their marks on the world music stage. Their exploits in various parts of the world have helped to broaden the knowledge of Nigeria and its music culture. Nigeria is, therefore, regarded as the musical heartbeat for popular music in Africa (Adedeji, 2016). In view of the growing preference for Nigerian brand of music, Erick (2017, p. 16) argues that, "over the last two decades, the demand for Nigeria's vibrant music content has risen dramatically both locally and internationally. It has become the music of choice in virtually all social events in Nigeria and Diaspora."

It is evident that Nigeria's Afro-pop music possesses soft power potential that the Nigerian government can exploit to resolve the lingering tensions that overshadow its relations with South Africa. In order to bring an end to the trend of Afrophobic attacks on its citizens, the Nigerian government needs to deploy the popularity and fondness of its music industry as a social tool for foreign policy conduct. To achieve this goal, it is important for the government to first understand that music can be used to shape public opinion and advance Nigeria's interest in Africa and beyond. Nigeria's Afro-pop music portrays an alternative narrative about Nigerians and Nigeria. A predominant feature of the Afrophobic attacks on Nigerian residents in South Africa is centered on the alleged bad image of Nigerians. They are widely accused of being the driving force behind the high rate of crime and other nefarious activities. Therefore, these musical stars are perfect models of changing the narratives about Nigeria and Nigerians abroad.

In the past, legendary Nigerian musicians such as the late Afro King Fela Anikulapo, Sunny Okosun, Ebenezer Obey, Victor Olaiya, Sunny Ade, Victor Uwaifo, Onyeka Onwenu, Christe Essien-Igbokwe among others supported Nigerian foreign policy pursuits and external relations through their music particularly in the fight against western imperialism, apartheid, and racism (Wapmuk, 2020b). However, contemporary Nigerian artists such as Tuface, M.I., D'Banj, 9ice, Wizkid, Burna Boy, Davido, Don Jazzy, Tiwa Savage, Simi, Yemi Alade, Flavour, Kiss Daniel, Runtown, Rema among others that have dominated the global airwaves with huge followership can play a vital role in portraying the image of Nigerians to abroad and in South Africa. These artists have also won huge international recognitions, awards and collaborations with top stars in the international scene. For example, in March 2020, Nigerian artists Burna Boy and Wizkid won the Grammy awards - one of the most prestigious musical awards on the planet. This provides a glimpse into the reach of Nigeria's Afro-pop music. To this end, it is expected that the Nigerian government can tap into the rich array of its music industry to sell the Nigerian brand to South Africans and beyond. For sure, there is great admiration globally for Nigerian music and leveraging on this fondness can help change the negative perception that often accompany Nigerians, drawing attention to the enterprising aspect of the Nigerian culture. Nigerian music is therefore a soft power potential which can be harnessed to improve Nigeria's influence and acceptance in South Africa. A recent case in point in the reprisal looting of South African owned businesses in Nigeria was the aftermath of the condemnation of the xenophobic violence in and around Gauteng province by some Nigerian musical celebrities such as Burna Boy, Teni, and Davido through their social media handles and calls to boycott events sponsored and hosted in South Africa. In a show of patriotic spirit, AKA a South African artist responding to Burna Boy's condemnation of South Africans following the Afrophobic attacks on Nigerians, defended his country and dared the Nigerian music celebrity never to come into South Africa again. Burna Boy pulled out of the African Unite concert which was to be hosted in South Africa, and eventually, the event was canceled. Following Burna Boy's Grammy award, however, AKA was quick to tweet "I always knew that guy (Burna Boy) was special. What a King. Just because I decided to defend my country doesn't mean I can't appreciate greatness." This is an apt illustration of how the voices of these major music artists in the creative industry can trigger responses and reaction from the peoples and their governments.

Given the above, it becomes paramount for the Nigerian and South African governments to both ride on the "wings" of its creative artists to mend fences that make it possible for xenophobic prejudice between them to thrive. As we have demonstrated, the Afro-music industry is not just an element of entertainment; rather, it is also a diplomatic infrastructure of soft power for regional integration, and in this case, with Nigeria and South Africa taking the lead.

Conclusion

The creative industry, as established above is a core source of Nigeria's soft power projection in Africa. The creative industry possesses inherent potentials that can help to correct the feelings of mistrust which occasion Afrophobic prejudice, thereby improving the social cohesion in Nigeria- South Africa relations. Thus far, we have maintained that while governmental measures and responses to the xenophobic violence are commendable, they remain "top-down approaches" which obviously have not addressed the underlying pervasive mistrust and mutual suspicion between Nigeria and South Africa. As such, we have analytically argued for cultural diplomacy as a panacea to the xenophobic prejudice, which breeds episodic diplomatic spats between Nigeria and South. That is, the strategic/diplomatic engagement of the creative industry such as film industry, afro-pop music, national festivals, and cultural troupes to enhance people-to-people interactions and mitigate the devastating effects of Afrophobia, and thereby changing the negative narratives of the two African powers, and by extension, promote the ideals of African Renaissance while re-positioning Africa in the global scene.

References

Adedeji, W. (2016). Nigerian music industry: Challenges, prospects and possibilities. *International Journal of Recent Research in Social Science and Humanities, 3*(1), 261–271.

Adegbulu, F. (2011). Pre-colonial west African diplomacy: Its nature and impact. *Journal of International Social Research, 18*(4), 1–20.

Adeoye, O. A. (2017). Introduction: Understanding xenophobia in Africa. In O. A. Adeoye (Ed.), *The political economy of xenophobia in Africa* (pp. 1–7). Springer Publisher.

Awosusi, O. E., & Ekpo, E. C. (forthcoming). Determinants of Nigeria's foreign policy: Making a case for religion. In O. O. Ogunnubi & S. Folarin (Eds.), *Global politics: Soft power in Nigeria and beyond*. Lexington Books.

Awosusi, O. E., & Fatoyinbo, F. C. (2019). Xenophobic prejudice in Africa: Cultural diplomacy as a panacea to the deteriorating inter-African relations. *International Journal of Research Publications, 40*(1), 1–26.

Chibuzor, et al. (2017). Xenophobia and Nigeria-South Africa relations. *Journal of Humanities and Social Science, 22*(10), 61–69.

Czarnowski, S. (2005). *Kultura*. Warsaw.

Ebegbulem, J. C. (2013). An evaluation of Nigeria—South Africa bilateral relations. *Journal of International Relations and Foreign Policy, 1*(1), 32–40.

Erick, O. (2014). *Nigerian film industry: Nollywood looks to expand to globally.* United States.

Fayomi, O. (2015). Transactional and integrative cultural roles of Nollywood entertainment media in West Africa: The case of Benin and Ghana. *International Journal of International Relations, 1*(1), 34–41.

Foreign Service. (2017). *Cultural diplomacy to ease xenophobia.* http://www.iol.co.za/capetimes/news/cultural-diplomacy-to-ease-xenophobia-9152343.

Frankel, J. (1963). *The making of foreign policy.* Oxford University Press.

Haynes, J. (2007). Nollywood in Lagos, Lagos in Nollywood films. *Africa Today, 54*(2), 131–150.

Hudson, V. (Ed.). (1997). *Culture and foreign policy.* Lynne Rienner.

Huntington, S. P. (1993). The clash of civilizations? *Foreign Affairs, 72*(3), 22–49.

Huntington, S. P. (1996). *The clash of civilizations and the remaking of the world order* (1st ed.). Simon & Schuster.

Iriye, A. (1979). Culture and power: International relations as intercultural relations. *Diplomatic History, 3*(2), 115–128.

Isike, C. & Isike, E. (2016). The human factor paradigm. *African Journal of Rhetoric, 8,* 175–203.

Kiewit, L. (2019). *The Nigerians who are bullish on SA.* http://mg.co.za/article/2019-10-04-00-the-nigerians-who=are-bullish-on-SA.

Lawal, L. (2007, September 27). *South Africa goes Shopping.* http://money.cnn.com/2007/09/26/news/international/south_africa_fortune/index.html

Lee, M. (2015). Seven of the biggest myth about South Africa and xenophobia-and how they drive attacks. *Mail & Guardian Africa.*

Lorngurum, D. S. & Tsevende, R. (2013). Nigerian dances and cultural diplomacy. *Global Advanced Research Journal of Peace, Gender and Development Studies, 2*(3), 54–60.

Mahe, I. G. (2012). Culture and foreign policy. In E. Anyaoku (Ed.), *Review of Nigerian foreign policy* (pp. 321–344). Nigerian Institute of International Affairs.

Morin, J. F., & Paquin, J. (Eds.). (2018). *Foreign policy analysis.* Palgrave Macmillan. https://doi.org/10.1007/978-3-319-61003-0

Ninkovich, F. A. (1981). *The diplomacy of ideas.* U.S. Foreign Policy and Cultural Relations 1938–1950.

Nye, J. S. (2004). *Soft power: The means to success in world politics.* Public Affairs.

Nye, J. S. (1990). *"Soft power", foreign policy.* Carnegie Endowment for Peace Press.

Odoh, I. (2019). *The challenges of Nigeria's citizen diplomacy.* http://businessday.ng/features/articles/the-challenges-of-nigerias-citizen-diplomacy/amp/.

Ogunnubi, O. (2014). *Hegemonic order and regional stability in Sub-Saharan Africa: A comparative study of Nigeria and South Africa* (Unpublished PhD thesis). University of KwaZulu-Natal, South Africa.

Ogunnubi, O. (2019): The ideational value of soft power and the foreign policy of African regional powers, *Politikon*, 1–22. https://doi.org/10.1080/02589346.2019.1641982

Ogunnubi, O., & Amusan, L. (2018). Nigeria's attitude towards South Africa's perceived Xenophobia: Exploring a shared hegemonic power for Africa's development. In A. O. Akinola (Ed.), *The Political Economy of Xenophobia in Africa* (pp. 53–68). Springer International Publishing.

Ogunnubi, O., & Ogbonna, C. (2020). Nigeria's creative industry: From soft power ideation to instrument of cultural diplomacy. In L. O. Eriomala & S. Wapmuk (Eds.), *Culture & Nigeria's foreign relations in a globalising world* (pp. 77–98). NICO.

Oni, E. O., & Okunade, S. K. (2018). The context of xenophobia in Africa: Nigeria and South Africa in comparison. In A. O. Akinola (Ed.), *The political economy of xenophobia in Africa*. Springer International Publishing.

Onuoha, J. (2008). *Beyond diplomacy: Contemporary issues in international relations*. Great AP.

Onuzulike, U. (2017). Nollywood: The Influence of the Nigerian industry on African culture. *Journal of Human Communications, 10*(3), 231–242.

Onyenankeya, O. M., Onyenankeya, K. U., & Osunkunle, O. (2017). The persuasive influence of Nollywood film in cultural transmission: Negotiating Nigerian culture in a South African environment. *Journal of Intercultural Communication Research, 46*(4), 297–313.

Ryhan, S. (2015). *Cultural diplomacy in International Relations: Understanding hidden barriers in cultural knowledge*, Yamagata University Bulletin.

Spotlight. (2017). *The Nigerian film industry*. PWC

Stelowska, D. (2015). Culture in international relations: Defining cultural diplomacy. *Polish Journal of Political Science, 1*(3), 50–72.

Tafira, H. K. (2018). Xenophobia in South Africa: A history. In T. Falola & M. M. Heaton (Eds.), *African histories and modernities* (pp. 15–35). Springer International Publishing.

Tella, O. (2016). Wielding soft power in strategic regions: An analysis of China's power of attraction in Africa and the Middle East. *Africa Review, 8*(2), 133–144.

Tella, O., & Ogunnubi, O. (2014). Hegemony or survival: South Africa's regional pursuit of soft power and the challenges of Xenophobia. *Africa Insight, 44*(3), 145–163.

Tylor, E. B. (1871). *Primitive culture: Researches into the development of mythology, philosophy, religion, language, art and custom*. J. Murray.

UNCTAD. (2010). *Strengthening the creative industries for development*. New York and Geneva.
UNESCO. (2001). *Universal declaration on cultural diversity*. Paris.
Vlahos, M. (1991). Culture and foreign policy author(s). *Foreign Policy, 18,* 59–78.
Wapmuk, S. (2020a). The Efficacy of culture as an operational instrument for promoting Nigeria's external relations. In L.O. Eriomala & S. Wapmuk (Eds.), *Culture & Nigeria's foreign relations in a globalising world* (pp. 19–42). NICO.
Wapmuk, S. (2020b). Harnessing Nigerian festivals, arts and crafts for economic benefits: Lessons from an emerging power. In L. O. Eriomala & S. Wapmuk (Eds.), *Culture & Nigeria's foreign relations in a globalising world* (pp 118–143). NICO.
Wendt, A. (1999). *Social Theory of International Politics*. CUP.
Zabadi, I. S., & Onuoha, F. C. (2012). Nigeria and South Africa: Competition or cooperation. In T. A. Imobighe & W. O. Alli (Eds.), *Perspectives on Nigeria's national politics and external relations: Essays in Honor of Professor A. Bolaji Akinyemi* (pp. 384–408). University Press Plc.

PART III

Cultural Performance and Sustainability

CHAPTER 15

Tumaini Festival: Cultural Production and Transnational Exchange at Dzaleka Refugee Camp in Malawi

Emmanuel Chima

Introduction

The Tumaini Festival, named after the Swahili word for hope, is an ingenious brainchild of Congolese refugee artist Trésor Nzengu Mpauni. It was first held in 2014 as a sister event to the Lake of Stars Festival which preceded it by a decade (Macfarlane, 2015; Perry, 2016). The latter festival was founded in 2004 by British national Will Jameson (Makhumula, 2019; Perry, 2016), and takes its name from Lake Malawi as described by Scottish missionary and explorer David Livingstone in 1859 (Ross, 2002; Thompson, 2013). The Tumaini Festival itself has gained particular recognition for its transnational, humanitarian reach and impact. It has received praise and recognition from international bodies

E. Chima (✉)
School of Social Work, Michigan State University, East Lansing, MI, USA
e-mail: chimaemm@msu.edu

© The Author(s), under exclusive license to Springer Nature Singapore Pte Ltd. 2022
T. Afolabi et al. (eds.), *Re-centering Cultural Performance and Orange Economy in Post-colonial Africa*,
https://doi.org/10.1007/978-981-19-0641-1_15

such as the World Bank, and the United Nations and its Global Refugee Forum (Africa Region Communications & Partnerships Unit, 2019, p. 5; United Nations High Commissioner for Refugees, 2019a). Held annually in either October or November at Dzaleka Refugee Camp in Malawi, the festival demonstrates public pedagogy in addressing refugee stigma and discrimination.

Burdick and Sandlin (2010) hold that, in a manner different from its initial conceptualization, public pedagogy has extended beyond public institutions to more public spheres and platforms to advance cultural critique and activism. Ultimately, what such spaces have in common is their counter-hegemonic practice (Sandlin, O'Malley et al., 2011; Sandlin, Schultz et al., 2010). Festival founder Mpauni writes, "The festival is an innovative cultural event, developed and delivered by refugees and the host community, which uses entertainment and artistic expression to promote economic empowerment, intercultural harmony, mutual understanding and peaceful co-existence" (Mpauni, 2019, "Breaking the mold for refugees," para. 6).

Residual echoes of colonization can be teased out from the strained socio-political context against which the festival emerged. In responding with art to the unwelcoming sentiment towards refugees that Mpauni himself experienced (Mpauni, 2015), he was remotely pushing back against a colonially instituted division predicated on national origin (Bernhard et al., 2004). This chapter explores how cultural production, as an interactional transformative practice (Burgess, 2014; Hesmondhalgh, 2006), has brokered a transnational exchange through the festival at Dzaleka (Levitt & Nyberg-Sørensen, 2004). It discusses how the festival has centred conversation on the experiences of refugees within and beyond Malawi. In addition, parallels are also drawn between prejudice towards refugees in Malawi, and the implicit, divisive elements of geopolitics and nationalism rooted in colonial history (Acemoglu & Robinson, 2010; Wengraf, 2018).

National Borders and the Postcolonial "Other"

The origins of Malawi as a nation can be traced back to the sixteenth century Maravi Kingdom (Pike, 1965). The kingdom's expanse covered present-day Malawi and parts of the neighbouring nations of Mozambique and Zambia. Its founding is credited to the Bantu people who migrated from the Congo basin as early as the thirteenth century. The

Maravi Kingdom was eventually eclipsed by Britain and Portugal's imperial expansion in the eighteenth century (Foeken, 1995). The area over which Britain exercised control was proclaimed British Central Africa Protectorate (Conroy, 2006). This was later renamed Nyasaland after Lake Nyasa, now Lake Malawi. Under British colonial rule, the Federation of Rhodesia and Nyasaland was formed, with Rhodesia comprising present day nations of Zambia and Zimbabwe (Posner, 2004).

Migration and multi-ethnic contact evidently underlies Malawi's political history. However, the nation now appears oblivious to such enduring history in responding to a growing refugee population (Mvula, 2010; Reiboldt, 2019). Malawi currently hosts more than fifty-four thousand refugees, with the majority ironically from the Democratic Republic of Congo (DRC) and others from Burundi, Rwanda and a few other countries in the region (UNHCR, 2021a). The camp at Dzaleka is located in a peri-urban area about fifty kilometres from the capital Lilongwe (Makhumula, 2019). It was set up in 1994 following civil unrest in the African Great Lakes region, particularly the Rwandan genocide and conflict in the Congo (Baker, 2011). Coincidently, this was also when Malawi held a referendum and transitioned from a post-independence, single-party rule lasting twenty-seven years to a multiparty political system (Mitchell, 2002).

The distinction made between post-colonial and postcolonial is significant. While the former refers to the period after decolonization, the latter entails the lasting impact of colonization (Burdick & Sandlin, 2010; Hitchcock, 1997). Postcolonial influence speaks to the persistence of colonial ideology and hegemony. Chaudhury (1994) cautions against a simplistic understanding of colonial hegemony as unidirectional. To the contrary, colonial hegemony operates in a cultural space that is co-created between the colonizer and the colonized. The othering of refugees in Malawi is most notably entrenched in national identity. Refugees are pejoratively called *maburundi* in the vernacular (Chima, 2020). This slur, which literally translates to Burundians, is used collectively for all refugees in Malawi regardless of national identity. This erases national affiliation while simultaneously othering refugees as an unwelcome people group in Malawi. Burundian as a distinct nationality construct has inadvertently also been antagonized.

The differences in nationality, on which the refugee stigma is predicated, are arguably rooted in the infamous 1884 Berlin Conference which culminated in the partition of Africa, also referred to as the Scramble for

Africa (Foeken, 1995). The territories controlled by the different European colonial powers were further divided, rather arbitrarily, resulting in borders that became the blueprint for African states during the wave of independence which had its apex in the 1950s and 1960s (Acemoglu & Robinson, 2010). These colonially imposed borders fragmented pre-existing tribal territories and redistributed people groups (Posner, 2004), something which the decolonial process cemented with the nations that emerged. National identity therefore became emphasized to the detriment of shared ethnic and cultural heritage which transcended politically defined boundaries.

The very essence of nationalism is the exclusive centring of national affiliation and interests (Wimmer & Schiller, 2003). In that vein, Malawi's own restrictive refugee policy gets at the idea of safeguarding the interests of citizens to the exclusion of "aliens" (Mvula, 2010). Thus, an unquestioning reliance on nationality in othering refugees is, by implication, a reinforcement of difference borne from colonialism. It is this ambivalence that the Tumaini Festival destabilizes in its appeal to the oneness of being and shared humanity through cultural production, while also offering up a critique of the stigma and discrimination that refugees face in Malawi. In the African context overall, the festival also serves as a decolonial strategy of representation (Zembylas, 2018). Issues of language and culture take centre stage through artistic display, spurring a celebration of diversity and multiculturalism. In brokering social engagement, the weekend-long festival brings together local, foreign and refugee artists, theatre ensembles, dancing troupes, and various other creatives. With a main stage set up next to the administrative centre of the camp and a smaller stage further into the camp, performances chronicle experiences of conflict, displacement, struggle, resilience, and hope. The thematic nature of the artistic work showcased mirrors how World Refugee Day, observed on June 20, is celebrated in the camp (UNHCR, 2007, 2016, 2021b). Popular acts at the festival include the Amahoro drummers whose red, green and white garb represents Burundi's national flag; the intricately choreographed Umushagiriro and Umushayayo women's dances from Rwanda; Congolese rumba; and Mganda, a traditional dance native to Malawi's central region in which the camp is located. It is common to see both residents and visitors to the camp cheer and ululate as the line-up of performances unfold.

Cultural Production and Transnational Exchange

Dzaleka Refugee Camp has been in existence for twenty-eight years, thereby making it a de facto protracted refugee situation. This is where forced displacement of twenty-five thousand people or more persists beyond five years (UNHCR, 2018). However, varying degrees of tension between refugee and host communities in Malawi have been reported since before the camp at Dzaleka was established in 1994 (Battiata, 1988, August 10; Eddings, 1992, November 10; Joint Assessment Mission, 2014; UNHCR, 2021a). The hardships of an extended stay at the camp are intensified by Malawi's refugee policy. The consolidation of a refugee framework was expedited by the Malawian government during the drawn out 1977–1992 civil war in Mozambique (Mvula, 2010). By 1986 Malawi was hosting up to eight-hundred thousand Mozambican nationals, the largest concentration of refugees in Africa at the time (Eddings, 1992; Englund, 1996). When Malawi enacted its Refugee Act of 1989, it incorporated previously adopted international agreements while also stipulating enforceable restrictions of the same at the local level (UNHCR, 2020). Limitations were placed on the personal freedoms that refugees could enjoy in Malawi. These included encampment, and restrictions on movement, place of residence, access to public education, and employment opportunities.

The Tumaini Festival has created a platform for public dialogue on the challenges emanating from Malawi's refugee framework and related issues surrounding political conflict, refugee protection, and local integration. This has been mediated by the cultural and creative arts showcased at the festival. While cultural performance denotes performative action (Schechner, 2010), cultural production presupposes intentionality of meaning-making in the performative process (Burgess, 2014; Hesmondhalgh, 2006). The visual and melodic aesthetics of the cultural artforms at the festival are seamlessly complemented by modern ones such as spoken word and drama skits which more readily give voice to the plight of life at Dzaleka and generally for refugees in Malawi. In claiming back and rewriting refugee narratives, the Tumaini Festival therefore functions as a form of artistic resistance (Sandlin, O'Malley et al., 2011; Sandlin, Schultz et al., 2010). The visibility brought to the refugee community has dispelled the myth of a refugee monolith. Patrons at the festival get to see and interact with refugees at the camp as individuals, this in itself has a humanizing effect (Zembylas, 2018). Beyond witnessing the immense talent in the community, visitors to the camp also get to participate in the normative experiences of the residents there. These include having *chai* at one of the many teahouses, shopping at the local markets, and getting custom made clothing by tailors renowned for their meticulousness (Chima, 2020; Makhumula, 2019).

The impact of the Tumaini Festival has been felt beyond the confines of the camp and the borders of Malawi to other parts of the world. The organization Tumaini Letu (our hope in Swahili) which runs the festival was the 2020 recipient of the Sharjah International Award for Refugee Advocacy and Support (The Big Heart Foundation, 2020). The coveted award included a cash prize of $136,000. As the face of the Tumaini Festival, Mpauni has become a de facto ambassador of goodwill for refugees. He has spoken at international gatherings like the 2019 Global Refugee Forum, and was featured in Al-Jazeera's documentary series "Witness" (Shaw, 2015). The way refugees are sometimes talked about merits attention as it leads to a rethinking of perception and reality. In humanizing refugees, the festival complexifies the relevance of national identity in humanitarian crises. Transnational actors of the festival include artists, patrons, volunteers, sponsors, expatriates, various organizations, and the media. As the festival's founder, Mpauni has also been recognized on the global stage for his contribution to furthering the wellbeing of refugees. He was named World Bank Africa Region's Social Inclusion Hero for 2018 (Africa Region Communications & Partnerships Unit, 2019, p. 5). Further to advocacy and increasing refugee visibility, the festival has created socioeconomic opportunities for camp residents and surrounding communities (Mpauni, 2019). Throughout the duration of the festival, there are food stalls for local delicacies, and vendors selling colourful, traditional fabrics, wooden curios, assorted art pieces, and other miscellaneous items as souvenirs. Hailed as an international event held in a refugee camp, the festival has additionally become a tourist attraction similar to its forerunner the Lake of Stars Festival (Macfarlane, 2015; Perry, 2016).

Conclusion

The Tumaini Festival has reasonably succeeded in promoting a more peaceful coexistence between refugees and the local hosting community. Its impetus for social inclusion has led it to stand out as worthy of emulation. The strength and resilience of the refugee community at Dzaleka has meaningfully contributed to the rewriting of refugee narratives. Through its cross-cultural platform, the festival offers up Pan-African and global citizen identities with which patrons and the refugee community alike can identify. The global engagement of Mpauni and Tumaini Letu completes a cycle of transnational exchange that began with the cultural capital and artistic talent that was brought to Malawi by the refugee community.

References

Acemoglu, D., & Robinson, J. A. (2010). Why is Africa poor? *Economic History of Developing Regions, 25*(1), 21–50.

Africa Region Communications & Partnerships Unit. (2019). *Social inclusion hero's competition 2018.* http://documents1.worldbank.org/curated/zh/257331573509983769/pdf/Social-Inclusion-Heroes-Competition-2018-Ten-Stories-of-Great-People-Serving-their-Communities.pdf

Baker, C. (2011). Come walk with me: Three Visits to Dzaleka. *The Society of Malawi Journal, 64*(1), 34–41.

Battiata, M. (1988, August 10). Mozambican refugee tide overwhelms Malawi; savage civil war drives hundreds of thousands to tiny African nation. *The Washington Post* (Pre-1997 Full text).

Bernhard, M., Reenock, C., & Nordstrom, T. (2004). The legacy of western overseas colonialism on democratic survival. *International Studies Quarterly, 48*(1), 225–250.

Burdick, J., & Sandlin, J. A. (2010). Inquiry as answerability: Toward a methodology of discomfort in researching critical public pedagogies. *Qualitative Inquiry, 16*(5), 349–360.

Burgess, D. (2014). Why Whistler will never be Sundance, and what this tells us about the field of cultural production. *Canadian Journal of Film Studies, 23*(1), 90–108.

Chaudhury, A. (1994). On colonial hegemony: Toward a critique of Brown orientalism. *Rethinking Marxism, 7*(4), 44–58.

Chima, E. (2020). Life in Malawi's prison-turned-refugee camp. African diaspora: Before and after COVID-19. *Africa in Fact,* 36–41. Good Governance Africa. https://gga.org/africa-in-fact-special-edition/

Conroy, A. (2006). The history of development and crisis in Malawi. In *Poverty, AIDS and Hunger* (pp. 14–32). Palgrave Macmillan.

Eddings, J. (1992, November 10). Mozambican war over, but refugees still crowd into tiny, dirt-poor Malawi. *The Sun.*

Englund, H. (1996). Waiting for the Portuguese: Nostalgia, exploitation and the meaning of land in the Malawi-Mozambique borderland. *Journal of Contemporary African Studies, 14*(2), 157–172.

Foeken, D. (1995). On the causes of the partition of Central Africa, 1875–1885. *Political Geography, 14*(1), 80–100.

Hesmondhalgh, D. (2006). Bourdieu, the media and cultural production. *Media, Culture & Society, 28*(2), 211–231.

Hitchcock, P. (1997). Postcolonial Africa? Problems of Theory. *Women's Studies Quarterly, 25*(3/4), 233–244.

Joint Assessment Mission. (2014). *Report: Dzaleka refugee camp, Malawi*. https://www.unhcr.org/5680f7d09.pdf

Levitt, P., & Nyberg-Sørensen, N. (2004). The transnational turn in migration studies. *Global Migration Perspectives, 6*, 2–13.

Makhumula, C. (2019). Re-imagining Dzaleka: The Tumaini Festival and refugee visibility. *Eastern African Literary and Cultural Studies, 5*(1), 1–18.

Macfarlane, C. (2015). The Malawi music festival bringing hope to its refugee residents. *The Guardian*. https://www.theguardian.com/world/2015/nov/17/malawi-tumaini-music-festivalrefugee-residents

Mitchell, M. (2002). Living our faith: The lentenpastoral Letter of the bishops of Malawi and the shift to multiparty democracy, 1992–1993. *Journal for the Scientific Study of Religion, 41*(1), 5–18.

Mpauni, T. (2015). *Breaking the mould for refugees*. Menes La Plume. TEDxLilongwe. https://youtu.be/i-7nKdX3KtE

Mpauni, T. (2019). *Breaking the mold for refugees: Founding the Tumaini Festival in Dzaleka refugee camp, Malawi*. WorldBank Blogs. Nasikiliza. https://blogs.worldbank.org/nasikiliza/breaking-mold-refugees-founding-tumaini-festival-dzaleka-refugee-camp-malawi

Mvula, L. D. (2010). *Refugee status determination and rights in Malawi*. Refugee Studies Centre, Oxford Department of International Development. University of Oxford. https://www.rsc.ox.ac.uk/publications/refugee-status-determination-and-rights-in-malawi

Perry, K. (2016). Malawi's Lake of Stars Festival: Banging the drum for Africa's musical heritage. *The Guardian*. https://www.theguardian.com/music/2016/oct/07/malawis-lake-of-starsfestival-dzaleka-refugees

Pike, J. (1965). A pre-colonial history of Malawi. *The Nyasaland Journal, 18*(1), 22–54.

Posner, D. N. (2004). The political salience of cultural difference: Why Chewas and Tumbukas are allies in Zambia and adversaries in Malawi. *American Political Science Review*, 529–545.

Reiboldt, M. L. (2019). *The power of labelling: A double-edged sword?-On the legal and social labels of asylum-seekers and refugees: A case study in Malawi* (Master's thesis).

Ross, A. C. (2002). *David Livingstone: mission and empire*. A&C Black.

Sandlin, J. A., Schultz, B. D., & Burdick, J. (Eds.). (2010). *Handbook of public pedagogy: Education and learning beyond schooling*. Routledge.

Sandlin, J. A., O'Malley, M. P., & Burdick, J. (2011). Mapping the complexity of public pedagogy scholarship: 1894–2010. *Review of Educational Research, 81*(3), 338–375.

Schechner, R. (2010). *Between theater and anthropology.* University of Pennsylvania Press.

Shaw, N. (2015). *Tresor and the camp musicians.* Filmmaker's view. Al-Jazeera. https://www.aljazeera.com/program/episode/2015/7/20/tresor-and-the-camp-musicians

The Big Heart Foundation. (2020). *Past winners.* Sharjah International Award. https://tbhf.ae/past-winners/#winnersId

Thompson, T. J. (2013). Lake Malawi, I presume? David Livingstone, maps and the 'discovery' of Lake Nyassa in 1859. *The Society of Malawi Journal, 66*(2), 1–15.

United Nations High Commissioner for Refugees. (2018). *Global trends: Forced displacement in 2018.* https://www.unhcr.org/5d08d7ee7.pdf

United Nations High Commissioner for Refugees. (2019a). *Refugee co-sponsors.* Global Refugee Forum. https://www.unhcr.org/refugee-co-sponsors.html

United Nations High Commissioner for Refugees. (2019b, October). *Submission for the Universal Periodic Review—Malawi.* UPR 36th Session. https://www.refworld.org/docid/5e17493a2.html

United Nations High Commission for Refugees. (2020). *Figures at a glance.* https://www.unhcr.org/en-us/figures-at-a-glance.html

United Nations High Commission for Refugees. (2021a). *Malawi.* Operations summary. https://data2.unhcr.org/en/country/mwi

United Nations High Commission for Refugees. (2021b). *World Refugee Day.* https://www.unhcr.org/en-us/world-refugee-day.html

Wengraf, L. (2018). Legacies of colonialism in Africa. Imperialism, dependence, and development. *The International Socialist Review*, 103.

Wimmer, A., & Schiller, N. G. (2003). Methodological nationalism, the social sciences, and the study of migration: An essay in historical epistemology 1. *International Migration Review, 37*(3), 576–610.

Zembylas, M. (2018). Decolonial possibilities in South African higher education: Reconfiguring humanising pedagogies as/with decolonising pedagogies. *South African Journal of Education, 38*(4).

CHAPTER 16

The Brave Musicians and "Bad-Ass Librarians" of Timbuktu: Culture Fuels Recovery from Conflict

Cynthia Schneider

INTRODUCTION

Torn apart by conflict and extremist violence, Mali, one of the poorest countries on earth, is held together by its rich cultural heritage and living culture. Mali's culture is the country's calling card to the world, and the membrane that connects its people to each other, to their shared history, and to a common vision for a peaceful future.

This matters because Mali offers a microcosm of the problems facing the global south—extremist and sectarian-caused violence and instability, loss of arable land due to climate change, corrupt and ineffective governance, and endemic poverty. Culture rarely figures in the myriad strategies

C. Schneider (✉)
Former US Ambassador to the Netherlands, Georgetown University, Washington, DC, USA
e-mail: schneidc@georgetown.edu

© The Author(s), under exclusive license to Springer Nature Singapore Pte Ltd. 2022
T. Afolabi et al. (eds.), *Re-centering Cultural Performance and Orange Economy in Post-colonial Africa*,
https://doi.org/10.1007/978-981-19-0641-1_16

and solutions proposed for these problems. But the example of northern Mali's Timbuktu suggests it should be.

Timbuktu? To many, this name evokes a place of epic remoteness. To others, it connotes an ancient crossroads of trade, exotic goods, and culture. And still others know it as the sacred intellectual capital of Africa and the Middle East, synonymous with universities, debate, and religious tolerance. Once a center of commerce and civilization on a par with Florence during the Renaissance, Timbuktu drew scholars from throughout Africa and the Middle East to its famed universities (Schneider et al., 2015) They penned manuscripts whose prescient ideas about good governance, human rights, women's rights, tolerance and plurality, astronomy, medicine, and other subjects testify to this mythic town's legacy, captured in a fifteenth-century Malian proverb: "Salt comes from the north, gold from the south, but the word of God and the treasures of wisdom are only to be found in Timbuctoo".

Anyone who listens to blues or rock n'roll can thank Timbuktu, the birthplace of the blues, or the "big bang of all the music we love," as Bono called it (Shields et al., 2014) The slave trade brought Timbuktu's rhythms to the Mississippi Delta, and from there they eventually spread to the world.

But Timbuktu's culture came under fire when al-Qaeda linked extremists invaded and occupied northern Mali in 2012. In June of that year, just a few months after thousands of music lovers—Malians, West Africans, Europeans, and Americans—had gathered in Timbuktu's desert for the renowned Festival au Désert, listening to Mali's greats such as Vieux Farka Touré, Khaira Arby, Tinariwen, and Bassekou Kouyaté, joined that year by Bono, the town fell into the iron grip of Ansar Dine, a West Africa-based offshoot of Al Qaeda. Months earlier Ansar Dine and other jihadist groups had joined forces with the Tuareg separatists of the National Movement for the Liberation of Azawad (MNLA), who were rising up again in their pursuit of independence from Mali's central government. This toxic mix of militants moved southward through Mali's vast desert north, occupying territory along the way. A military coup in March 2012 that deposed President Amadou Toumani Touré had left a power vacuum that opened the way for this incursion of separatists and extremists ("Destabilization of Mali").

Tensions between the Tuareg and Ansar Dine factions grew as the latter moved to impose strict Sharia law, anathema to Mali's tolerant and pluralistic society. By June 2012, the Tuareg separatists (MNLA) split with the extremists, leaving Timbuktu in the hands of Ansar Dine and under the thumb of Sharia law.

The occupiers of Timbuktu did the unthinkable. They banned music in Mali's music mecca. Ironically, the mastermind of Ansar Dine's rule of terror Iyad Ag Ghali was a school classmate of Manny Ansar, the founder of the Festival Au Désert.

The extremists who invaded northern Mali in 2012 and occupied Timbuktu targeted living culture—music—and cultural heritage—monuments to Timbuktu's revered scholar saints. Why? As Malians, members of Ansar Dine knew the indispensable role of music in their country, where most of the population is illiterate, and they would have realized that historic Timbuktu's identity is grounded in its sacred monuments. As an essential component of every celebration, especially marriages, music communicates the stories of Mali's past, as well as family histories and even gossip (Denselow, 2013; Fernandes, 2013). Music and Mali's regional and national identities are inextricably linked. For it is through song that the Tuaregs of the north or the Bambara of the south express their traditions and pass on their stories. By the same token, music conveys Mali's national identity, knit together from multiple ethnic groups. Music may not seem to be a matter of life or death in the west, but in Mali it is. Fadimata Walet Oumar, lead singer of the Tuareg group Tartit, declared, *"They want to ban music? They will have to kill us first* (Shields et al, 2014)." For Ansar Dine, forbidding music was a pragmatic divide and conquer strategy that also conformed to the fundamentalist ideas that underlie a strict interpretation of Sharia law.

After French-led forces expelled the occupying extremists, and restored northern Mali to local control, what Timbuktu, devastated psychologically and economically, bereft of tourism which provided so many livelihoods, really needed was a public concert (Smith, 2014). Not your textbook solution for recovering from conflict, but for Timbuktu—just right. *Festival Au Desert* founder Manny Ansar knew that music would be able to heal the divisions and distrust left in the wake of the occupation. From the refugee camp to which he had fled the invading extremists, Ansar hatched a plan with his friend, entrepreneur Chris Shields, for a Malian music tour, the "Festival in Exile" to raise awareness of Mali's plight.

After the successful Festival in Exile tour, Ansar and Shields brought Malian entrepreneur Salif Niang and me on board, and together we planned a brainstorming session to develop a strategy to assist Mali's recovery from conflict through support for her culture. At the Brookings Institution's 2014 U.S.- Islamic World Forum in Doha, Qatar, we brought together an unprecedented meeting of Mali's cultural leaders—musicians, historians, manuscript experts—with American counterparts and backers. Due to Ansar's deft behind-the scenes diplomacy, Mali's newly elected President Ibrahim Boubacar Keita delivered a keynote at the Forum. He and his accompanying Cabinet members attended every one of our working group sessions and endorsed the action plan that emerged to establish the *Timbuktu Renaissance (TR)*, as a Malian association (nonprofit) with the goal of supporting Mali's culture as a means of advancing post-conflict unity, development, and peace.

Beginning in 2017, the *Timbuktu Renaissance* (http://www.timbukturenaissance.org/) has revived public concerts in Timbuktu, bringing the country's different ethnic groups together and, in the words of attendees "breaking down barriers and rebuilding trust and social cohesion between people of different backgrounds" (MacLean, 2018). In the face of continued attacks from extremists, audience members told us that the Timbuktu population views music as "a form of cultural resistance."

From the first *Timbuktu Renaissance* concert to the present, participants have emphasized how important these joyful communal events have become in rebuilding social cohesion in Timbuktu. Following the occupation, citizens of Timbuktu, a city famous for its tolerance and hospitality, did not trust each other. No one knew who had sided with the invading extremists, or who had a family member who did. There was uncertainty about how long the peace would last, and whether the invaders would return.

Townspeople from the youth to Timbuktu's *eminence gris,* the revered historian Salem Oud El Haj, have felt the impact of the *Timbuktu Renaissance* concerts, which have been held almost monthly since December 2017. Members of the *TR* team have interviewed concert goers to gauge the impact of the musical gatherings. For youth leader Yehia Bore, the *TR* concerts restored his sense of hope: «Si vide d'espoir était mon mode à Tombouctou avant que je ne connaisse ces concerts de musique. Une musique qui en moi a éveillé amour et espoir de même que dans l'âme de tout Tombouctien.» (I had no hope whatsoever before I experienced these music concerts. The music awakened love and hope in me and in the souls of all Timbuktu people.)

Salem Oud El Haj explained the importance of music as a messenger of peace, especially in Mali, with its high rates of illiteracy. "C'est une très bonne chose d'organiser des concerts pour la paix. Surtout on s'intéresse au publique dans sa langue, partant des réalités qu'ils connaissent. Chez nous la musique draine le maximum de monde surtout les illettrés. Un morceau de musique à Tombouctou devient une leçon permanente parce qu'on ne cesse de le chanter» (It is a very good thing to organize concerts for peace, especially when the messages are transmitted in local languages and highlight realities that they know. In Timbuktu, music is capable of attracting the maximum of people, especially those who are illiterate. A piece of music in Timbuktu becomes a permanent lesson because we keep singing the songs»).

Jumpstarting public concerts in Timbuktu did not solve the city's dire economic state but bringing the diverse population together began to heal divisions, rebuild trust, and social cohesion, and to give people hope of a better future, and the strength to fight for it.

Sometimes big impacts can be measured in seemingly small things. The morning after the first *Timbuktu Renaissance* concert in December 2017, which brought the "nightingale of Timbuktu" Khaira Arby back to her hometown for her first public concert since the occupation, the driver at the Auberge Du Désert told me that he had slept soundly for the first time since the occupation.

The *Timbuktu Renaissance* partners with other entities such as the Festival Vivre Ensemble (https://www.facebook.com/VivreEnsembleBo uctou/), organized by Timbuktu youth leaders with the support of MINUSMA (United Nations Multidimensional Integrated Stabilization Mission), the UN peacekeeping missions in Mali, and Cultural Caravan for Peace, a touring re-incarnation of Manny Ansar's Festival au Désert, to amplify messages of peace through music. For the second edition of the Festival Vivre Ensemble (February 2018), which offers a weekend of conversations, workshops, artisanal displays and shops, and concerts, the *Timbuktu Renaissance* hosted a concert featuring a Tuareg band *Imiktane* from the M'berra refugee camp in Mauritania where people from northern Mali fled during the 2012 occupation.

This choice of a band made up of Tuareg refugees reflected a deliberate strategy to help re-integrate Tuaregs into the local population in Timbuktu, a challenging task since Tuaregs were regarded with suspicion because some sided with the occupying extremists in 2012–13. *Imitkane's* desert blues soon had people dancing and swaying to the music. In Mali enjoying music is what brings different ethnic groups together and reminds people of their distinctive Malian identity (vs. foreign extremist ideology).

The US Embassy in Mali has recognized this capacity of music and has awarded significant grants with the purpose of countering violent extremism to the NGO Instruments4Africa (https://i4africa.org/), led by Paul Chandler. The mandate is to organize concerts and accompanying discussions and workshops on peacebuilding, economic development, and related topics. Both Instruments4Africa and the *Timbuktu Renaissance* allow the messages of peace to come directly from the musicians, whose words and ideas are respected by the Malian public. At one concert, I heard Khaira Arby, from Timbuktu, literally embody the unity in diversity that is Mali by singing in the different local dialects "I am from Segou; I am from Mopti: I am from Gao," etc. The music breaks the ice. After they have been singing and dancing together, Malians of all ages and backgrounds feel ready to sit down and talk about their similarities and differences, and their shared goals for a peaceful future for their country.

In addition to bringing people together through song and dance, public concerts in Mali also support an important part of the local economy—live music. Even in the best of times, it is not easy to make a living as a musician in Mali. But without the staples of weddings and festivals to provide income, musicians have suffered dramatically during the pandemic. Both Instruments4Africa and the *Timbuktu Renaissance* hire and provide training and mentorship in music production and distribution to technicians, so the economic benefits of the concerts extend beyond the musicians themselves.

Not only the banning of music, but also Ansar Dine's destruction of historic monuments in Timbuktu devastated the local population. "I couldn't believe it when I saw on the television: the destruction of the shrines of the saints of Timbuktu. I was traumatized, upset beyond words at these cataclysmic acts that were an enormous sin against God, against Islam, and against the history of Timbuktu" (Schneider & Djitteye, 2017). The dismay historian Salem Oud El Hadj felt upon seeing that the jihadists were destroying the tombs of Timbuktu's revered scholars/saints, reveals everything about why the occupiers tore down the tombs. In attacking the shrines, the jihadists attacked Timbuktu's very foundation. But if they thought that this desecration would defeat the people of Timbuktu, they were mistaken.

Five years later, the shrines had been rebuilt with the support of UNESCO, and the International Criminal Court had convicted Ahmad

Al-Faqi Al-Mahdi for the desecration of the tombs. This dramatic conviction represented the first time that destruction of cultural heritage had been recognized as a war crime (Bokova, 2016; Domonoske, 2016).

In Timbuktu the news of the historic sentence was met with a measured response. While citizens were overjoyed to have the shrines of their beloved scholar saints restored, and gratified that the destruction of their cultural heritage had received global attention, they were frustrated that the crimes against humanity—rapes, torture, assaults had not yet been punished (Schneider & Djitteye, 2017). This changed with the 2020 trial of Al Hassan Ag Abdoul Aziz for rape, torture, and sexual slavery, as well as demolishing sacred monuments (van den Berg, 2020). Additionally, the people of Timbuktu knew Al-Faqi Al-Mahdi, as a person of no great distinction, a sometime schoolteacher—a follower, not a leader. Attracted by the money and power offered by Ansar Dine, Al-Faqi al-Mahdi was then used by the occupiers to help them target the most important monuments for destruction. At his sentencing Al-Faqi Al-Mahdi expressed remorse for betraying his townspeople and heritage (Domonoske, 2016).

Arguably Timbuktu's most precious heritage, the hundreds of thousands of manuscripts penned by the scholars from the eleventh to the nineteenth centuries, also risked destruction at the hands of the jihadists. Through extraordinary acts of courage that have earned them the moniker, the "Bad-Ass Librarians of Timbuktu" (Hammer, 2016), Dr. Abdel Kader Haidara and his colleagues saved over three hundred thousand texts. Dr. Haidara master-minded a courageous scheme that secreted the manuscripts out of Timbuktu right under the noses of the occupying jihadists. In 2012, over a period of six months, every night a dozen or so cases of manuscripts were removed from secret storage locations, loaded into cars, trucks, donkey carts, or boats—whatever seemed safest—and sent on their way to the capital Bamako. With the nocturnal curfew imposed by the militants, the librarians and their assistants risked apprehension and punishment every night, and indeed, were briefly jailed by Ansar Dine. But the extremists never caught on to the ingenious scheme.

While the astonishing story of the rescue of the manuscripts is well known, the content of these extraordinary documents is not. The *Timbuktu Renaissance* worked with Google Arts and Culture (GAC) and Dr. Abdel Kader Haidara and his NGO Savama to make a selection of the most important of the Timbuktu manuscripts available to the general public—in English, Arabic, French, and Spanish—on Google Arts and Culture's monumental web platform celebrating Mali's culture MALI MAGIC (https://artsandculture.google.com/project/mali-heritage). Brief explanations that put the writings of Timbuktu in a global historical context will accompany the manuscript passages. With humanistic ideas on a par with the Italian Renaissance and advanced scientific and medical thought comparable to Islam's Golden Age, these manuscripts reveal the depth and breadth of knowledge cultivated in Timbuktu.

The manuscript exhibitions form part of the larger Google Arts and Culture Mali site -MALI MAGIC which makes the extraordinary accomplishments of Mali's Golden Age (eleventh-seventeenth centuries) as well as the richness of Mali's contemporary culture accessible with one click. The Mali GAC site should help dispel two myths: (1) that Africa has little or no literary history; and (2) that Islamic societies shun knowledge and science.

Timbuktu's illustrious past as a historic capital of commerce, culture, and education for much of the Islamic world gives it a special role in fostering national unity and social cohesion in Mali, and indeed throughout the entire Sahel. With its symbolic stature and actual experience of occupation, Timbuktu can become a "Best Practice" example of how culture can help to rebuild social cohesion and resilience, and stave off extremism, an ongoing threat to Mali and the region.

References

Bate, F., & Fletcher, P. (2012, April 2). Timbuktu: From city of myth to rebel stronghold. *Reuters.* https://www.reuters.com/article/us-mali-timbuktu-myth/timbuktu-from-city-of-myth-to-rebel-stronghold-idUSBRE8330GB20120404

Bokova, I. (2016, June 22). Ending impunity for war crimes for cultural heritage: The Mali Case. *Arguendo.* https://www.international-criminal-justice-today.org/arguendo/ending-impunity-for-war-crimes-on-cultural-heritage-the-mali-case/.

Denselow, R. (2013, January 15). Mali Music ban by Islamists' crushing culture to impose rule. *The Guardian.* https://www.theguardian.com/music/2013/jan/15/mali-music-ban-islamistscrushing#:~:text=Nowhere%20does%20music%20have,controlled%20by%20Islamic%20rebel%20groups

"Destabilization of Mali". n.d. *Council on Foreign Relations, Global Conflict Tracker.* https://www.cfr.org/global-conflict-tracker/conflict/destabilization-mali

Domonoske, C. (2016, September 27). For the first time destruction of cultural sites leads to war crime conviction. *NPR.* https://www.npr.org/sections/the two-way/2016/09/27/495606932/for-first-time-destruction-of-cultural-sites-leads-to-war-crime-conviction

Fernandes, S. (2013, May 19). The day the music died in Mali. *New York Times.* https://www.nytimes.com/2013/05/20/opinion/the-day-the-music-died-in-mali.html

Hammer, J. (2016). *The bad-ass librarians of Timbuktu: And their race to save the world's most precious manuscripts.* Simon and Shuster.

MacLean, R. (2018, January 18). Islamists banned their music. Now Timbuktu is singing again. *The Guardian.* https://www.theguardian.com/world/2018/jan/18/timbuktu-begins-to-sing-again-mali-music-jihadists

Schneider, C., & Djitteye, E.H. (2017, October 3). The word on the street in Timbuktu (About the ICC Trial). *Huffington Post.* https://www.huffpost.com/entry/the-word-on-the-street-in_b_12187738

Schneider, C., Shields, C., Ansar M. A., & Niang, S. R. (2015, June 3). *The Timbuktu renaissance: One year later.* Brookings Institution, Markaz. https://www.brookings.edu/blog/markaz/2015/06/03/the-timbuktu-renaissance-one-year-later/

Shields, C., Schneider, C., Ansar, M. A., & Niang, S. R. (2014, August 4). *Culture at the heart of peace-building and socio-economic development.* Brookings Institution Up-Front. https://www.brookings.edu/blog/up-front/2014/08/04/timbuktu-renaissance-culture-at-the-heart-of-peace-building-and-socio-economic-development/

Smith, A. D. (2014, September 16). Life in Timbuktu: How the ancient city of gold is slowly turning to dust. *The Guardian.* https://www.theguardian.com/cities/2014/sep/16/-sp-life-timbuktu-mali-ancient-city-gold-slowly-turning-to-dust#:~:text=There%20are%201%2C200%20assigned%20for,estimated%20at%20less%20than%2015%2C000

van den Berg, S. (2020, July 14). Malian accused of Timbuktu war crimes refuses to enter plea. *Reuters.* https://www.reuters.com/article/us-mali-war crimes/malian-accused-of-timbuktu-war-crimes-refuses-to-enter-plea-idUSKCN24F1OA

CHAPTER 17

Tapping into Africa's Environmental and Cultural Heritage: The Role of Theatre for Development

Patricia N. Nkweteyim

Introduction

Africa is a very rich continent blessed with an affluent ecological and cultural heritage. She has coasts, rainforests, mountains, savannah, deserts and wildlife and is also a cornucopia of culture. Unfortunately, these riches are hardly being exploited by Africans. Shakur (2006, para. 16) makes it clear that Africa is the cradle of civilization. She reports that when Europeans "began exploring and trading with Africans... the beauty of Africa and the efficiency in which the Africans governed their land and peoples" amazed them and so they embarked on an "evil" scheme to take their land and resources. Slavery and colonialism were instituted and

---

P. N. Nkweteyim (✉)
Department of Performing and Visual Arts, University of Buea, Buea, Cameroon
e-mail: patricia.nkweteyim@ubuea.cm

© The Author(s), under exclusive license to Springer Nature Singapore Pte Ltd. 2022
T. Afolabi et al. (eds.), *Re-centering Cultural Performance and Orange Economy in Post-colonial Africa*,
https://doi.org/10.1007/978-981-19-0641-1_17

through these they raped Africa, her people and her riches under the guise that they were "civilizing the dark African continent". White supremacy thus elevates the European culture while downplaying and attempting to destroy that of Africa. Consequently, the African continent *has over the years been perceived and represented as plagued with backwardness, hunger and starvation, civil wars, diseases, corruption, poverty and aid-dependency. The Africans themselves, unfortunately, have helped to propagate this negative image as it is not uncommon for them to portray such when seeking foreign aid or loans. There is also a high rate of emigration, via dangerous routes, of Africans to Europe, North America and recently Asia. All these only go to accentuate this prejudice and inform the world that Africa is really not worth living in and that nothing good can come out of it.*

Using Woteva, a village in Buea, Cameroon as a model, an online survey was conducted on 106 Cameroonians by this researcher in August 2020 to find out what they, and by extension Africans, think about African cultural and environmental riches, why African youths were leaving the Continent, as well as what could be done in the continent, to create the opportunities Africans were looking for outside. The findings indicate that Africans were aware of their rich environmental, cultural and natural resources which if well-harnessed, will make the Continent very great. Secondly, the youths were leaving the Continent because of their hope for job opportunities and better standards of living. Thirdly, to create the opportunities the youths were looking for, it necessary for African Governments to embark on the following: (a) Review and professionalize the educational system. (b) Financially empower youths through loans. (c) Support people's constructive efforts. (d) Patriotism. (e) Break free from colonial masters and foreign aid. (f) Focus more on industrialization. (g) Think and practice accountability and transparency. (h) Stop the exploitation of natural and environmental resources by foreigners, and, (i) Tap into youths' potentials.

This chapter seeks to establish the fact that if Cameroonians, and by extension African citizens, could stop waiting on their governments for everything, and start tapping into their rich environmental and cultural resources, the continent will so develop its soft power that they will no longer see reason to migrate. By so doing, those abroad, together with citizens of the other continents, would start seeking ways to immigrate to Africa. Soft power, according to Nye (2017, p. 2), is the "ability to affect others and obtain preferred outcomes by attraction and persuasion rather than coercion or payment". One tool that could be employed to put

Africans on the rails of developing their soft power is theatre, particularly Theatre for Development (TfD).

Theatre for Development

This is a participatory kind of theatre resulting from a dialogical process in which community members create a story to be acted, by discussing their problems, needs and aspirations, as well as possible solutions to the problems raised. The resulting play created and which is performed by the members of the community, is a theatre of "songs, stories, dance and dialogue" that draws from the everyday life of the people. This performance style is the result of the "performative instincts and practices of the communities" (Abah & Okwori, 2005, pp. 7–8). According to Samba (2005, p. 37), this kind of theatre challenges people to "view their world from alternative perspectives", creating an awareness of their "potentialities to seek change from an existing situation of oppression and deprivation to one of freedom and multiple possibilities, from a situation of abject poverty and degradation to one of both economic and psychological freedom". It was pioneered by a group of radical scholars and artists in the 1970s and 1980s whose intention was to enable "marginalised people to discuss issues of importance to them, either among themselves, or with 'experts', to resolve community difficulties and/or to critique power: familial, local, or national" (Plastow, 2015, p. 107). As a community-based theatre which seeks to liberate people from all forms of social and economic oppression, its preoccupation is to "set communities on fire" (Iorapuu, p. 357), making it an "instrument for instigating people-centred development… an instrument for mobilization and for instigation of participation in the development process" (Abah, 2005, p. xiv). Adie (2016, p. 24) calls it "a tool for galvanizing people for critical consciousness" which enables them to "take action towards solving some of their problems". The people themselves are the "protagonist generating the themes and infusing the drama with conflicts from their daily lives" (Abah, p. 101). It does this by "building confidence and solidarity, stimulating discussion, exploring alternative options for action, and building a collective commitment to change; starting with people's urgent concerns and issues; it encourages reflections on these issues and possible strategies for change" (Kidd, 1984, p. 264).

Epskamp (2006, p. 43) submits that TfD is about learning together through arts and using the arts to inform and to teach. In corroboration, Akashoro et al., (2010, p. 111) state that TfD "offers an alternative approach and medium by which theatre can be of direct service to the marginalized urban and peasant masses". Examples include its use in development work ranging from health, water, agriculture, sanitation, community mobilization and information dissemination. Therefore, TfD is necessary to galvanize Cameroonians and Africans in general, to take up their destinies and that of their continent in their hand, by engaging in activities that will develop the soft power of their countries and continent.

It is worthy of note that TfD is not an activity per se but is used to describe a "range of theatrical practices and participatory methods" (Espkamp, p. 43) in a bid to improve the quality of life of the people. It can be used both as a process and a product. When used as a process, workshops are run in which development agents and members of the community engage in a "learning and discovery process made up of a sequence of social practices seen as interconnected", and meant to "create a critical consciousness and raise the awareness of the participants" (Espkamp, p. 44) which will propel them to take action towards solving their problems, hence achieving development. In this light, TfD is always a work in progress. The entire process includes preliminary visits or advocacy, information gathering or research, analysis/interrogation of findings or data analysis and prioritization, scenario making or play creation and rehearsal, performance, post-performance discussions, community action plans or follow-up and evaluation of impact. On the other hand, when TfD is used as a product, plays aimed at providing information and instructions on sustainable behaviour change that would improve living condition and quality of life are performed before the targeted audience. Worthy of note is the fact that a combination of process and product can be used.

Whatever the case, at the end of the intervention, discussions are held and a sustainable community action plan agreed upon by the community members. Because of the potential of TfD, the notion can be extended to other performing arts like music and film, hence, Music or Film for Development. When appropriately exploited, TfD can be used to galvanize and mobilize Cameroonians, and by extension, Africans, to tap into their cultural and environmental wealth for the sustainable development of their nation and continent.

Culture, Environment and Sustainable Development

Culture and environment intersect in diverse and complex ways with each being determined by the other such that a change in one directly or indirectly affects the other. It is in a particular environment that one learns and picks up particular habits, values, beliefs and ways of doing things. Man equally meets his basic needs by harvesting and using resources in his environment, viz, water, air, earth, flora and fauna. As this happens, the environment is in turn impacted, positively or negatively. This is so because as man continues to interact with his environment, diverse social, economic and technological developments take place. Development is a process that culminates in growth, progress and positive change in a society through the addition of physical, economic, environmental, social and demographic components. It should however be noted that over the years, attempts at development have severely harmed or destroyed the environment and supplier of resources, hence, limiting the environment's capacity to satisfy human demands. As a result, the quality life diminishes every day. Therefore, man's attempts at development, together with factors such as carelessness and ignorance of the harm his actions may cause on the environment, leads him to continue to exert pressure on the same environment. The result is a vicious circle of the adoption of new habits and behaviours, which in turn, impact on local cultures and the very environment on which man depends, what ecologists call "the self-destructive or suicidal motive that is inherent in our prevailing and paradoxical attitude towards nature" (Rueckert, 1996, p. 107).

The diverse destructions, not only on the ecosystem but also on man's health as well, is an indication that development cannot be measured only in terms of economic or technological advancements. No wonder there is a global planetary emergency to ensure sustainability in development endeavours.

The concept of sustainability can be traced back to the earliest human civilizations when man started interacting with resources in his environment to make life better. The industrial revolution of eighteenth and early nineteenth centuries saw purely agrarian, rural communities becoming mechanized and urban. While industrialization brought about an increase in the volume and variety of manufactured goods and an improved standard of living for some on the one hand, it brought about grim employment and poor living conditions for the poor and working classes on the other. Pollution and other social and environmental problems became the order of the day, leading to untold misery and the death of many (Galbi, 1994; Haradhan, 2019). The imbalance "civilisation and progress" have caused in the ecosystem over the years has led to many dissenting voices condemning the destruction of the environment and advocating a return to the care and protection of nature. In December 1983, for instance, the World Commission on Environment and Development, headed by Gro Brundtland, was asked to formulate "a global agenda for change". That is, identify long term environmental strategies for the international community. The term, "sustainable development", widely used in their report and which has become a catch phrase in today's world, is defined as "development that meets the needs of the present without compromising the ability of future generations to meet their own needs" (Brundtland, 1987, p. 43). The world is so ecologically devastated by the Western nations' (where Africans are flocking to) uncontrolled pursuit of material wealth and technological advancement that the REDD+ (Reducing Emission from Deforestation and forest Degradation in developing countries, and the role of conservation, sustainable management of forest carbon stocks) mechanism has been put in place as an attempt to encourage developing countries to contribute to climate change mitigation efforts.

Worthy of note is the fact that Africa has the greatest number of countries (28) participating in REDD+ . Latin America has 17 and Asia–Pacific 20. This alone is an indication that Africa has a lot to offer the rest of the world. It is for this reason that this study is advocating a reawakening for Africa. Africans must arise and engage with the environment and cultural vitality if the continent must rebrand itself and come out of the negative labels it has been tagged with. Environmental engagement in this context refers to Africans culturally connecting to their environment and developing it with a commitment to sustainable environmental practices. *Cultural vitality on the other hand, is "evidence of creating, disseminating, validating and supporting arts and culture as a dimension of everyday life"* (Jackson, Kabwasa-Green & Herranz, p. 13). Africa may not have the money or good policies as other continents but her environment and culture are enough wealth she can harness to achieve this. *When such becomes the case, Africa will so develop sustainably that it will become the envy of other continents.* According to Rabie (2016, p. 8), development is "a comprehensive societal process to move the underdeveloped nations from their state of economic backwardness and slow sociocultural change to a dynamic state characterized by sustained economic growth and sociocultural and political transformation that improves the quality of life of all members of society".

It is in this light that a review of the views of Cameroonians, as far as African culture, environment and sustainable development are concerned, is paramount at this juncture.

The Views of Cameroonians

It is evident from the online survey that many Cameroonians believe that the citizens of other continents see opportunities in Africa more than Africans do. That is why their governments pass through African Governments and the elite to exploit Africa's riches which they are using to develop their countries. As to the role ordinary citizens can play in promoting Africa's environmental and cultural richness, Cameroonians think that Africans ought to (a) get back to the roots and learn the basics of culture and environment, (b) be active in the protection and promotion of the environment and culture and showcase these in and out of Africa, (c) create awareness through exhibitions and videos, (d) develop necessary technical skills to sustainably exploit the resources, (e) sensitize and create awareness in communities on the importance of the natural resources the continent has and the importance of good governance, (f) be more environmentally conscious and disciplined by promoting hygiene, sanitation and effective waste management, as well as planting more trees and cutting less, (g) believe in Africa, consume Africa and be proud of Africa, (h) freely express self through cultural elements like music, dance or costume and be ambassadors of their country and continent's rich cultural heritage to the outside world, (i) use smart phones to document and share the environmental beauty, cultural diversity and other potentials of Africa on touristic and other websites, (j) teach kids their heritage (mother tongue, culture) so that the West will not completely wipe out what is left, (k) advocate change to get rid of colonial and greedy leaders still linked to the West that continue to drain Africa, (l) organize wider cultural events and build products and services that can serve a greater number of people, and (n) invest in the cultural sector and make the community aware of the importance of culture.

The above notwithstanding, some Cameroonians however, do not think there is much individuals can do to promote Africa's environmental and cultural richness. Their reasons are as follows: first of all Africans, particularly Cameroonians, need a lot of education as far as the environment is concerned, especially in the areas of constructions, agriculture, deforestation and waste management. Secondly, Africans do not know that they are special and can help themselves. Thirdly, they don't have the opportunity to control what they have or the platform to express their ideas and promote their efforts. Therefore, it is the government that has to organize wider cultural events, or build products and services that can serve a maximum number of people. One respondent thought it would be unfair to ask citizens to be responsible for this. According to him, many have used their personal finances and resources, but were frustrated when they approached leadership for additional support and got nothing. To him, African leadership should catch and promote any vision or ideas which have the potential to develop environmental and cultural richness. In support of this view, others said the African Governments should launch, promote and support initiatives and start-ups as well as set up industries to create job opportunities for citizens. Some others think that NGOs should take up the challenge.

Finally, participants of the online survey were asked what sustainable solutions for Africa's development they would propose if given the opportunity. Their responses have been summarized and categorized under the four pillars of sustainable development, viz, society, economy, environment and culture, in Table 17.1 as follows.

It can be deduced from the above that most Cameroonians, and by extension Africans, look up to their governments for everything. They don't have the mindset of taking initiative. They mostly wait to be employed. This is a very big challenge. In Cameroon for instance, the government is the highest employer of labour. The Cameroon Development Corporation was the second but with the ongoing socio-political crisis in the Northwest and Southwest Regions, thousands of their workers have become redundant. The private sector also exists but is not vibrant enough to do much in term of employment. That is the reason why it is believed that the majority of youths who go out go in search of jobs and better standards of living. Also, the school curriculum is mostly knowledge-oriented and not skill-based. If the curriculum were designed differently, the exploitation of the rich heritage by Africans themselves would have been possible. In line with the suggestion of one respondent, this study is of the opinion that if Africans would stop looking up to their governments for everything and embark on projects by themselves through NGOs, CBOs, CSOs, CIGs and cultural associations, things

Table 17.1 Proposed sustainable solutions for Africa's development

Society	Economy	Environment	Culture
Ensure good leadership and political stability through power decentralization and democratic and accountable governments	Technological advancement, Innovations, Industrialization and Exports rather than imports	Environmental sustainability and eco-cultural identity	Go back to roots and adopt an African language and writing system like the Asians (China, Japan, India) Make people understand that civilisation started in Africa (Egypt)
Break free from colonial rule and stop Chinese invasion of Africa	Use a value chain approach to develop and promote sustainability of all kinds of activities	Go for waste management and afforestation	Identify and promote core African cultural and environmental values
Reform the political landscape to promote good governance, diversity, meritocracy and innovation. Adopt an ethno-philosophical approach to African developmental initiatives	Transform natural resources to finished products thereby creating employment, reducing cost of living and increasing standard of living	Sustained environmental policies	Teach youths and women entrepreneurial skills for sustainability
A good dose of citizenship education. Once there's love for country, sustainable solutions will flow naturally	Invest in agriculture because it employs people, solves hunger and provides export, hence, generating an excellent GDP	Potable water and agricultural incentives	Introduce STEM education in primary school
A united Africa free from European intervention. Replicate the EU system of working internally together and negotiating with other states in a block	Encourage small and medium size enterprises, and the consumption of locally produced goods. This will create more jobs	Sustainable low cost shelters	Youth and women's empowerment and their inclusiveness in policy making
Professionalize the educational sector and fashion educational policies after African cultures and way of thinking to meet the needs of the masses	Encourage entrepreneurs and reduce importation and taxes	Good farm to market roads	Youths should be given a chance to handle strategic positions in government and be given forums to showcase their talents

(continued)

Table 17.1 (continued)

Society	Economy	Environment	Culture
A real democratic and accountable electoral system			Institute the mother tongue at home and educate the girl child

would be better for them, especially considering the rich environmental, cultural and natural resources which the continent possesses. This is where Theatre for Development (TfD) comes in.

Way Forward

To resolve the problem of negative labels for Africa and youth emigration, Africans should tap into their environmental and cultural riches by harnessing the collective power of the people (we-the-people approach) through NGOs, CBOs, CSOs, CIGs, etc., and become agents of their own development rather than waiting for their governments. This study uses Woteva as a model.

Woteva, a village situated on the east foot of Mount Cameroon, at an altitude ranging from 650 to 1300 m above sea level, is the habitat of rare species of plants and animals as well as many natural resources. In 1997, the Woteva Village Traditional Council embarked on a painstaking mission to get government's approval of a Community Forest. This they finally got in 2011. The villagers have since then planted trees (cedrela mexicana) to revive the local forest, and at the same time, are conserving and encouraging the regeneration of plant and animal species in the area. The Woteva Community Forest also has some of the most attractive Eco-touristic sites in the Southwest Region. These include lava flow craters, caves, valleys, gigantic tree species, medicinal and carnivorous plants, wild animals (monkeys, baboons, chimpanzees, snakes, birds, etc.) (http://treff-end.com/ecotourism-woteva-village).

The initiative of the Woteva community caught the interest of Cameroon Vision Trust (CamVision). CamVision, of which this researcher is a member, is a scientific, technical and awareness-building Cameroon based NGO. It is interested in contributing to international efforts to combat the escalating environmental and water crisis as well as promote sustainable development. Partnering with the Woteva Traditional Council, CamVision is poised to carry out sustainable development projects in the village. This will comprise transforming Woteva into an eco-village, setting up community schools (nursery, primary and vocational), hospital, organic farms, as well as enhancing eco-tourism. The village has already been mapped out for the various projects. A large expanse of land, at least five hectares, has equally been reserved for agriculture and expansion in the future.

TfD is the approach adopted. Still at the introductory stage of the project, CamVision has carried out preliminary visits and advocacy at the level of Woteva, NGOs engaged with the environment, and the Buea Council. Lots of information about Woteva, her environmental and cultural riches, have been gathered and analyzed. Partnerships, collaboration and Memoranda of Understanding are also being signed with key stakeholders like the Cameroon Opportunity and Industrialization Centre (a vocational training centre), Mount Cameroon Project and the Buea Council. The next phase will be play creation and performances. Plays are meant to "transmit the pain and suffering that is all around us, but also to glimpse a ray of hope in the chaos and nightmare of our daily lives" (Rascón-Banda, 2006, p. 1). This will obviously galvanize the people and other stakeholders to action. As proposed by CamVision, OIC is in the process of creating the Department of Agriculture to complement the already existing Catering and Hotel Management Department, while Mount Cameroon Project, an organization aimed at encouraging the conservation and sustainable use of forests, has come up with a plan to create a school of tourism (to be hosted in OIC). Again, AMABO Cameroon, an NGO that fabricates cost-efficient, eco-responsible and near indestructible, 100% recyclable, world-class roofing tiles, by mixing post-consumer plastic waste and sand, as well as some craftsmen interested in recycling and up-cycling, have been contacted for collaboration and training. Plans are equally underway for the Council to open and grade the road leading to Woteva. All this is in preparation for the sustainable development work at Woteva, notably the Eco-village Project. It is hoped that OIC and the NGOs will supply skilled youths to construct the eco houses, work on the farms, manage the hotels and tourists, teach in the vocational school, etc.

The next stage of the TfD process is play creation and production. This is a very important aspect as it takes into account the people's culture. TfD is participatory and against the top-down model of development.

Because of this, and despite the fact that CamVision has held lengthy discussions with the gatekeepers of Woteva, the feelings and contributions of the common man must be taken into consideration. At the appropriate time, members of the Woteva community will be brought together in a workshop wherein they will talk about their specific problems and propose solutions to these problems. Enfolded in the people's culture (song, dance, language, rituals, history, etc.) plays with sensitization messages will then be created and performed before the rest of the community. At the end of the productions, issues raised in these plays will be discussed by the community members and the development agents. Community action plans will then be set up and integrated in the CamVison overall project.

At the end of the day, the entire community will work as one people to protect their village with all its projects because they contributed in one way or the other, to its establishment. Nkweteyim (2019, p. 91) posits that when a people are made to take part in deciding about a project, rather than having it imposed on them, they will "feel important and see the project as their own and would do everything to protect it" and not wait for some outsider to do it. In addition, the youths, both village youths and others from around the country, will feel a sense of belonging and will have no reason to migrate from the village as there will be gainful employment for them as well as a platform to freely express themselves. The cultural industry (cuisine, crafts, costume, music, dance, cinema, etc.) will flourish because of the natural environment and the influx of tourists. The success of Woteva will be replicated in other communities and nations of Africa and before long, the emigration rate would have been greatly reduced and Africa will become a safe haven to which people of other continents will flock to for tourism, residence, etc.

African Governments could equally facilitate this process by cutting links with their colonial masters and the West as many of the online respondents proposed. Rwanda did just that and tapped into what she had, and today, a little above two decades after the genocide, she has emerged as a great and strong nation everyone wants to go to.

Conclusion

The foregoing discussions have proven that Africa is blessed and has all what it takes to be great again. All the people need is game changing initiatives. The era of African Governments looking up to their colonial masters for directives has passed. The era of African people waiting on their governments for everything has also passed. Now is the time for community action and self-help projects. The environmental and cultural resources are bountiful. Vocational education for the youths that takes into consideration the African environment and culture, will go a long way to make this happen. Only Africans can rebuild Africa!

References

Abah, O. S. (2005). *Performing life: Case studies in the practice of theatre for development.* Tamaza Publishing.

Abah, O. S., & Okwori, J, Z. (2005). A nation in search of citizens: Problems of citizenship in the Nigerian context. In N. Kabeer (Ed.), *Inclusive citizenship: Meanings and expressions* (pp. 7–8). ZED. [FlipHTML5 Guset User]. https://fliphtml5.com/ijja/mgbv

Adie, E. U. (2016). Critical issues and criticism in the praxis of theatre for development: An experiential discourse in Nigeria. *JOTAMS, 1*(2), 23–33.

Akashoro, O. G., Kayode, J., & Husseini, S. (2010). Theatre and development: Opportunities and challenges in a developing world. *Journal of Communication, 1*(2), 107–112.

Brundtland, G. H. (Ed.). (1987). *Our common future: Report of the world commission on environment and development.* WCED, OUP.

Epskamp, K. (2006). *Theatre for development: An introduction in context, application and training.* Zed Books.

Galbi, D. A. (1994). Child labor and the division of labour in the early English cotton mills. *Journal of Population Economics, 10*(4), 357–375.

Haradhan, M. (2019). The first industrial revolution: Creation of a new global human era. *Journal of Social Sciences and Humanities, 5*(4), 377–387.

Iorapuu, T. J. (2013). From Zaria to everywhere: Community performance with Oga Steve Abah in Nigeria. In S. A. Kafewo, T. J. Iorapuu, & E. S. Dandaura (Eds.), *Theatre unbound: Reflections on theatre for development and social change: A Festschrift in honour of Oga Steve Abah* (pp. 355–369). SONTA.

Jackson, M. R., Kabwasa-Green, F., & Herranz, J. (2006). *Cultural vitality in communities: Interpretation and indicators.* The Urban Institute.

John. (2018/2019). *Ecotourism and sustainable development in Woteva village.* Retrieved from http://treff-end.com/ecotourism-woteva-village/

Kidd, R. (1984). Popular theatre and non-formal education in the third world: Five strands of experience. *International Review of Education, 30*(3), 267–287.

Nkweteyim, P. (2019). *Preserving culture and environment through theatre and new media in Buea Municipality, Cameroon* (Unpublished doctoral thesis). University of Calabar, Calabar, Nigeria.

Plastow, J. (2015). Embodiment, intellect, and emotion: Thinking about possible impacts of theatre for development in three projects in Africa. In F. Alex & T. Jonas (Eds.), *Anthropology, theatre, and development: The transformative potential of performance* (pp. 107–126). Macmillan.

Rabie, M. (2016). *A Theory of sustainable sociocultural and economic development*. Macmillan.

Rueckert, W. (1996). Literature and ecology: An experiment in ecocriticism. In C. Glotfelty & H. Fromm (Eds.), *The ecocriticism reader: Landmarks in literary ecology* (pp. 105–123). University of Georgia Press.

Nye, J. (2017). Soft power: The origins and political progress of a concept. *Palgrave Communications, 3*, 17008. https://doi.org/10.1057/palcomms.2017.8

Samba, E. N. (2005). *Women in theatre for development in Cameroon: participation, contributions and limitations*. Pia Thielmann & Eckhard Breitinger.

Shakur, A. (2006, December 4). *Africa is the cradle of civilization*. Retrieved from http://www.thepatrioticvanguard.com/africa-is-the-cradle-of-civilization

CHAPTER 18

Problematic Leisure: The Consequences of Engaging European Chess in African/Black Schools' Curriculum

Adewonuola A. Ajayi

Introduction

As at 2019, more than 25 Nigerian schools boasted of chess-assisted mathematics programs (PedaChess, 2019). Berkman (2004), Boruch (2011), and Bart's (2014) studies found a positive correlation between chess-playing and improved math-solving abilities. Similarly, Gobet and Simon (1996), Ericsson and Kintsch (1995), and Trinchero (2013) found a positive correlation between chess-playing and improved general problem-solving abilities.

These positive results notwithstanding, this chapter argues that engagement in European chess could cause African/black students to develop

---

A. A. Ajayi (✉)
Department of Sociology and Anthropology, Obafemi Awolowo University (OAU), Ile-Ife, Nigeria
e-mail: adewonuola.negus@gmail.com

© The Author(s), under exclusive license to Springer Nature Singapore Pte Ltd. 2022
T. Afolabi et al. (eds.), *Re-centering Cultural Performance and Orange Economy in Post-colonial Africa*,
https://doi.org/10.1007/978-981-19-0641-1_18

the malaises of cultural incoherence and de-culturization, both of which can be negative for African culture. This concern stems from an understanding of chess as not just a mentally stimulating board game, but also as a platform to showcase culture. Unfortunately, the chess played in African/black schools does not espouse African culture, but fifteenth-century European social realities.

This critique of European chess' engagement in African/black schools is couched within the ideological framework of African-centered pedagogy, an educational approach that entails the investigation, interpretation, and explication of all reality through an African-centered lens or from a perspective grounded in African-centered values (Merry & New, 2008). African-centered pedagogy aims to cultivate a positive cultural identity for African/black students by ensuring that African history, culture and social realities permeate the entire education process (i.e., both the curricular and the extra-curricular) whenever possible.

Chess: More Than Mental Stimulation

Taken at face value, chess is simply a strategic board game that promotes mental stimulation. However, below the surface and within the ambit of cultural studies, it should be understood as more than just a game. To the culture scholar, chess should be understood as a playable, visual representation of a people's culture that depicts their socio-political hierarchies, conflict theories, and occupation types, among many other unique cultural elements. This characterization of chess means that aside from being a cognition-improving game, it also doubles as a platform to showcase culture. Indeed, as Ajayi (2020a) asserts in *More than leisure: the case for the adoption of an African chess variant*; one would struggle to find another game that reflects/showcases as many elements of a culture in a single fixed medium. Specific cultural elements like weapon types, fauna, flora, fashion types, and religious beliefs, among others, are typically depicted in chess sets, making the game a veritable cultural artifact and an appropriate tool for cultural diplomacy.

Chess' life-imitating/culture-reflecting abilities are largely due to:

1. Its Anthropomorphic Pieces on Which Representations of Cultural Attire, Occupational Equipment, Weaponry and Adornments Etc., Are Depicted; and

2. The expanse of a game board that can easily be imagined as a real "land mass" on which one can showcase the flora, fauna, architecture, landmarks, etc., of a subject culture's environment.

It is instructive to note that while chess may be one of the most popular board games in world history, it is but one of more than 2,000 descendants of the Indian strategic board game known as Chaturanga that was invented more than 1,500 years ago (Murray, 1913). Of the more than 2,000 variants of the game, 15 are culture-based, e.g., Xiangqi (Chinese variant), Shogi (Japanese variant), Chess (European variant), and Shatrang (Iranian variant). All these variants modified the original Chaturanga game to reflect their own culture's unique sociopolitical structures, monarchical systems, fashion, religions and conflict theories. Because of their strong cultural foundations, these variants are very widely played in their respective culture areas and engaged as part of their schools' extra-curricular activities (Gralla, 2005; Matake, 2016). However, this is not the case with Africa and African schools.

In Chinese schools, Xiangqi is the staple strategic board game (Jiangsu, 2020), as is European chess in European/western schools and Shogi in Japanese schools (JSA, 2016). However, European chess is played in African schools. Therefore, while the Chinese, Europeans and the Japanese exhibit cultural coherence in that they engage their own cultural chess variants in their schools, Africa and African schools appear to suffer from cultural incoherence.

EUROPEAN CHESS IN AFRICAN/BLACK SCHOOLS: A CULTURALLY INCOHERENT ENGAGEMENT

In African-centered pedagogy, the concept of cultural coherence primarily focuses on shaping the African/black student's cultural identity through a consistent set of cultural beliefs, practices, and representations in the education process; both curricular and extra-curricular (Merry & New, 2008). Thus, for cultural coherence to be observed in the education process; it is crucial that all learning accessories and accompaniments are representative of African culture, with every opportunity to reflect African culture adequately utilized. When representations do not match the African/black student's cultural reality, cultural incoherence can be said to have occurred. This is precisely the case when the game of European chess is juxtaposed against African cultural reality.

A cursory overview of the version of chess currently played in many African/black schools does not reveal an African variant but a European one. From the Anglicized look of the game's pieces (a cross-crown wearing king, a fish-hat wearing bishop), to Anglo-Saxon piece-names (rook, bishop, knight, pawn, etc.) and even game tactics (the *en passant* rule, castling, check, etc.), a picture of fifteenth-century Western Europe is formed. Because chess reflects European culture so well, it is a perfect extra-curricular activity in European schools and cultural spheres; however, it is culturally problematic for African/black students in African culture spheres, because all its imagery and depictions of cultural elements like ethnic fashion, weapon systems, and occupation types do not match African/black students' cultural realities. As seen in Fig. 18.1, the game's religious-leader piece (the bishop) is not representative of any African traditional religious leader, nor is the crucifix-crown wearing king piece representative of any African royal.

The cultural incoherence extends beyond non-African imagery in European chess, to non-African hierarchical arrangements and family structures. For instance, in European chess, the royal spouse (the queen) is more powerful than the actual monarch (the king). This rule, which was invented to honor Queen Isabella of fifteenth century Spain (Gralla, 2005), is at odds with the cultural realities of African/black students socialized into largely patriarchal cultures. There is also the very Christianized depiction of marriage as a monogamous union (the European chess king piece has just one queen). Thus, European chess fails to adequately capture the cultural realities of African/black students, some of who might find monogamy a foreign concept, and polygamy the traditional norm. Finally, the characterization of the European chess king as the weakest piece in 'town' is certainly at odds with African/black students' understanding of African royals as the most powerful personages in society. Indeed, many African kings are believed to be so powerful that they are second only to the gods, as is the case in Yoruba culture, Zulu culture, and Benin culture, among others.

The simple image and narrative analysis above points to the visual and ideological differences between the culture espoused by chess and the cultural realities of the African player. These disconnects in cultural representation help to make the case that European chess' inclusion in

Fig. 18.1 Two chess pieces

African/black schools is culturally inappropriate since it generates incoherence. Such incoherence could have very profound consequences not only for the positive cultural identity of the African/black student, but African culture at large.

Possible Consequences of European Chess Engagement in African/Black Schools' Curriculum

To evaluate the possible consequences of the engagement of European chess in African/black schools, it is important to understand that images, narratives, and ideologies create representations as central signifying practices for producing shared meaning (Hall, 1997). These representations are constitutive of cultural communications that help to create reality and normalize specific world-views or ideologies (Fursich, 2010).

Thus, as a cultural-communication device within institutions devoted to mind-molding and socialization (e.g., schools), European chess has the power to indoctrinate, direct thought and shape the imagination of young African/black students. And what does European chess communicate? European social hierarchy, European rules of military engagement, and European religious systems, among other cultural elements. Nothing African is communicated. This perhaps translates the game of European chess from a harmless cognition-improving device to a tool for culture transference and even cultural imperialism. Engaging in such a game within the confines of powerful socialization centers such as schools may have dire consequences for an African culture already buffeted by the winds of westernization and globalization (Merry, 2007).

The first potential consequence of such cultural incoherence is mental colonization. In this case, mental colonization refers specifically to preclusion of thought about the existence of other culture-based chess variants or the real position of European chess as merely one of more than 2,000 Chaturanga variants. In 2018, I conducted an ethnographic study of a Nigerian university-based European chess club that was introduced to an African chess variant (Ajayi, 2021). The study, involving 46 participants, was conducted over a period of about seven months (between May and December 2018) at Obafemi Awolowo University chess club. One of the most profound findings was that the all-African members of the club appeared to suffer from the form of mental colonization described above. Of the 46 participants, more than 82% were not aware of the existence of other chess variants or that chess was not the primary game but a descendant of an Indian strategic board game. Furthermore, asked to imagine an African culture variant of chess, more than 73% of the participants imagined a game with the same operations as European chess, but with Africanized game pieces; they could not see past the European conflict theory and narrative. I inferred that these results are evidence of the preclusion of thought and mental colonization resulting from regular exposure to the game of European chess. Shifman (2015) asserts that, the more a culturally based leisure activity/product is engaged; the more the root culture is reflected upon, showcased and enlivened. This basically means that when African/black students engage with European chess, they are not thinking of Africa, but Europe. Given this, the knowledge base of European culture can be expected to grow at the expense of Africa's.

The second potential consequence of engaging European chess in African/black schools is the problem of low cultural patriotism. A sub-consequence of mental colonization, this describes a situation where a culture actor comes to view his/her culture as inferior to another and consequently loses regard for it. Low cultural patriotism is typified by reduced patronage of the native culture in favor of a foreign one. In the case of European chess engagement in African/black schools, the seeds of low cultural patriotism are planted once students realize that the game chosen to improve their cognition and academic performance is a European culture-based game and not an African game. This runs the risk of reinforcing western superiority tropes in the minds of the African/black students. This consequence was also encountered in this author's aforementioned ethnographic study. When participants were asked; "*would you rather invent an African variant of chess or become a European-chess grandmaster* (the highest player rank)?" more than 60% chose to become European chess grandmasters. Asked if they would play an authentic African variant of chess, at least one participants replied in the negative, stressing that an African variant couldn't possibly be better than European chess, while another simply asked, "*what is the need for it?*" implying that since European chess already exists, why create an African variant? Of those who said they would play an authentically African variant, more than 52% believed that it would not thrive because European chess is already ubiquitous across the world (Ajayi, 2021). This low cultural patriotism stemming from mental colonization extends beyond the walls of schools into the mainstream. In many African music videos and movies where attempts are made to show that the subject(s) possess high intelligence, it is not uncommon to see a European chess set displayed as an exemplar of the subject(s)' high intellect. Mainstream acceptance of European chess in African culture areas and schools, as the ultimate board game to make individuals smart is concerning because European chess cannot be divorced from its western culture. Reverence for the game's intelligence-boosting quality is automatically extrapolated to westerners, inadvertently reinforcing unfounded tropes of western intellectual superiority.

The cumulative result of these consequences is ultimately the creation of a de-culturized African/black student, somewhat akin to the culturally hollowed-out individual described by Frantz Fanon as having black skin but wearing a white mask (Fanon, 1967). As defined by Boateng (1990: 73), de-culturization is "*a process by which the individual is deprived of his or her culture and then conditioned to other cultural values.*" It is thus understood as an erosion of an individual's culture as a result of the proliferation and acceptance of another culture. With this understanding, engaging in European chess within African/black schools and cultural spheres can be seen as a subtle instrument of de-culturization of the African, which should be cause for concern among African culture stakeholders across the continent.

Addressing Cultural Incoherence in Chess

Mental colonization, a cultural inferiority complex and de-culturization pose grave threats to the continued existence of African culture and should be given due attention by culture stakeholders. The solution may lie in the adoption and application of an African-centered pedagogy by all-African/black schools. According to Grills (2004: 173), in order to efficiently apply an African-centered paradigm, one must be prepared to *"examine or analyze the phenomena with a lens consistent with an African understanding of reality; African values; African logic; African methods of knowing; and African historical experiences."*

This means that, as far as possible, all educational accessories engaged within African/black schools should be African culture-enhancing in their imagery, ideology and narratives, things European chess clearly isn't. The answer is obviously not the wholesale removal of the game of chess and its cognition-improvement benefits, but the adoption of an African chess variant. This would enable African/black students to enjoy not just the mental stimulation of the game, but also cultural coherence and cultural affirmation. The result would be culturally grounded African/black scholars with improved cognitive, math and general problem-solving skills.

On the cultural diplomacy front, an African chess variant would be an effective ambassador to showcase and promote African culture to the world. For centuries, the cultural exchange between Africa and Europe has been largely one-sided, with European culture, language, religions and even games dominating the exchange. An African chess variant would be a significant step toward righting the balance of "mutuality and exchange" that Jora (2013) espouses as typifying true cultural diplomacy.

Fortunately, creating an African variant of chess is not a very complicated process. Indeed, in the seventeenth century, an Ethiopian chess variant known as Senterej existed, which is unfortunately largely extinct (Pankhurst, 1971). The Europeans, Chinese, Japanese, Koreans, Iranians, and the Thai, among other cultures, boast local chess variants. Local cultural elements (conflict theories, monarchical systems, socio-political structures, military tactics and personnel, etc.) are superimposed on the

18 PROBLEMATIC LEISURE: THE CONSEQUENCES OF ENGAGING ... 297

original Chaturanga game to birth a local chess variant. Following this simple system, an authentic African chess variant could be created, as demonstrated in the prototype I invented in 2014 called Nubia African chess (Fig. 18.2).

Nubia African chess is a chess variant that utilizes imagery and operations that mirror African traditional conflicts. The game's pieces are representative of the four cardinal regions of Africa; from the East African

Fig. 18.2 Nubia African chess

High Chief, to the North African War Chief, South African Advisor, and the West African Mystic, with the king and queen pieces both being Nubian/Egyptian royalty. All Nubia African chess game pieces depict the way prominent ethnic groups (Yoruba, Zulu, Kikuyu, and Tuareg) from the four cardinal regions typically attire themselves, giving the game a culturally appropriate look. In terms of war tactics, elements of traditional African mysticism are featured as part of the game's moves. Game moves like the "EDI" or Hypnosis attack (performed by a piece that causes opponent pieces to turn on each other), and "GBESELE" (a telepotent move that allows the king piece's capture without having to leave a spot) are prime examples of some of the African mystical war tactics that make Nubia African chess an authentically African strategic board game vis-à-vis European chess (Ajayi, 2020a, 2020b). The game has received endorsement from the Centre for Black Culture and International Understanding (CBCIU), the Centre for Black and African Arts and Civilizations (CBAAC), and the Institute of Cultural Studies (ICS). However, it is just one iteration of what an African chess variant can look and play like. Other iterations are welcome as long as an African chess variant is ultimately adopted for African/Black schools.

In the creative and expressive space, Africans already watch home-grown movies, listen to home-grown music, and laugh at home-grown comedy. Why not home-grown chess? To reiterate, no other board game has been shown to showcase as many cultural elements in a single fixed medium as chess. Therefore, in seeking to combat westernization, neo-colonization, and one-sided cultural diplomacy, the adoption of an African chess variant is more important than ever for African/Black scholars, the African continent and the African diaspora at large.

REFERENCES

Ajayi, A. (2020a). More than leisure: The case for the adoption of an African chess variant as a tool for African culture showcase and propagation. In "*Social Sciences and National Development: perspectives in contemporary Nigeria society*". A 2020a festschrift in honor of Prof. Olakunle Abiona Ogunbameru

Ajayi, A. (2020b). *The Game of Nubia: Rethinking chess in inventing an authentically African variant*. On the culturally-revisionist process behind the invention of the game of Nubia African Chess. An unpublished manuscript.

Ajayi, A. (2021). *Mental colonization, stirred imaginations and the need for an African chess variant*. An ethnographic study of a Nigerian university's

European chess club introduced to an African chess variant. A forthcoming publication.

Bart, W. M. (2014). On the effects of chess training on scholastic achievement. *Frontiers in Psychology*, 5, Article 762.

Berkman, R. M. (2004). The chess and mathematics connection: More than just a game. *Mathematics Teaching in the Middle School, 9*, 246–250.

Boateng, F. (1990). Combating deculturalization of the African-American child in the public school system: a multicultural approach. In: Ko Lomotey, *Going to school: The African-American experience*. SUNY Press.

Boruch, R. (2011). *Does playing chess improve math learning? Promising (and inexpensive) results from Italy*. Unpublished manuscript.

Ericsson, K., & Kintsch, W. (1995). Long-term working memory. *Psychological Review, 102*, 211–245.

Fanon, F. (1967). Black skin, white mask. Grove Press.

Fursich, E. (2010). Media and the representation of others. *International Social Science Journal*. https://doi.org/10.1111/j.1468-2451.2010.01751.x

Gobet, F., & Simon, H. (1996). The roles of recognition processes and look-ahead search in time-constrained expert problem-solving: Evidence from grandmaster-level chess. *Psychological Science, 7*, 52–55.

Gralla, R. (2005). Interview with Prof. David, H. Li. www.en.chessbase.com/post/give-up-he-siy-version-play-chinese-chess.htm

Grills, C. (2004). African psychology. In R. L. Jones (Ed.), *Black psychology* (pp. 243–265). Cobb and Henry Publishers.

Hall. S., ed. (1997). *Representation: Cultural representation and signifying practices*. Sage

Jiangsu. (2020). *International students compete in Chinese chess*. http://subsites.chinadaily.com.cn/jiangsuedu/2019-06/17/C_383061.htm

Jora, L. (2013). New practices and trends in cultural diplomacy. *Political Science and International Relations, X,* 1,43–52.

JSA. (2016). *Japan Shogi Association*. www.shogi.or.jp

Matake, K. (2016). Shogi and artificial intelligence. *Japan policy forum. Culture*. No. 32. japanpolicyforum.jp/culture/pt20160516000523

Merry, M. S. (2007). *Culture, identity and Islamic schooling: A philosophical approach*. Palgrave Macmillan.

Merry, M. S., & New, W. (2008). Constructing an authentic self: 'the challenge and promise of African-centered Pedagogy': *American Journal of Education, 115*.

Murray, H. J. R. (1913). *A history of chess*. Clarendon Press.

Pankhurst, R. (1971). History and principles of Ethiopian chess. *Journal of Ethiopian Studies*, XI, (2).

Pedachess. (2019). *Statistics on schools offering chess-assisted mathematics programs.* PedaChess Educational Services. www.findglocal.com/NG/Lagos/127086710637278/Pedachess-educational-service.htm

Shifman, R. (2015). *Delving deeper: The relationship between culture, leisure, and wellbeing.* A thesis presented to the University of Waterloo in fulfillment of the degree of Master of Arts in Recreation and leisure studies. Waterloo, Ontario, Canada. 2015

Trinchero, R. (2013). Can chess training improve PISA scores in mathematics? An experiment in Italian primary schools. *Kasparov Chess Foundation Europe*

Index

A

Africa, vii, viii, x, xii, xiii, 10, 25, 43, 47, 52, 60–69, 73, 102, 113–116, 118–122, 125–127, 132, 136, 142, 145, 146, 148–153, 169–172, 174, 180–182, 210–213, 218–220, 230, 234, 236–243, 245–248, 257, 259, 266, 272, 275, 276, 280–284, 286, 291, 294, 296, 297

Africa and Cultural Manifesto, 61, 62, 64, 66, 67, 69

African/black schools, xii, 290, 292–296, 298

Africanize, 180, 187, 294

Afrophobia, xi, 238–240, 248

Agency, x, xiii, 35, 50, 78, 99, 101, 102, 107, 119, 130, 143, 162, 170, 171, 180, 187, 191, 192, 195, 202, 204, 205, 212, 220, 243

Aviation, 160, 166

C

Chess, xii, 289–298

Community museum, ix, 26, 28–30, 32–36

Conflict, xii, 31, 47, 122, 126, 127, 144, 153, 218, 231, 237, 241, 257–259, 265, 267, 268, 277, 290, 291, 294, 296, 297

Content, 42, 48, 60, 61, 64, 69, 72, 73, 77, 134–136, 143, 151, 160, 162–164, 166, 242, 243, 246, 271

Cultural and creative industries (CCI), 143–145

Cultural beliefs, 27, 28, 30, 31, 33–35, 291

Cultural diplomacy, ix–xi, 42–44, 48, 49, 71–73, 75, 78, 92, 97–101, 103–108, 125–128, 131, 135, 136, 152, 210, 213–216, 219, 225, 234, 240, 241, 248, 290, 296, 298

© The Editor(s) (if applicable) and The Author(s), under exclusive license to Springer Nature Singapore Pte Ltd. 2022
T. Afolabi et al. (eds.), *Re-centering Cultural Performance and Orange Economy in Post-colonial Africa*,
https://doi.org/10.1007/978-981-19-0641-1

INDEX

Cultural exchange, xiii, 71–78, 83, 98–104, 114–116, 118, 119, 121, 122, 296
Cultural heritage, ix, xii, 6, 36, 46, 48, 53, 54, 62, 66, 69, 86, 98, 100, 102, 104–106, 118, 120, 126, 130, 131, 180, 230, 242, 244, 258, 265, 267, 271, 275, 281
Cultural identity, xi, xii, 119, 209, 221, 283, 290, 291, 293
Cultural objects, 26–36
Cultural performance, viii, x–xiii, 191, 192, 211, 213, 219–222, 224, 225, 259
Cultural policy/cultural policies, viii, ix, xiii, 3–9, 11, 12, 19, 21, 22, 43, 45, 46, 48–51, 53, 60–62, 64–71, 75, 76, 81, 83, 91, 92, 99, 107, 130, 233
Cultural production, xi, 43, 256, 258, 259
Cultural relations, 44, 62, 71–74, 78, 89, 92, 99, 116, 127, 128, 234, 235
Culture, vii, viii, x, xii, xiii, 4–11, 13, 14, 19–22, 25–29, 31, 33, 35, 36, 41–54, 60–74, 76–81, 86, 89–92, 97–107, 112–118, 121, 126, 128–134, 145, 148–153, 160, 163, 165–167, 170, 171, 174, 181, 184, 185, 210, 211, 230–235, 241–243, 245–247, 258, 265–268, 272, 275, 276, 279–287, 290–296
Curriculum, xii, 20, 282, 293

D

Darmasiswa, 112, 113, 116, 117, 119, 120, 122
Diplomacy, viii, x, xiii, 8, 44, 97–102, 105, 115, 116, 118, 120, 126–128, 130, 145, 150, 152, 183, 205, 206, 215, 231, 234, 268
Dzaleka refugee camp, xi, 256, 259

E

Ecological heritage, 275
Evaluation, vii, ix, 47, 278
Exchanges, ix–xi, 42–45, 49, 53, 67, 72, 73, 76, 78, 80, 81, 86, 89–91, 97–99, 101, 104, 106, 113, 120, 128, 133, 166, 193, 206, 215, 219, 231, 234, 235, 245, 256, 259, 261, 296

F

Film, vii–ix, xiii, 41–54, 79, 80, 106, 127, 130, 132, 134–136, 143, 145, 146, 148, 162–164, 214, 230, 235, 241–243, 248, 278
Folktale, 121, 170, 180
Foreign policy, x, 10, 99, 100, 105–107, 116, 126, 128, 133, 142, 148, 150, 152, 213, 231–236, 246

G

Geopolitics, xi, xii, 256
Ghana, 43, 60, 61, 64, 66, 68, 69, 103, 148, 151, 173, 181, 218

I

Identity, x, 11, 21, 28–30, 33–35, 44, 60, 61, 65, 66, 69, 70, 114, 116, 119, 121, 134, 170, 174–176, 180, 183, 187, 212, 231–233, 235, 241–245, 257, 258, 260, 267, 270
Image, vii, x, xii, 10, 22, 43, 47, 48, 53, 70, 100, 106, 122, 125, 126,

134–136, 142, 143, 145, 148, 150–153, 165, 174, 180–182, 184, 185, 230, 244, 246, 276, 292, 293
Indonesia, x, 112, 113, 116–121
Inflight entertainment (IFE), x, 159–167

J
Job security, 216

L
Leisure, xii, 294

M
Malawi, xi, 256–261
Mali, xii, 173, 181, 265–270, 272
Morocco, ix, 22, 73, 74
Movies, 42, 44, 48, 51, 128, 132, 136, 142, 145–152, 159–161, 163–166, 214, 215, 241–244, 295, 298
Music, xii, 4, 5, 7, 9, 12–16, 18–22, 42, 78–80, 99, 100, 104, 106, 119, 132, 142, 143, 145, 146, 164, 165, 193, 194, 202, 210, 214, 217, 218, 222, 230, 231, 235, 241, 242, 245–248, 266–270, 281, 286, 295, 298

N
National integration, 26–30, 34–36, 53
Nationalism, xi, xii, 232, 256, 258
National Troupe of Nigeria (NTN), xi, 99–104, 106, 107, 130, 210, 211, 213–216, 219–222, 224
Niger and festival, x, xi, 100, 245
Nigeria, ix–xi, 25–31, 33–36, 43, 45–50, 52–54, 60, 61, 64, 66–69, 98–107, 116, 121, 126–129, 131, 133–136, 142–148, 150–153, 195, 210–217, 219, 221, 224, 225, 230, 235–242
Nigeria-South Africa, xi, 236, 238, 239, 244
Nollywood, ix, x, 42–45, 47–54, 106, 127, 131, 132, 134–136, 142, 143, 145–153, 214, 241–244
North Africa, 75

O
Orange economy, viii, x, xiii, 125–127, 131, 132, 136, 142, 143, 146, 153

P
Pan-Africanism, ix, xii, 59–64, 66–69
Passenger, x, 159–163, 165–167
Pedagogical initiative, 210, 213
Performance/performances, vii, xi, 13–15, 26, 27, 30, 42, 47, 81, 83, 86, 90, 101–105, 160, 162, 191–194, 196, 199, 203–206, 214, 216, 219, 221, 223, 224, 258, 277, 278, 285, 295
Performative culture, 26
Policy, viii, ix, 4, 5, 7, 10–12, 15, 16, 18, 19, 21, 22, 45, 46, 48, 50, 53, 54, 66, 72, 73, 76–78, 80, 81, 83, 86, 89–92, 105, 106, 129, 130, 143, 144, 150, 192, 232, 236, 258, 259, 283
Post-colonial, ix, 53, 60, 114–116, 118, 120, 122, 257
Post-colonial Africa, viii, 47, 114, 115, 121
Postcolonialism, 74, 210–213, 219, 220

Post-independence, viii, 5, 15, 21, 214, 257
Power, x, xi, 26, 27, 29, 33, 34, 36, 44, 60, 91, 98, 101, 114–117, 122, 126, 127, 132, 133, 148, 149, 170–172, 174–179, 182–187, 191, 192, 196, 197, 199, 200, 205, 212, 225, 229, 232, 234, 266, 271, 277, 283, 284, 294

R
Regional powers, 230, 239

S
Sculptural materials, 26–36
Single story, 113–115, 121, 142
Soft power, viii–xiii, 22, 26, 43, 44, 47, 48, 71, 73, 90, 91, 97, 98, 102, 104, 114–120, 122, 127, 132, 133, 136, 142, 143, 148–153, 169–171, 173, 175–178, 180–187, 213, 225, 229, 230, 233, 235, 240, 241, 243, 245–248, 276–278
Sustainability, viii, xi–xiii, 28, 29, 73, 90, 91, 204, 279, 283

T
Theatre, vii, ix, xiii, 42, 46, 78, 79, 99, 101–107, 130, 145, 213, 214, 219, 258, 277, 278
The Netherlands, ix, xii, 73–78, 80, 81, 83, 86, 89, 91, 92
Timbuktu, xii, 266–272
Tumaini Festival, 255, 258–260
Tunisia, viii, 3–5, 7–16, 20–22

W
Will, x, 147, 166, 173–175, 179–181, 183–187, 225

Printed in the United States
by Baker & Taylor Publisher Services